A Reader on Reading

Alberto Manguel

A Reader
on Reading

Yale UNIVERSITY PRESS
New Haven and London

Published with assistance from the Mary Cady Tew
Memorial Fund.

Designed by Sonia Shannon
Set in Fournier type by Tseng Information Systems, Inc.
Printed in the United States of America.

Excerpts from *Into the Looking-Glass Wood: Essays on
Words and the World* by Alberto Manguel copyright © 1998
by Alberto Manguel. Reprinted by permission of Knopf
Canada.

The Library of Congress has cataloged the hardcover edition
as follows:
Manguel, Alberto.
A reader on reading / Alberto Manguel.
p. cm.
Includes bibliographical references and index.
ISBN 978-0-300-15982-0 (alk. paper)
1. Books and reading. 2. Manguel, Alberto —
Books and reading. I. Title.
Z1003.M2925 2010
028'.9 — dc22

                                    2009043719

ISBN 978-0-300-17208-9 (pbk.)

A catalogue record for this book is available from the British
Library.

10 9 8 7 6 5 4 3 2 1

To Mavis Gallant,
always in search of the evidence.

"Give your evidence," said the
King; "and don't be nervous, or I'll
have you executed on the spot."
Alice's Adventures in Wonderland,
Chapter 11

Contents

IV. WORDPLAY

V. THE IDEAL READER

VI. BOOKS AS BUSINESS

VII. CRIME AND PUNISHMENT

VIII. THE NUMINOUS LIBRARY

Preface

"You ought to return thanks in a neat speech," the Red Queen said, frowning at Alice as she spoke.

Through the Looking-Glass, Chapter 9

THE SUBJECT OF THIS BOOK, as of almost all my other books, is reading, that most human of creative activities. I believe that we are, at the core, reading animals and that the art of reading, in its broadest sense, defines our species. We come into the world intent on finding narrative in everything: in the landscape, in the skies, in the faces of others, and, of course, in the images and words that our species creates. We read our own lives and those of others, we read the societies we live in and those that lie beyond our borders, we read pictures and buildings, we read that which lies between the covers of a book.

This last is of the essence. For me, words on a page give the world coherence. When the inhabitants of Macondo were afflicted with an amnesia-like sickness which came to them one day during their hundred years of solitude, they realized that their knowledge of the world was quickly disappearing and that they might forget what a cow was, what a tree was, what a house was. The antidote, they discovered, lay in words. To remember what their world meant to them, they wrote out labels and hung them from beasts and objects: "This is a tree," "This is a house," "This is

a cow, and from it you get milk, which mixed with coffee gives you café con leche." Words tell us what we, as a society, believe the world to be.

"Believe to be": therein lies the challenge. Pairing words with experience and experience with words, we, readers, sift through stories that echo or prepare us for an experience, or tell us of experiences that will never be ours, as we know all too well, except on the burning page. Accordingly, what we believe a book to be reshapes itself with every reading. Over the years, my experience, my tastes, my prejudices have changed: as the days go by, my memory keeps reshelving, cataloguing, discarding the volumes in my library; my words and my world—except for a few constant landmarks—are never one and the same. Heraclitus's bon mot about time applies equally well to my reading: "You never dip into the same book twice."

What remains invariable is the pleasure of reading, of holding a book in my hands and suddenly feeling that peculiar sense of wonder, recognition, chill, or warmth that for no discernible reason a certain string of words sometimes evokes. Reviewing books, translating books, editing anthologies are activities that have provided me with some justification for this guilty pleasure (as if pleasure required justification!) and sometimes even allowed me to make a living. "It is a fine world and I wish I knew how to make £200 a year in it," wrote the poet Edward Thomas to his friend Gordon Bottomley. Reviewing, translating, and editing have sometimes allowed me to make those two hundred pounds.

Henry James coined the phrase "the figure in the carpet" for the recurrent theme that runs through a writer's work like a secret signature. In many of the pieces I have written (as reviews or memoirs or introductions) I think I can see that elusive figure: it has something to do with how this art I love so much, the craft of reading, relates to the place in which I do it, to Thomas's "fine world." I believe there is an ethic of reading, a responsibility in how we read, a commitment that is both political and private in the act of turning the pages and following the lines. And I believe that sometimes, beyond the author's intentions and beyond the reader's hopes, a book can make us better and wiser.

In the "neat speech" returning thanks, I want to acknowledge the generous reading of Ileene Smith and Susan Laity, the careful proofreading of Dan Heaton, and the meticulous indexing of Marilyn Flaig. Also the splendid cover design of Sonia Shannon.

Craig Stephenson, who for the past twenty years has been the first reader of everything I've written, suggested the structure, order, and selection for this book (as he did earlier for *Into the Looking-Glass Wood*, the 1998 volume from which a few of the essays here included were taken, as well as a few of the lines in this preface). He curbed my inclination to keep occasional pieces to which I was attached for sentimental reasons, reminded me of others that I had forgotten but insisted that I revise certain paragraphs or examples that now seemed dated, and spent far more time reflecting on the appropriateness of each piece than I myself, in my impatience, would have done. For this, and for more things than he would ever be willing to acknowledge, my loving thanks.

PART ONE

Who Am I?

"I *am* real!" said Alice, and began to cry.

"You won't make yourself a bit realer by crying," Tweedledee remarked: "there's nothing to cry about."

"If I wasn't real," Alice said—half-laughing through her tears, it all seemed so ridiculous—"I shouldn't be able to cry."

"I hope you don't suppose those are real tears?" Tweedledum interrupted in a tone of great contempt.

Through the Looking-Glass, Chapter 4

A Reader in the Looking-Glass Wood

"Would you tell me, please, which way I
ought to go from here?"

"That depends a good deal on where you want
to get to," said the Cat.

Alice's Adventures in Wonderland, Chapter 6

WHEN I WAS EIGHT OR NINE, in a house that no longer stands, someone gave me a copy of *Alice's Adventures in Wonderland and Through the Looking-Glass*. Like so many other readers, I have always felt that the edition in which I read a book for the first time remains, for the rest of my life, the original one. Mine, thank the stars, was enriched by John Tenniel's illustrations and was printed on thick, creamy paper that reeked mysteriously of burnt wood.

There was much I didn't understand in my first reading of Alice, but that didn't seem to matter. I learned at a very early age that unless you are reading for some purpose other than pleasure (as we all sometimes must for our sins), you can safely skim over difficult quagmires, cut your way through tangled jungles, skip the solemn and boring lowlands, and simply let yourself be carried by the vigorous stream of the tale.

As far as I can remember, my first impression of the adventures was that of a physical journey on which I myself became poor Alice's companion. The fall down the rabbit hole and the crossing through the looking-glass were merely starting points, as trivial and as wonderful as boarding a bus. But the journey! When I was eight or nine, my disbelief was not so much suspended as yet unborn, and fiction felt at times more real than everyday fact. It was not that I thought that a place such as Wonderland actually existed, but that I knew it was made of the same stuff as my house and my street and the red bricks that were my school.

A book becomes a different book every time we read it. That first childhood *Alice* was a journey, like the *Odyssey* or *Pinocchio,* and I have always felt myself a better Alice than a Ulysses or a wooden puppet. Then came the adolescent Alice, and I knew exactly what she had to put up with when the March Hare offered her wine when there was no wine at the table, or when the Caterpillar wanted her to tell him exactly who she was and what was meant by that. Tweedledee and Tweedledum's warning that Alice was nothing but the Red King's dream haunted my sleep, and my waking hours were tortured by exams in which Red Queen teachers asked me questions like "Take a bone from a dog: what remains?" Later, in my twenties, I found the trial of the Knave of Hearts collected in André Breton's *Anthologie de l'humour noir,* and it became obvious that Alice was a sister of the surrealists; after a conversation with the Cuban writer Severo Sarduy in Paris, I was startled to discover that Humpty Dumpty owed much to the structuralist doctrines of *Change* and *Tel Quel.* And later still, when I made my home in Canada, how could I fail to recognize that the White Knight ("But I was thinking of a plan / To dye one's whiskers green, / And always use so large a fan / That they could not be seen") had found a job as one of the numerous bureaucrats that scurry through the corridors of every public building in my country?

In all the years during which I've read and reread Alice, I have come across many other different and interesting readings of her books, but I can't say that any of these have become, in any deep sense, my own. The readings of others influence, of course, my personal reading, offer new points of view or color certain passages, but mostly they are like the comments of the Gnat who keeps naggingly whispering in Alice's ear, "You might make a joke on that." I refuse; I'm a jealous reader and will not allow others a *jus primae noctis* with the books that I read. The intimate sense of kinship established so many years ago with my first *Alice* has not weakened; every time I reread her, the bonds strengthen in very private and unexpected ways. I know other bits by heart. My children (my eldest daughter is, of course, called Alice) tell me to shut up when I burst, yet again, into the mournful strains of "The Walrus and the Carpenter." And for almost every new experience, I find a premonitory or nostalgic echo in her pages, telling me once again, "This is what lies ahead of you" or "You have been here before."

One adventure among many does not describe for me any particular experience I have had or may one day have but rather seems to address something vaster, an experience or (if the term is not too grand) a philosophy of life. It takes place at the end of chapter 3 of *Through the Looking-Glass*. After passing through her reflection and making her way across the chessboard country that lies behind it, Alice reaches a dark wood where (she has been told) things have no names. "Well, at any rate it's a great comfort," she says bravely, "after being so hot, to get into the—into the—into *what?*" Astonished at not being able to think of the word, Alice tries to remember. "'I mean to get under the—under the—under *this*, you know!' putting her hand on the trunk of a tree. 'What *does* it call itself, I wonder? I do believe it's got no name—why, to be sure it hasn't.'" Trying to recall the word for the place she is in, accustomed to putting into words her experience of reality, Alice suddenly discovers that nothing actually *has* a name: that until she herself can name something, that thing will remain nameless, present but silent, intangible as a ghost. Must she remember these forgotten names? Or must she make them up, brand new? Hers is an ancient conundrum.

After creating Adam "out of the dust of the ground" and placing him in a garden east of Eden (as the second chapter of Genesis tells us), God went on to create every beast of the field and every fowl of the air, and brought them to Adam to see what he would call them; and whatever Adam called every living creature, "that was the name thereof." For centuries, scholars have puzzled over this curious exchange. Was Adam in a place (like the Looking-Glass Wood) where everything was nameless, and was he supposed to invent names for the things and creatures he saw? Or did the beasts and the fowl that God created indeed have names, which Adam was meant to know, and which he was to pronounce like a child seeing a dog or the moon for the first time?

And what do we mean by a "name"? The question, or a form of the question, is asked in *Through the Looking-Glass*. A few chapters after crossing the nameless wood, Alice meets the doleful figure of the White Knight, who, in the authoritarian manner of adults, tells her that he will sing a song to "comfort" her. "The name of the song," says the Knight, "is called '*Haddocks' Eyes*'":

"Oh, that's the name of the song, is it?" Alice said, trying to feel interested.

"No, you don't understand," the Knight said, looking a little vexed. "That's what the name is *called*. The name really is '*The Aged Aged Man*.'"

"Then I ought to have said 'That's what the *song* is called'?"
Alice corrected herself.

"No, you oughtn't: that's quite another thing! The song is called
'*Ways And Means*': but that's only what it's *called*, you know!"

"Well, what *is* the song then?" said Alice, who was by this time
completely bewildered.

"I was coming to that," the Knight said. "The song really is
'*A-sitting On A Gate*': and the tune's my own invention."

As it turns out, the tune *isn't* his own invention (as Alice points out) and
neither are the Knight's careful distinctions between what a name is called,
the name itself, what the thing it names is called, and the thing itself; these
distinctions are as old as the first commentators of Genesis. The world into
which Adam was inducted was innocent of Adam; it was also innocent of
Adam's words. Everything Adam saw, everything he felt, as everything he
fancied or feared, was to be made present to him (as, eventually, to every one
of us) through layers of names, names with which language tries to clothe the
nakedness of experience. It is not by chance that once Adam and Eve lost their
innocence, they were obliged to wear skins "so that," says a Talmudic com-
mentator, "they might learn who they were through the shape that enveloped
them." Words, the names of things, give experience its shape.

The task of naming belongs to every reader. Others who do not read must
name their experience as best they can, constructing verbal sources, as it were,
by imagining their own books. In our book-centered societies, the craft of
reading signals our entrance into the ways of the tribe, with its particular codes
and demands, allowing us to share the common source of recorded words; but
it would be a mistake to think of reading as a merely receptive activity. On
the contrary: Stéphane Mallarmé proposed that every reader's duty was "to
purify the sense of the words of the tribe." To do this, readers must make books
theirs. In endless libraries, like thieves in the night, readers pilfer names, vast
and marvelous creations as simple as "Adam" and as far-fetched as "Rumpel-
stiltskin." Dante describes his encounter with the three beasts in a dark forest,
"in the middle of the road of life"; for his readers that half-run life becomes
their own, and also a mirror of another forest, a place they once saw in childhood, a forest that fills their dreams with scents of pine and fox. John Bunyan
describes Christian running from his house with his fingers in his ears so as
not to hear the pleas of his wife and children, and Homer describes Ulysses,

bound to the mast, forced to listen to the sirens' song; the reader of Bunyan and Homer applies these words to the deafness of our contemporary, the amiable Prufrock. Edna St. Vincent Millay calls herself "domestic as a plate," and it is the reader who renames the daily kitchen china, the companion of our meals, with a newly acquired meaning. "Man's innate casuistry!" complained Karl Marx (as quoted by Friedrich Engels in *The Origins of the Family*): "To change things by changing their names!" And yet, *pace* Marx, that is exactly what we do.

As every child knows, the world of experience (like Alice's wood) is nameless, and we wander through it in a state of bewilderment, our heads full of mumblings of learning and intuition. The books we read assist us in naming a stone or a tree, a moment of joy or despair, the breathing of a loved one or the kettle whistle of a bird, by shining a light on an object, a feeling, a recognition and saying to us that this here is our heart after too long a sacrifice, that there is the cautionary sentinel of Eden, that what we heard was the voice that sang near the Convent of the Sacred Heart. These illuminations sometimes help; the order in which experiencing and naming take place does not much matter. The experience may come first and, many years later, the reader will find the name to call it in the pages of *King Lear*. Or it may come at the end, and a glimmer of memory will throw up a page we had thought forgotten in a battered copy of *Treasure Island*. There are names made up by writers that a reader refuses to use because they seem wrongheaded, or trite, or even too great for ordinary understanding, and are therefore dismissed or forgotten or kept for some crowning epiphany that (the reader hopes) will one day require them. But sometimes they help the reader name the unnamable. "You want him to know what cannot be spoken, and to make the perfect reply, in the same language," says Tom Stoppard in *The Invention of Love*. Sometimes a reader can find on a page that perfect reply.

The danger, as Alice and her White Knight knew, is that we sometimes confuse a name and what we call a name, a thing and what we call a thing. The graceful phantoms on a page, with which we so readily tag the world, are not the world. There may be no names to describe the torture of another human being, the birth of one's child. After creating the angels of Proust or the nightingale of Keats, the writer can say to the reader, "Into your hands I commend my spirit," and leave it at that. But how are readers to be guided by these entrusted spirits to find their way in the ineffable reality of the wood?

Systematic reading is of little help. Following an official book list (of clas-

sics, of literary history, of censored or recommended reading, of library catalogues) may, by chance, throw up a useful name, as long as we bear in mind
the motives behind the lists. But the best guides, I believe, are the reader's
whims — trust in pleasure and faith in haphazardness — which sometimes lead
us into a makeshift state of grace, allowing us to spin gold out of flax.

Gold out of flax: in the summer of 1935 the poet Osip Mandelstam was
granted by Stalin, supposedly as a favor, identity papers valid for three months,
accompanied by a residence permit. According to his wife, Nadezhda Mandelstam, this little document made their lives much easier. It happened that a
friend of the Mandelstams, the actor and essayist Vladimir Yakhontov, chanced
to come through their city. In Moscow he and Mandelstam had amused themselves by reading from ration books, in an effort to name paradise lost. Now
the two men did the same thing with their identity papers. The scene is described in Nadezhda's memoir *Hope Against Hope:* "It must be said that the
effect was even more depressing. In the ration book they read off the coupons
solo and in chorus: 'Milk, milk, milk . . . cheese, meat . . .' When Yakhontov
read from the identity papers, he managed to put ominous and menacing in-
flections in his voice: 'Basis on which issued . . . issued . . . by whom issued . . .
special entries . . . permit to reside, permit to reside, permit to re-side . . .'"

All true readings are subversive, against the grain, as Alice, a sane reader,
discovered in the Looking-Glass world of mad name givers. The Duchess calls
mustard "a mineral"; the Cheshire Cat purrs and calls it "growling"; a Canadian prime minister tears up the railway and calls it "progress"; a Swiss businessman traffics in loot and calls it "commerce"; an Argentinean president
shelters murderers and calls it "amnesty." Against such misnomers readers can
open the pages of their books. In such cases of willful madness, reading helps
us maintain coherence in the chaos. Not to eliminate it, not to enclose experience within conventional verbal structures, but to allow chaos to progress cre-
atively on its own vertiginous way. Not to trust the glittering surface of words
but to burrow into the darkness.

The impoverished mythology of our time seems afraid to go beneath the
surface. We distrust profundity, we make fun of dilatory reflection. Images of
horror flick across our screens, big or small, but we don't want them slowed
down by commentary: we want to watch Gloucester's eyes plucked out but not
to have to sit through the rest of *Lear.* One night, some time ago, I was watching television in a hotel room, zapping from channel to channel. Perhaps by
chance, every image that held the screen for a few seconds showed someone

being killed or beaten, a face contorted in anguish, a car or a building exploding. Suddenly I realized that one of the scenes I had flicked past did not belong to a drama series but to a newscast on war in the Balkans. Among the other images which cumulatively diluted the horror of violence, I had watched, unmoved, a real person being hit by a real bullet.

George Steiner suggested that the Holocaust translated the horrors of our imagined hells into a reality of charred flesh and bone; it may be that this translation marked the beginning of our modern inability to imagine another person's pain. In the Middle Ages, for instance, the horrible torments of martyrs depicted in countless paintings were never viewed simply as images of horror: they were illumined by the theology (however dogmatic, however catechistic) that bred and defined them, and their representation was meant to help the viewer reflect on the world's ongoing suffering. Not every viewer would necessarily see beyond the mere prurience of the scene, but the possibility for deeper reflection was always present. After all, an image or a text can only *offer* the choice of reading further or more profoundly; this choice the reader or viewer can reject since in themselves text and image are nothing but dabs on paper, stains on wood or canvas.

The images I watched that night were, I believe, nothing but surface; like pornographic texts (political slogans, Bret Easton Ellis's *American Psycho*, advertising pap), they offered nothing but what the senses could apprehend immediately, all at once, fleetingly, without space or time for reflection.

Alice's Looking-Glass Wood is not made up of such images: it has depth, it requires thought, even if (for the time of its passing) it offers no vocabulary to name its proper elements. True experience and true art (however uncomfortable the adjective has become) have this in common: they are always greater than our comprehension, even than our capabilities of comprehension. Their outer limit is always a little past our reach, as the Argentinean poet Alejandra Pizarnik once described:

And if the soul were to ask, Is it still far? you must answer:
On the other side of the river, not this one, the one just beyond.

To come even this far, I have had many and marvelous guides. Some overwhelming, others more intimate, many vastly entertaining, a few illuminating more than I could hope to see. Their writing keeps changing in the library of my memory, where circumstances of all sorts — age and impatience, different skies and different voices, new and old commentaries — keep shifting the volumes, crossing out passages, adding notes in the margins, switching jackets, inventing titles. The furtive activity of such anarchic librarians expands my limited library almost to infinity: I can now reread a book as if I were reading one I had never read before.

In Bush, his house in Concord, the seventy-year-old Ralph Waldo Emerson began suffering from what was probably Alzheimer's disease. According to his biographer Carlos Baker: "Bush became a palace of forgetting. . . . [But] reading, he said, was still an 'unbroken pleasure.' More and more the study at Bush became his retreat. He clung to the comforting routine of solitude, reading in his study till noon and returning again in the afternoon until it was time for his walk. Gradually he lost his recollection of his own writings, and was delighted at rediscovering his own essays: 'Why, these things are really very good,' he told his daughter."

Something like Emerson's rediscovery happens now when I take down *The Man Who Was Thursday* or *Dr. Jekyll and Mr. Hyde* and meet them like Adam greeting his first giraffe.

Is this all?

Sometimes it seems enough. In the midst of uncertainty and many kinds of fear, threatened by loss, change, and the welling of pain within and without for which one can offer no comfort, readers know that at least there are, here and there, a few safe places, as real as paper and as bracing as ink, to grant us roof and board in our passage through the dark and nameless wood.

Room for the Shadow

"That's very important," the King said, turning to the jury.
They were just beginning to write this down on their slates,
when the White Rabbit interrupted: "*Un*important, your Majesty
means of course," he said, in a very respectful tone, but frowning
and making faces at him as he spoke.

"*Un*important, of course, I meant," the King hastily said,
and went on to himself in an undertone, "important — unimportant —
unimportant — important — " as if he were trying which word
sounded best.

Some of the jury wrote down "important," and some
"unimportant." Alice could see this, as she was near enough to look
over their slates; "but it doesn't matter a bit," she thought to herself.
Alice's Adventures in Wonderland, Chapter 12

For Connie Rooke

I WASN'T GOING TO WRITE. For years the temptation kept itself at bay,
invisible. Books had the solid presence of the real world and filled my every
possible need, whether read out loud to me at first, or later read silently on
my own, but always repeating their assurance that what they told me would
not change, unlike the rooms in which I slept and the voices heard outside the
door. We traveled much, my nurse and I, because my father was in the Argentinean diplomatic service, and the various hotel rooms, and even the embassy
house in Tel Aviv, lacked the familiarity of certain pages into which I slipped
night after night.

After I learned to read, this story-land homecoming no longer depended on my nurse's availability, weariness, or mood, but on my own whim alone, and I would return to the books I knew by heart whenever the fancy or the urge took me, following on the page the words recited in my head. In the morning, under one of four palm trees set in a square in the walled embassy garden; during the car drive to the large wild park where wild tortoises crept along the dunes planted with oleander bushes; especially at night, while my nurse, thinking I was asleep, sat at her electric knitting machine and, suffering from mysterious stomach pains that kept her agonizingly awake, worked until well past midnight, I read. To the metronomic rasp of her machine, as she rolled the handle back and forth, in the dim yellow light that she kept on to work by, I would turn to the wall with my open book and follow an Aladdin-like hero called Kleine Muck, the adventurous dog Crusoe, the robber bridegroom who drugged his victims with three-colored wine, the ill-fated Kay and Gerda, and the wicked Snow Queen.

It never occurred to me that I might add something of my own to the books on my shelf. Everything I wanted was already there, at arm's reach, and I knew that if I wished for a new story, the bookshop only a short walk from the house had countless more to add to my stock. To invent a story, impossible as the task then seemed to me, would have felt like trying to create another palm tree for the garden or model another tortoise to struggle across the sand. What hope of success? Above all, what need?

We returned to Buenos Aires when I was seven, to a large, dark, cool house on a cobblestoned street, where I was given my own room perched on the back terrace, separate from the rest of the family. Until then, I had spoken only English and German. I learned to speak Spanish, and, gradually, Spanish books were added to my shelves. And still nothing prompted me to write.

Homework, of course, did not count. "Compositions," as they were called, required one to fill a couple of pages on a given subject, keeping always closer to reportage than to fiction. Imagination was not called for. "Portrait of Someone in Your Family," "What I Did on Sunday," "My Best Friend" elicited a sugary, polite prose, illustrated in colored pencils with an equally cordial depiction of the person or event concerned, the whole to be scrutinized by the teacher for accuracy and spelling mistakes. Only once did I diverge from the imposed subject. The title given to us was "A Sea Battle," the teacher no doubt imagining that his students, all boys, had the same enthusiasm for war games that he had. I had never read the books on airmen and soldiers that several of my schoolmates enjoyed, the "Biggles" series for instance, or the abridged histories of the world wars, full of pictures of airplanes and tanks, printed on spongy, coarse paper. I realized that I completely lacked the requisite vocabulary for the task. I decided therefore to interpret the title differently, and wrote a description of a battle between a shark and a giant squid, no doubt inspired by an illustration from one of my favorite books, *Twenty Thousand Leagues Under the Sea*. I was surprised to discover that my inventiveness, instead of amusing, angered the teacher who told me (quite rightly) that I knew very well that this was not what he had meant. I think that this was my first attempt at writing a story.

Ambition prompted my second attempt. Every year, just before the summer holidays, the school put on a vaguely patriotic play, exemplary and dull. I decided that I could write something at least not worse than these pedagogical dramas, and one evening after dinner, I sat down and composed a play about the childhood of one of our ancient presidents, famous, like Washington, for having never told a lie. The first scene opened with the boy facing the dilemma of denouncing a playmate or lying to his parents; the second portrayed him inventing a story to protect his friend; in the third, my hero suffered the pangs of a tormented conscience; in the fourth, his loyal friend confessed to the awful crime; the fifth showed our hero repenting of his lie, thus adroitly circumventing the real dilemma. The play bore a title that had the virtue of being, if not inspiring, at least clear: *Duty or Truth*. It was accepted and staged, and I experienced for the first time the thrill of having the words I had written read out loud by somebody else.

I was twelve at the time, and the success of the experience prompted me to try and repeat it. I had written *Duty or Truth* in a few hours; in a few more hours I tried to write an imitation of *The Sorcerer's Apprentice* (inspired by Disney's *Fantasia*); a religious drama in which Buddha, Moses, and Christ were the main protagonists; and an adaptation of "Falada, the Talking Horse," taken from the Brothers Grimm. I finished none of them. I realized that if reading is a contented, sensuous occupation whose intensity and rhythm are agreed upon between the reader and the chosen book, writing instead is a strict, plodding, physically demanding task in which the pleasures of inspiration are all well and good, but are only what hunger and taste are to a cook: a starting point and a measuring rod, not the main occupation. Long hours, stiff joints, sore feet, cramped hands, the heat or cold of the workplace, the anguish of missing ingredients and the humiliation owing to the lack of knowhow, onions that make you cry, and sharp knives that slice your fingers are what is in store for anyone who wants to prepare a good meal or write a good book. At twelve I wasn't willing to give over even a couple of evenings to the writing of a piece. What for? I settled comfortably back into my role as reader.

Books continued to seduce me, and I loved anything that had to do with them. During my Buenos Aires adolescence, I was lucky enough to come across a number of well-known writers. First in an English-German bookstore where I worked between school hours, and later at a small publishing company where I apprenticed as an editor, I met Jorge Luis Borges, Adolfo Bioy Casares, Silvina Ocampo, Marta Lynch, Marco Denevi, Eduardo Mallea, José Bianco, and many others. I liked the company of writers and yet I felt very shy among them. I was, of course, almost invisible to them, but from time to time one would notice me and ask: "Do you write?" My answer was always "No." It was not that I didn't wish, occasionally, to be like them and have my name on a book that other people would admire. It was simply that I was aware, very clearly, that nothing that I could produce would ever merit sitting on the same shelf as the books I loved. To imagine a book that I might write rubbing covers with a novel by Joseph Conrad or Franz Kafka was not only unthinkable but incongruous. Even an adolescent, in spite of all his overwhelming arrogance, has a sense of the ridiculous.

But I listened. I heard Bioy discuss the need to plot carefully the successive episodes in a story so as to know exactly where the characters are headed, and then cover the tracks, leaving only a few clues for the readers to think that they are discovering something invisible to the writer. I heard Ocampo explain why the tragedy of small things, of ordinary people, was more moving than that of complex and powerful characters. I heard Lynch speak passionately, enviously, of Chekhov, Denevi of Dino Buzzati, Mallea of Sartre and Dostoyevsky. I heard Borges break down a Kipling story into its many parts and reassemble it, like a clockmaker inspecting a precious ancient instrument. I listened to these writers tell me how the stuff that I read and loved had been made. It was like standing in a workshop and hearing the master craftsmen argue about the strongest materials, the best combinations, the tricks and devices by which something can be made to balance at a difficult angle or keep on ticking indefinitely, or about how something can be built to look impossibly slim and simple and yet hold a myriad complex springs and cogwheels. I listened not in order to learn a new craft but better to know my own.

In 1969, having decided not to follow a university career, I left for Europe and did desultory freelance work for a number of publishers. The pay was abysmal, and I seldom had enough money for more than a few meals a week. One day, I heard that an Argentinean paper was offering a five hundred dollar prize for the best short stories. I decided to apply. I quickly wrote, in Spanish, four stories that were readable, formally correct, but lifeless. I asked Severo Sarduy, whom I had met in Paris and who wrote in a rich, exuberant, baroque Spanish that resonated with literary allusions, to read them over for me. He told me they were awful. "You use words like an accountant," he said. "You don't ask words to perform for you. Here you have a character who falls and loses one of his contact lenses. You say that he lifts himself 'half blind' from the floor. Think harder. The word you want is 'Cyclops.'" I obediently wrote *Cyclops* in the story and sent the lot off. A few months later, I heard that I had won. I felt more embarrassed than proud, but was able to eat properly for a couple of months.

Still I would not write. I scribbled a few essays, a few poems, all forgettable. My heart wasn't in it. Like someone who loves music and tries his hand at the piano, I undertook the experience less out of passion than out of curiosity, to see how it was done. Then I stopped. I worked for publishers, I selected manuscripts and saw them through the press, I imagined titles for other people's books and put together anthologies of different kinds. Everything I did was always in my capacity as reader. "David was talented and knew how to compose psalms. And I? What am I capable of?" asked Rabbi Ouri in the eighteenth century. His answer was: "I can recite them."

I published my first book in 1980. *The Dictionary of Imaginary Places* was the result of a collaboration with Gianni Guadalupi, an inspired editor whom I had met when we were both working for the same Italian publisher. The idea for the book was Gianni's: a serious guide to fictional countries, for which we read more than two thousand books, with an energy that one only possesses when one is young. Writing the *Dictionary* was not what I would today call writing: it was more like glossing the books we read, detailing the geography, customs, history, flora, and fauna of places such as Oz, Ruritania, Christianopolis. Gianni would send me his notes in Italian, I would write my own and translate his into English and then recast the lot into dictionary entries, always sticking to our preestablished Baedeker style. Because we use words for a vast number of things, writing is easily confused with other activities: recounting (as in our *Dictionary*), scribbling, instructing, reporting, informing, chatting, dogmatizing, reviewing, sweet-talking, making pronouncements, advertising, proselytizing, preaching, cataloguing, informing, describing, briefing, taking notes. We perform these tasks with the help of words, but none of these, I am certain, constitutes writing.

Two years later, in 1982, I arrived in Canada. On the strength of the *Dictionary*, I was asked to review books for newspapers, talk about books on the radio, translate books into English, and adapt books into plays. I was perfectly content. Discussing books that had been familiar to my friends when I was young but were new to the Canadian reader, or reading for the first time Canadian classics that mysteriously mirrored others from my past, I found the library that I had begun when I was four or five kept growing nightly, ambitiously, relentlessly. Books had always grown around me. Now, in my house in Toronto, they covered every wall, they crowded every room. They kept growing. I had no intention of adding my own to their proliferation.

Instead, I practiced different forms of reading. The possibilities offered by books are legion. The solitary relationship of a reader with his or her books breaks into dozens of further relationships: with friends upon whom we urge the books we like, with booksellers (the few who have survived in the Age of Supermarkets) who suggest new titles, with strangers for whom we might compile an anthology. As we read and reread over the years, these activities multiply and echo one another. A book we loved in our youth is suddenly recalled by someone to whom it was long ago recommended, the reissue of a book we thought forgotten makes it again new to our eyes, a story read in one context becomes a different story under a different cover. Books enjoy this modest kind of immortality.

Then, by chance, because of an unanswered question, my attitude towards writing changed. (I've told the story in another essay included here, "In Memoriam.") A friend who had gone into exile during the military dictatorship in Argentina revealed to me that one of my high school teachers, someone who had been essential in fostering my love of literature, had willingly denounced his students to the military police, knowing that they would be taken and tortured and sometimes killed. This was the teacher who had spoken to us of Kafka, of Ray Bradbury, of the murder of Polyxena (I can still hear his voice when I read the lines) in the medieval Spanish romance that begins

A la qu'el sol se ponía
en una playa desierta,
yo que salía de Troya

por una sangrienta puerta,

delante los pies de Pirro

vide a Polyxena muerta . . .

After the revelation, I was left with the impossibility of deciding whether to deny the worth of his teaching or close my eyes to the evil of his actions, or (this seemed impossible) to grasp the monstrous combination of both, alive in the same person. To give a shape to my question I wrote a novel, *News from a Foreign Country Came.*

From what I've heard, most writers know from a very early age that they will write. Something of themselves reflected in the outside world, in the way others see them or the way they see themselves lending words to daily objects, tells them they are writers, like something tells their friends that they are veterinarians or pilots. Something convinces them that they are chosen for this particular task and that when they grow up their name will be stamped on the cover of a book, like a pilgrim's badge. I think something told me I was to be a reader. The encounter with my exiled friend happened in 1988; it was therefore not till I turned forty that the notion of becoming a writer appeared to me as firmly possible. Forty is a time of change, of retrieving from ancient cupboards whatever we have left behind, packed away in the dark, and of facing its latent forces.

My intention was clear. That the result wasn't successful doesn't change the nature of my purpose. Now, at last, I wanted to write. I wanted to write a novel. I wanted to write a novel that would put into words—literary words, words like the ones that made up the books on my shelves, incandescent words—what seemed to me impossible to be spoken. I tried. In between my bread-and-butter jobs, early in the morning or late at night, in hotel rooms and in cafés when an assignment forced me to travel, I cobbled together the story of a man of two natures, or of a single divided nature. *Dr. Jekyll and Mr. Hyde,* read during one terrified night when I was thirteen, was never far from my thoughts. I felt desperate for a long chunk of time to work continuously on my novel, so as not to lose the pace, the sequence, the logic, and, above all, the rhythm. I convinced myself that I could recapture the thread after days or weeks of interruption. I pretended that the lack of concentration didn't matter and that I'd be able to pick up where I'd left off, just as I'd pick up a story I was reading at the place where I'd left my bookmark. I was wrong, but lack of uninterrupted time was not the only reason for my failure. The lessons from the masters during my adolescence seemed to be now almost useless. A few scenes worked. The novel didn't.

There was a lack of craft. Readers can tell when a sentence works or doesn't, when it breathes and rises and falls to the beat of its own sense, or when it lies stiff as if embalmed. Readers who turn to writing can recognize this too, but they can never explain it. The most writers can do is learn the rules of grammar and spelling, and the art of reading. Beyond this, whatever excellence they may achieve will be the result of simply doing what they are trying to learn, learning to write by writing, in a beautiful vicious circle that illuminates itself at each new turn. "There are three rules for writing a good book," said Somerset Maugham. "Unfortunately, no one knows what they are."

Experience of life everyone has; the knack for transforming it into *literary* experience is what most of us lack. And even if one were granted that alchemical talent, what experience is a writer allowed to use in trying to tell a story? The death of her mother, like the narrator in Alice Munro's "Material"? His guilty desire, as in Thomas Mann's *Death in Venice*? The blood of a loved one, like the master who sees his disciple beheaded and thinks how beautiful the scarlet color is on the green floor, in Marguerite Yourcenar's "How Wang Fo Was Saved"? Is he entitled to use even the intimate secrets of his family, his friends, of those who trusted in him and might be horrified to find themselves speaking private words in front of a reading public? When the novelist Marian Engel, in the company of other authors, heard of something that appealed to her, however confidential, she would shout out, "Called it!" claiming for her writing the juicy tidbit. Apparently in the realm of writing there are no moral restrictions on hunting and gathering.

I, too, tried to work from experience, seeking moments and events to furnish the thing I was calling up from the shadows. I chose for my main character the face of a man I had once seen in the paper, a gentle, knowledgeable, kindly face which I later discovered belonged to Klaus Barbie. That misleading face suited my character perfectly, as did the name, Berence, a name I borrowed from a strange gentleman I met on the ship from Buenos Aires to Europe, a writer who was in the habit of traveling back and forth across the Atlantic, never spending time in the port of destination, and who one night, when I was suffering from a bad cold and a high fever, told me the story of Lafcadio, who commits the gratuitous act of pushing the unworldly Amédée off a moving train in Gide's *Les Caves du Vatican*. I depicted Algiers according to my memories of Buenos Aires (another pseudo-French city on the sea),

and northern Quebec according to my memories of a visit to Percé. In order
to bring the story to its close, I needed to describe the workings of a torturer,
but not the torture itself. I imagined someone applying the brutal methods not
to a person but to something inert, lifeless. My unattended fridge contained
an old celery stalk. I imagined what it would be like to torture it. The scene,
mysteriously, turned out to be exactly right. But I still had to give words to
the torturer's self-justification. I didn't know how to do it. "You have to bring
yourself to think like him," my friend, the novelist Susan Swan, advised. I
didn't think I was capable. Humiliatingly, I realized that I could think the torturer's thoughts.

But in spite of a few successful moments, the writing hesitated, stumbled,
fell flat. Attempting to say that a man enters a room, or that the light in the
garden has changed, or that the child felt that she was being threatened, or any
simple, precise thing that we communicate (or believe we communicate) every
moment of every day, is, I discovered, one of the most difficult of literary endeavors. We believe the task is easy because our listener, our reader, carries
the epistemological weight and is supposed to intuit our message, to "know
what we mean." But in fact, the signs that stand for the sounds that spark the
thoughts that conjure up the memory that dredges up the experience that calls
upon the emotion crumble under the weight of all they must carry and barely,
hardly ever, serve the purpose for which they were designed. When they do,
the reader knows the writer has succeeded and is grateful for the miracle.

G. K. Chesterton observes in one of his essays that "somewhere embedded
in every ordinary book are the five or six words for which really all the rest
will be written." I think every reader can find them in the books he or she truly
loves; I am not certain that every writer can. As to my novel, I have a vague
notion of what those words might be, and now (so many years after the fact)
I feel that they would have sufficed if they had come to me then, at the beginning of the process.

The book I finished was not what I had imagined, but now I too was a
writer. Now I too was in the hands (in a very literal sense) of readers who had
no proof of my existence except my book, and who judged me, cared for me,
or, more likely, dismissed me without any consideration for anything else I
could offer beyond the strict limits of the page. Who I was, who I had been,
what my opinions were, what my intentions, how deep my knowledge of the
subject, how heartfelt my concern for its central question were to them immaterial excuses. Like a hovering and persistent ghost, the writer wishes to tell

the reader "you might laugh at the absurdity of this passage" or "you might weep over this scene," but then the reader is bound to answer: "If you're so anxious to have a point made, why don't you make one yourself?" Whatever I had not managed to convey in my novel wasn't there, and no self-respecting reader would supply, out of nothing, the laughter and sorrow that I had left out. In this sense I'm always puzzled by the generosity with which certain readers agree to mend the deficiencies of dismal writers. Perhaps a book has to be not just mediocre but outright bad to elicit this Samaritan response.

I don't know what — from the mass of advice given to me by the masters, of the books that set examples, of the exemplary events I witnessed and the cautionary gossip heard throughout my life — was responsible for my few successful pages. The process of learning to write is heartbreaking because it is unaccountable. No amount of hard work, splendid purpose, good council, impeccable research, harrowing experience, knowledge of the classics, ear for music, and taste for style guarantee good writing. "No pen, no ink, no table, no room, no time, no quiet, no inclination," wrote James Joyce to his brother on 7 December 1906. Indeed.

Something, driven by what the ancients called the Muse and we bashfully call inspiration, chooses and combines, snips, stitches, and mends a coat of words to clothe whatever it is that stirs in our depths, ineffable and immaterial, a shadow. Sometimes, for reasons that never become clear, everything fits: the shape is right, the point of view is right, the tone and coloring are right, and, for the space of a line or a paragraph, the shadow can be seen fully fledged in all its awful mystery, not translated into anything else, not in service of an idea or an emotion, not even as part of a story or an essay, but as sheer epiphany: writing that is, as the old metaphor has it, exactly equivalent to the world.

During the first half of the eighteenth century, it was customary in France for theatergoers, if they were rich, to pay for seats not in the orchestra or the boxes but directly onstage, a practice so popular that often this intrusive public outnumbered the cast. During the premiere of Voltaire's *Sémiramis,* there were so many spectators onstage that the actor playing King Ninus's ghost stumbled and nearly fell, thus spoiling a key dramatic scene. Among the ensuing peals of laughter, Voltaire is said to have stood up and cried out, "Place à l'ombre!" "Make room for the shadow!"

The anecdote is useful. Like the stage, the writing life is made up of carefully balanced artifice, exact inspirational lighting, right timing, precise music, and the secret combination of craft and experience. For reasons of chance, money, prestige, friendship, and family duties, the writer allows onto the stage, to sit in on the performance, a crowd of intruders who then become involuntary participants — taking up space, spoiling a good effect, tripping the actors — and who eventually turn into excuses, reasons for failure, honorable distractions, and justifiable temptations. Success in writing (I mean, writing something good) depends on tiny, brittle things, and while it is true that genius can override all obstacles — Kafka wrote masterpieces in a corridor of his father's hostile house and Cervantes dreamt up his *Quixote* in prison — mere talent requires less crowded, less constrained mental settings than those that most writers usually enjoy. The shadow needs room. And even then, nothing is promised.

For the time being, the reader I am judges the writer I managed to become with amused tolerance, as he invents strategies for his new craft. The shadow flitting in the gloom is infinitely powerful and fragile, and immensely alluring and a little frightening, and beckons (I think it beckons) as I cross from one side of the page to the other.

On Being Jewish

"Well, now that we *have* seen each other," said the Unicorn,
"if you'll believe in me, I'll believe in you. Is that a bargain?"
Through the Looking-Glass, Chapter 7

I SELDOM READ BOOKS WITH titles such as *The French Identity, An Essay on Masculinity,* or *What It Means to Be a Woman*. It was therefore with some considerable hesitation that, a few years ago, I picked up a copy of Alain Finkielkraut's cautionary essay *The Imaginary Jew*. Through one of those curious autobiographical associations that a book sometimes conjures up, I suddenly recalled an event I had forgotten from far away and long ago. One afternoon when I was seven, on the bus back from the Buenos Aires English high school that I had started to attend, a boy whose name I never knew called out at me from the back seat, "Hey, Jew! So your father likes money?" I remember being so bewildered by the question that I didn't know what to answer. I didn't think my father was particularly fond of money, but there was an implied insult in the boy's tone that I couldn't understand. Above all, I was surprised at being called "Jew." My grandmother went to the synagogue, but my parents were not religious, and I had never thought of myself in terms of a word I believed was reserved for the old people of my grandmother's generation. But since the epithets applied to us imply a definition, in that moment (though I didn't know it then) I was forced into a choice: to accept this vast, difficult identity or to deny it. Finkielkraut in his book tells of a similar moment and acknowledges the universality of such an experience, but his subject is not the inheritance of hatred. "I myself," writes Finkielkraut, "would like to address and meditate upon the opposite case: the case of a child, an adolescent who is not only proud but happy to be Jewish and who came to question, bit by bit, if there were not some bad faith in living jubilantly as an exception and an exile." These individuals of assumed identity, the inheritors of a suffering to which they have not been personally subjected, Finkielkraut, with a flair for the mot juste, calls "imaginary" or "armchair" Jews.

I am struck by how useful this notion is to address a question that troubles me: How does the perception of who I am affect my perception of the world around me? How important is it for Alice to know who she is (the Victorian child that the world perceives her to be) when wandering through the Looking-Glass Wood? Apparently, very important, since this knowledge determines her relationship to the other creatures she encounters. For instance, having forgotten who she is, Alice can become friends with a fawn who has forgotten it is a fawn. "So they walked on together through the wood, Alice with her arms clasped lovingly round the soft neck of the Fawn, till they came out into another open field, and here the Fawn gave a sudden bound into the air, and shook itself free from Alice's arm. 'I'm a Fawn!' it cried out in a voice of delight. 'And, dear me! you're a human child!' A sudden look of alarm came into its beautiful brown eyes, and in another moment it had darted away at full speed."

Around this notion of constructed identity, Finkielkraut has assiduously elaborated a sequence of questions about what it means to be Jewish (or, I would add, to be Alice or a fawn), and, since every definition is a limitation, he has refused to give these questions definitive answers. Central to Finkielkraut's interrogation is the seemingly trite statement that the Jews *exist*, that whatever their identity may be, individually or as a group, they have a presence that not even the Nazi machinery was able to erase. This existence is not easily borne, let alone categorized. "Listen, Doctor," wrote Heinrich Heine, "don't even talk to me about Judaism, I wouldn't wish it on my worst enemy. Slurs and shame: that's all that comes of it. It's not a religion, it's a misfortune." The cry "Why me?" uttered by every persecuted Jew, the imaginary Jew picks up with a sigh of ennui. Using himself as an example, Finkielkraut confesses that on the one hand he broadcasts his wish to be a Jew while on the other he de-Judaizes himself, transforming himself into the "other" and becoming a messenger of his gentile companions: in this I vividly recognize myself. When his parents refer to the Holocaust, he responds with Vietnam; when they mention antisemitism, he points out that there are no Jewish garbage collectors in France. "Why me?" has become "Why am I not someone else?"

In this Looking-Glass Wood, the imaginary Jew has lost all sense of belonging; for this Jew there is no possible Jewish "we." The conventions of prejudice understand this "we" to mean a secret society of infamous plots and world domination; the imaginary Jew's response has been to deny solidarity, to declare, "There is no 'we,' for Judaism is a private affair" — even though today it once again widely recognizes itself as a community. But why, Finkielkraut asks pointedly, must collective expression "always remain the exclusive province of politics? Why would anything that is not 'I' necessarily be a question of power or of state?" Why can the Jew not be "I" without either going into hiding or making claims to belonging to the slaughtered millions of the past?

These are dangerous waters. Perhaps it is not the necessity to remember the ancestral persecution that is called into question, but the illusion of heroism it so often entails. Those who profess contempt for their fellows living "in the forgetfulness of history," forget in turn that their own precarious identity rests on "the phantasm of history." On the vaporous webbing of such a past, a past that blesses all Jews with a multitudinous family far in time and vast in space, younger Jews sometimes feel they are nothing but spectators. Watching my grandmother light the Shabbat candles, say the ritual prayers as her hands drew opposing circles over the startled light, I felt no connection to the dark, ancient places of wood and winter mist and ancient languages from which she had come. She was my grandmother, but her existence started and ended in my present; she rarely spoke of other ancestors or of the place where she was born, so that in my mythology her brief, piecemeal stories had far less bearing on my life than the landscapes of Grimm and Alice.

If Judaism has a central injunction, Finkielkraut argues, it should be not "a matter of identity, but of memory: not to mimic persecution or make theater of the Holocaust, but to honor its victims," to keep the Holocaust from becoming banal, so that the Jews are not condemned to a double death: by murder and by oblivion. Even here, my connection to those horrors was vicarious: to my knowledge, we lost no immediate family to the Nazis; both my mother's and my father's parents had immigrated long before World War I to one of the colonies set up by Baron Hirsch for Jewish exiles in the north of Argentina, where gauchos with names like Izaak and Abraham called out to their cattle in Yiddish. I did not learn about the Holocaust until well into my adolescence, and then only by reading André Schwarz-Bart and Anne Frank. Was this horror then part of my history too, mine beyond the call of a shared humanity? Did the epithet hurled at me insultingly on that remote school bus grant me citizenship in that ancient, beleaguered, questioning, stubborn, wise people? Was I — am I — part of Them? Am I a Jew? Who am I?

Alice, a human child, and the fawn, cne of the hunted, echo this last question, and like me are tempted to answer it not with words born from what they know themselves to be but with words coined by those who stand outside and point. Every group that is the object of prejudice has this to say: we are the language in which we are spoken, we are the images in which we are recognized, we are the history we are condemned to remember because we have been barred from an active role in the present. But we are also the language in which we question these assumptions, the images with which we invalidate the stereotypes. And we are also the time in which we are living, a time from which we cannot be absent. We have an existence of our own, and we are no longer willing to remain imaginary.

Meanwhile, in Another Part of the Forest

"The Seventh Square is all forest—however, one of the Knights will show you the way."
Through the Looking-Glass, Chapter 2

IN THE DAYS WHEN I WAS an avid reader of comic books, the line that thrilled me most, because it promised to reveal something that had been taking place beyond the more obvious bits of the plot, was "Meanwhile, in another part of the forest . . ."—usually inked in capital letters in the top left-hand corner of the box. To me (who like any devoted reader wished for an infinite story) this line promised something close to that infinity: the possibility of knowing what had happened on that other fork of the road, the one not taken, the one less in evidence, the mysterious and equally important path that led to another part of the adventurous forest.

MAPPING THE FOREST

Damn braces. Bless relaxes.
William Blake

In the middle of the third century B.C., the Cyrene poet Callimachus under-took the task of cataloguing the half-million volumes housed in the famous Library of Alexandria. The task was prodigious, not only because of the number of books to be inspected, dusted, and shelved, but because it entailed the conception of a literary order that was supposed somehow to reflect the vaster order of the universe. In attributing a certain book to a certain shelf—Homer to "Poetry" or Herodotus to "History," for example—Callimachus had first to determine that all writing could be divided into a specific number of categories, or, as he called them, *pinakes*, "tables"; and then he had to decide to which category each of the thousands of unlabeled books belonged. Callimachus divided the colossal library into eight tables, which were to contain every possible fact, conjecture, thought, imagination ever scrawled on a sheet of papyrus; future librarians would multiply this modest number to infinity. Jorge Luis Borges recalled that in the numeric system of the Institut Bibliographique in Brussels, number 231 corresponded to God.

No reader who has ever derived pleasure from a book has much confidence in these cataloguing methods. Subject indexes, literary genres, schools of thought and style, literatures classified by nationality or race, chronological compendiums, and thematic anthologies suggest to the reader merely one of a multitude of points of view, none comprehensive, none even grazing the breadth and depth of a mysterious piece of writing. Books refuse to sit quietly on shelves: *Gulliver's Travels* jumps from "Chronicles" to "Social Satire" to "Children's Literature" and will not be faithful to any of these labels. Our reading, much like our sexuality, is multifaceted and fluid. "I am large," wrote Walt Whitman, "I contain multitudes."

The notion of "gay literature" is guilty on three counts: first, because it implies a narrow literary category based on the sexuality of either its authors or its characters; second, because it implies a narrow sexual category that has somehow found its definition in a literary form; third, because it implies a narrow political category that defends a restricted set of human rights for a specific sexual group. And yet the notion of "gay literature," albeit recent, doubtless exists in the public mind. Certain bookstores have "gay literature" shelves, certain publishers publish "gay literature" series, and there are magazines and papers that regularly bring out stories and poems under the rubric of "gay literature."

What then is this "gay literature"?

At the risk of committing a tautology, what is in general understood by "gay literature" is literature concerned with gay subjects. This can swing from obscure hints about "the love that dare not speak its name," in Lord Alfred Douglas's self-silencing phrase, apparent in some nineteenth-century writing, to explicit chronicles of gay life in our time by authors who may or may not be gay. Sometimes books dealing with nongay subjects by gay writers (E. M. Forster's *A Passage to India*, Edward Albee's *Who's Afraid of Virginia Woolf?* for instance) are put on the same "gay literature" shelf as books with an explicitly gay content—Marguerite Yourcenar's *Alexis* or Manuel Puig's *Kiss of the Spider Woman*—as if the critic, editor, or bookseller were deliberately attempting to catalogue the person, not the person's work. Certain writers refuse to have their work labeled "gay" (Patrick Gale, Timothy Findley) and refer to it as "books by a writer who happens to be gay." As usual with this kind of labeling, the exceptions to any proposed definition make the process finally useless, so that every time the label is applied it must be redefined.

Claude J. Summers, in his collection of essays *Gay Fictions*, defines his subject as "the fictional representation of male homosexuals by gay male and lesbian writers." This leaves out a fair number of works by nongay writers, which are thus excluded simply by reason of their authors' sexuality. A writer's sexual preferences probably color the text, but a reader does not require careful study of the *National Enquirer* to be able to read literature. Being told that D. H. Lawrence was attracted to older women may or may not inform the enjoyment of *Lady Chatterley's Lover*, but it is in no way essential for reading that too-famous novel. A study of Melville's life might shed light on homoerotic elements in *Moby-Dick*, but is such a study essential in order to discover those same elements? And is a short story by William Faulkner on a gay subject readable only if we have proof of his experience in this field? Doesn't the word *fiction* imply the creation of an imagined rather than a physically experienced world? And if knowledge of the author's inclinations is essential to the understanding of a text, wouldn't reading anonymous literature (and so much erotic literature is anonymous) be ultimately impossible?

PATHS THROUGH THE FOREST

The fairy way of writing which depends only upon the force of imagination.
John Dryden, *King Arthur*

Every genre creates its own prehistory. Edgar Allan Poe invented the detective story, and in doing so allowed us to include in the definition tales as old as the Bible. The label "gay literature" is a recent creation, probably no older than the founding of the gay magazine *Christopher Street* in 1975, but it now includes much earlier work. An anthology of English-language gay poetry would feature many names from the traditional canon, from Shakespeare to Lord Byron; examples of English-language gay fiction are not as venerably old, perhaps because poetry lends itself more readily to an ambiguous reading and (as is the case in many spurious explanations of Shakespeare's homoerotic sonnets) to a bigoted interpretation, while prose can be less easily subverted for the sake of social decorum. Thomas Hardy suggested that a writer could "get away with things in verse that would have a hundred Mrs. Grundys on your back if said in prose."

A chronological list of gay fiction in English might begin with obscure novels such as Bayard Taylor's *Joseph and His Friend* (1871) or Theodore Winthrop's *Cecil Dreme* (1876), or with better-known works such as Oscar Wilde's "The Portrait of Mr. W.H." (a short story written circa 1890); it might continue with Henry James's almost too subtle depiction of a gay infatuation, "The Pupil" (1891), E. M. Forster's posthumously published *Maurice* (finished in 1914), D. H. Lawrence's "The Prussian Officer" (also 1914), and Ronald Firbank's *Concerning the Eccentricities of Cardinal Pirelli* (1926), up to Gore Vidal's *The City and the Pillar*, one of the earliest mainstream fictional accounts of gay life, published in 1948 — the year that also saw the publication of two other gay classics: Truman Capote's *Other Voices, Other Rooms* and Tennessee Williams's collection *One Arm and Other Stories*. Similar lists could be made in the literature of other languages.

By 1950, two main trends in English-language gay literature had been established: one apologetically addressing a "straight" audience, trying to justify and atone for the fact of being gay; the other unabashedly celebrating another, equally vital sexuality and speaking mainly to an enlightened reader. *The City and the Pillar*, which follows both trends to some degree, is the first novel to make use of an important device (suggested perhaps by André Gide's *Si le grain ne meurt* of 1926) evident in almost all the gay fiction that follows it: the autobiographical voice. Edmund White, himself the author of one of the most influential gay autobiographical fictions in North America, *A Boy's Own Story* (1982), has remarked that "since no one is brought up to be gay, the moment [a boy] recognizes the difference he must account for it." Nongays learn about their sexual mores (mostly from conservative, sexist sources) in hundreds of different places: home, school, workplace, television, film, print. Gays are, by and large, deprived of any such geography. They grow up feeling invisible and must go through the apprenticeship of adolescence almost invariably alone. Gay fiction — especially autobiographical gay fiction — therefore serves as a guide that both reflects and allows comparison with the reader's own experience.

Much of this factual prose is illuminating and encouraging (something much needed in the age of AIDS) and allows the reader to admit the fact of being gay as part of everyday life. Camille Paglia has commented that most gays, unlike other minority groups, do not reproduce themselves, and therefore, like artists everywhere, "their only continuity is through culture, which they have been instrumental in building." Authors such as Christopher Isherwood (*A Single Man*), David Leavitt (*The Lost Language of Cranes*), and Armistead Maupin (in his soap-opera saga *Tales of the City*) make this "continuity through culture" explicit: they place their gay characters in the midst of a multifaceted society, so that their reality is not "other" but "another," part of a historical cultural whole, with no reigning central entity determining what is normal according to his own image.

Because of the instructional use to which gay literature can be put, gay stories that bow to prejudice, implicitly accepting the patriarchal verdict about the wages of sin, commit literary terrorism and deserve to be housed on the same shelf as moralistic Victorian fables. A number of good writers fall into this category: Dennis Cooper, for instance, whose fiction depicts necro-homoerotic longings and explores the aesthetics of sickness and decay, with death as the inevitable end; and at times the timorous Gide, who believed that homosexuality was "an error of biology," and whose heroes are so terribly ridden by Catholic angst.

Because it needs to instruct, because it needs to bear witness, because it needs to affirm the right to exist of a group that the power-holding majority of society wishes to ignore or eliminate, most gay literature has been staunchly realistic. Lagging behind the rights demanded and partly achieved by other oppressed groups, gay men are depicted in a literature that is still largely at an informative or documentary stage. Women's literature can produce fantasies, such as Margaret Atwood's *The Handmaid's Tale* or Jeanette Winterson's *The Passion*, black literature can invent ghost stories, such as Toni Morrison's *Beloved;* with one or two superb exceptions (Wilde's *The Picture of Dorian Gray* and Genet's *Our Lady of the Flowers* come immediately to mind) gay literature has no fantastic stories, no imaginary worlds. Instead, its strength lies in the subversive possibilities of its language.

Appropriating everyday language, undermining the bureaucratic use of common words, using the guerrilla tactics of the surrealists to fill the commonplace with a sense of danger — these are the things gay literature, like any literature of the oppressed, can do best. Jean Genet, the French poet, playwright, and novelist who died in 1985, created, better than any other gay writer in any language, a literary voice to explore the gay experience. Genet understood that no concession should be made to the oppressor. In a hypocritical society that condemns gay sexuality but condones the exploitation of women, arrests pickpockets but rewards robber barons, hangs murderers but decorates torturers, Genet became a male prostitute and a thief, and then proceeded to describe the outcast's vision of our world as a sensual hallucination. This vision was so unsettling that when Jean Cocteau showed Paul Valéry the manuscript of Genet's *Our Lady of the Flowers*, Valéry's response was "Burn it." In English, Oscar Wilde, Joe Orton, William Burroughs—all forced or voluntary outsiders of society—set social language against its overlords.

Perhaps the literature of all segregated groups goes through similar stages: apologetic, self-descriptive, and instructive; political and testimonial; iconoclastic and outrageous. If that is the case, then the next stage, which I think can be recognized in certain novels by Alan Gurganus or Alan Hollinghurst, introduces characters who *happen to be gay* but whose circumstances are defined well beyond their sexuality, which is once again seen as part of a complex and omnivorous world.

MARKING THE TREES

Years hence, perhaps, may dawn an age,
More fortunate, alas! than we,
Which without hardness will be sage,
And gay without frivolity.
Matthew Arnold, "Stanzas from the Grande Chartreuse"

Naked except for a fur-trimmed gauze negligee and waddling about in bare feet, Cary Grant announced to an enquiring May Robson that he was thus attired because he had gone "gay." With this pronouncement in the 1938 film *Bringing Up Baby* the word *gay*, meaning "male homosexual," publicly entered the English language of North America.

It was not an auspicious beginning. Grant's usage reflected a stereotype: that being gay somehow involves dressing up in women's clothing, wishing to be the other sex, and consequently becoming an involuntary parody of a woman. Certainly some gay men dress up in drag, but all transvestites are not homosexual, and all homosexuals are certainly not transvestites. Society, for the majority of Grant's audience, appeared to be an immutable reality in which men and women fulfilled certain specific roles, dressed in specific ways, and reacted in a specific manner, and the questioning of the necessity of these roles and styles was seen as deviant—and therefore wrong. Today, some of these perceptions have changed, but the changes have been mostly superficial. Beneath the apparently tolerant manners of Grant's new audiences, the same traditional standards continue to rule and the same old discomfort continues to be felt.

The historical origins of this meaning of the word *gay* are somewhat dubious. *Gai savoir* meant "poetry" in thirteenth-century Provençal, and as some troubadour poems were explicitly homosexual, it is possible that the word came to designate this particular aspect of their repertoire. Other inquisitive etymologists have traced its origins to Old English, where one of the meanings of the word *gal* was "lustful," as in modern German *geil*. Whatever the sources, by the early twentieth century *gay* was commonly used in English homosexual subculture as a password or code, and quickly *gay* or *gai* became the usual term for "male homosexual" in French, Dutch, Danish, Japanese, Swedish, and Catalan.

Gay is usually reserved for male homosexuality. Female homosexuality—lesbianism, to use the term still ignored in the 1971 edition of the *Oxford English Dictionary*—has a vocabulary and career of its own. In spite of the prejudice that views all unconventional sexualities as part of the same herd of sinners, and in spite of the common political force that results from being the object of such a prejudice, male and female homosexualities differ in their public image, their vocabularies, and their histories. Lesbianism, for instance, is empowered by its association with feminism—gay males have no such support from any equivalent male group—and lesbian acts are ignored in certain heterosexual codes of law; Britain's notorious anti-homosexual laws of the past century were designed exclusively for males, as Queen Victoria (tradition has it) refused to believe "that women did such things." In most countries, female couples are considered "respectable" while male couples are unthinkable except as an abomination, perhaps because in the heterosexual male imagination that dominates most societies, two women living together do so only because they haven't been able to acquire a man and are either to be pitied for this shortcoming or praised for undertaking on their own tasks that are normally a man's responsibility. Similarly, lesbian images are accepted—in fact, encouraged—in heterosexual male pornography, the fantasy being that these women are making love among themselves in expectation of the male to come. The heterosexual male code of honor is thereby preserved.

A person not complying with these preset codes seemingly threatens the received identity of the individuals who uphold them in their society. In order to dismiss the transgressor with greater ease, it is best to caricature him (as the success of such pap as *La Cage aux Folles* seems to prove), thereby creating the myth of the Good Homosexual. The Good Homosexual, as in Harvey Fierstein's *Torchsong Trilogy*, is the man who deep down inside wants to be like his mother — have a husband, have a child, putter around the house — and is prevented from doing these things by a quirk of nature. Underlying the myth of the Good Homosexual is the conviction (upheld by the American Psychological Association until 1973) that a homosexual is a heterosexual gone wrong: that with an extra gene or so, a little more testosterone, a dash of tea and sympathy, the homosexual will be cured, become "normal." And if this cannot be achieved (because in some cases the malady is too far advanced), then the best thing for the creature to do is assume the other, lesser role designed by society in its binary plan, that of an ersatz woman. I remember a psychological test set for my all-boys class by a school counselor concerned with "particular friendships." A previous class had warned us that if we drew a female figure, the counselor would assume that our fantasy was to be a woman; if we drew a male figure, that we were attracted to a man. In either case we would be lectured on the terrors of deviancy. Deviants, the counselor had told the other class, always ended up murdered by sailors on the dockside. When my turn came, I drew the figure of a monkey.

The Forest in History

And warming his hands to the fire exclaimed, "Now where would we be without fagots?"
Sir Walter Scott, *Kenilworth*

Homosexuality is not always socially condemned. In other societies human sexuality was known to cover a larger spectrum. In ancient Greece and Rome, no moral distinction was made between homosexual and heterosexual love; in Japan, gay relationships were formally accepted among the samurai; in China, the emperor himself was known to have male lovers. Among the native people of Guatemala, gays are not seen as outsiders: "Our people," said the native leader Rigoberta Menchú, "don't differentiate between people who are homosexual and people who aren't; that only happens when we go out of our society. What's good about our way of life is that everything is considered a part of nature."

In European society, hostility against gays did not become widespread until the mid-twelfth century. "The causes of this change," wrote the Yale historian James Boswell, "cannot be adequately explained, but they were probably closely related to the increase in intolerance of minority groups apparent in ecclesiastical and secular institutions throughout the thirteenth and fourteenth centuries." And yet in spite of this hostility, until the nineteenth century the homosexual was not perceived as someone distinct, someone with a personality different from that of the heterosexual, someone who could be persecuted not only for a specific act *contra naturam* but merely for existing. Until then, noted Michel Foucault in his *History of Sexuality*, "the sodomite had been a temporary aberration; the homosexual was now a species."

With the invention of the species "homosexual," intolerance created its quarry. Once a prejudice is set up, it traps within its boundaries a heterogeneous group of individuals whose single common denominator is determined by the prejudice itself. The color of one's skin, one's varying degrees of alliance to a certain faith, a certain aspect of one's sexual preferences can and do become the obverse of an object of desire — an object of hatred. No logic governs these choices: prejudice can couple an Indonesian lawyer and a Rastafarian poet as "colored people" and exclude a Japanese businessman as an "honorary white"; revile an Ethiopian Jew and an American Hassid, yet pay homage to Solomon and David as pillars of the Christian tradition; condemn a gay adolescent and poor Oscar Wilde, but applaud Elton John and ignore the homosexuality of Leonardo da Vinci and Alexander the Great.

The group created by prejudice comes into existence not by the choice of the individuals forming it but by the reaction of those outside it. The infinitely varying shapes and shades of sexual desire are not the pivot of everyone's life, yet gay men find themselves defined through that single characteristic — their physical attraction to others of the same sex — notwithstanding that those who attract them run the gamut of the human male: tall, short, thin, fat, serious, silly, rough, dainty, intelligent, slow-witted, bearded, hairless, right wing, left wing, young, old, with nothing in common except a penis. Once limited and defined by this grouping, the quarry can be taunted, excluded from certain areas of society, deprived of certain rights, sometimes arrested, beaten, killed. In England the promotion of homosexuality was illegal until recently; in Argentina, gays are routinely blackmailed; in the United States and Canada their inclusion in the armed forces is contested; in Cuba they are imprisoned; in Saudi Arabia and Iran they are put to death. In Germany many homosexuals who were victimized by the Nazis are still denied restitution, on the grounds that they were persecuted for their criminal, not political, activities.

A group, a category, a name may be formed and transformed throughout history, but direct experience of this is not necessary for a writer to express that experience in artistic terms — to compose a poem, to write a novel. Many stories touching on a gay theme stem from writers forced to exist within the gay ghetto. But many others have been written by men and women who have not been condemned to such enclosures. As works of fiction, they are thankfully indistinguishable from one another.

VARIATIONS IN THE LANDSCAPE

Variety is the soul of pleasure.
Aphra Behn, *The Rover*, Part 2

The fourth book of the *Odyssey* tells of Proteus, king of Egypt, known as "the Ancient One of the Sea," who was able to tell the future and to change shape at will. According to one version of the story, he was the first man, imagined by the gods as a creature of endless possibilities. Like the apparent shapes of that ancient king, our desire need not be limited. Heterosexuality and homosexuality were no doubt two of those protean forms, but they are neither exclusive nor impermeable. Like our literary tastes, our sexual affinities need only declare allegiance and define themselves under duress. In the moment of pleasure, we are as indefinable as the moment itself. Perhaps that generous sense of pleasure will ultimately prevail.

Our social organizations, however, still demand labels, require catalogues, and these unavoidably become hierarchies and class systems in which some assume power and others are excluded. Every library has its shadow: the endless shelves of books unchosen, unread, rejected, forgotten, forbidden. And yet the exclusion *of any* subject from literature, whether by design of the reader or of the writer, is an inadmissible form of censorship that degrades everyone's humanity. The groups ostracized by prejudice may be, and usually are, cut off, but not forever. Injustice, as we should have learned by now, has a curious effect on people's voices. It lends them potency and clarity and resourcefulness and originality, which are all good things to have if one is to create a literature.

The Further off from England

"What matters it how far we go?" his scaly friend replied.

"There is another shore, you know, upon the other side.

The further off from England the nearer is to France —

Then turn not pale, beloved snail, but come and join the dance."

Alice's Adventures in Wonderland, Chapter 10

BETWEEN THE END OF HIGH school in Buenos Aires and the beginnings of a full-time publishing career in Europe, I spent a splendid decade in Paris and London reading in an almost perfectly haphazard way, dipping into books that were too expensive for me to buy, skimming over others that incautious friends had lent me, borrowing a few from public libraries for company rather than for instruction's sake, and hardly ever finishing anything. No method, erudite order, sense of duty, or rigorous curiosity ruled my reading. In body as in mind, I drifted.

The year of the Beatles' last LP I left Paris, where I had been living happily for a year or so, and settled for a few months in London, sharing a house with three other guys and paying five pounds a week. My Argentinean passport made it impossible for me to get a work permit in Europe, so I made a living selling painted leather belts, which I hawked on Carnaby Street and later in a store called Mr. Fish. My hour of glory came when Mick Jagger Himself bought one of my belts and wore it onstage during a concert. Life was never that magnanimous again.

But we trifle with Fortune. On the spur of the moment, I accompanied a friend back to Paris and spent a few days nursing a coffee at the Café de Flore and wondering why I had ever left this most rousing of cities; then, having visions of irate clients storming beltless up and down Piccadilly, I decided it was time to get back to London. This was in the prehistoric days before the

Eurostar, and the train fare was fairly inexpensive. I bought my ticket and set off for Calais in the late afternoon.

The caramel-colored coach of the express Garde-du-Nord–Calais, with cracked leatherette seats and curiously encrusted window frames, was not the most welcoming of places. I tried to read but felt distracted, uneasy. As we left the gray neighborhoods and started crossing the ugly districts of the northern *banlieues,* the entire coach seemed to be momentarily possessed by a mood of collective melancholy: the woman in the corner seat stopped humming, the baby stifled its crying, the rowdy group of adolescents talked no more, and in eerie silence we entered the flat countryside of Normandy under cover of darkness. We sped through Arras, a town I never visited, and which in my imagination carried the copyright of Saint-Exupéry. Then the air became musty and salty, and the signs along the platform announced that we had reached Calais.

Crossing what the British like to call the English Channel is, as everyone knows, a sickening experience, unrelieved by the sight of the white cliffs of Dover, which, in the pale moonlight, greet the nauseated traveler like huge piles of slightly off cottage cheese. I walked unsteadily up the gangplank and waited in line for passport control.

French ticket controllers are strict but just. One imagines them writing sonnets in the evening and tending to their fruit trees on weekends, rigorous in the application of both rhyme and aphid poison. Immigration officials are different. Whether French or British (especially in those days before the now quasi-borderless European Community), these clerks are ruled not by the Spirit of Justice but by the Phantom of Power, and they delight, like butchers, in holding in their cold hands your identity papers as if it were your liver or your shank. The officer behind the passport desk looked very much like Peter O'Toole in *Lawrence of Arabia.* He cast pale blue eyes on my passport, raised them to look at me, looked back at the passport, and once again at me. What he saw seemed to make him immensely sad.

I was dressed in the style appropriate to Carnaby Street at the time, in clothing found at the Marché aux Puces of Clignancourt. My sandals and flowing white cotton shirt were Indian, my cerise-colored trousers had bell bottoms, I was wearing a belt of my own design on which I had painted *Leda and the Swan* in the exact style (if I say it myself) of Poussin. My hair curled coquettishly over my shoulders.

"What is the purpose of your visit?" asked Peter in a low, pained voice.

Suddenly I realized that, just as if I'd been confronted by his namesake in Heaven above, I had to give Peter a good reason to let me into his kingdom. My brain made a quick deduction. This man was a bureaucrat. Bureaucrats are impressed by officialdom. My father had been, fifteen years earlier, the Argentinean ambassador. There are few people more official than ambassadors. In my best pseudo-Argentinean accent, I told him that I had come to meet my father, the ex-Argentinean ambassador.

Peter's eyebrows arched ever so slightly.

"And where are you to meet the . . . ehm . . . ambassador?"

Again, my brain desperately scrambled for an answer. Once I had stayed at a Salvation Army hostel in London, just across from (what seemed to me at the time) a very chic hotel. I remembered the name.

"Hotel St James,'" I said.

(Years later I found out that the St James is what the French call a *hôtel de passe*, lodging an inordinate number of Mr. and Mrs. Smiths.)

"Have you got a reservation at the . . . ehm . . . St James?" asked Peter.

"I think . . . father made reservation."

"Let us phone then, shall we?" said Peter.

By now the other passengers had drifted past and were boarding the ferry. I had no idea how I'd get across the Channel and on to London. I had ten francs and two pounds in my pocket. Hitchhiking in England didn't have a good reputation.

Peter put the phone down.

"At the St James they have no reservation for . . . ehm . . . Ambassador Manguel."

Another officer joined us. The hint of a smile appeared on Peter's face, dispelling some of the sadness.

"This gentleman says his father is an Argentinean ambassador and that he is to meet him in London, at the St James."

"At the St James?"

The other officer's eyes rolled up and down.

"I see."

"But they have no reservation under the name of Manguel. Perhaps we should call the Argentinean embassy."

I argued that there would be no one at this hour. It was shortly before midnight.

"We'll try, shall we?" said the other officer.

He tried and someone answered who obviously only spoke Spanish. The other officer handed me the phone.

"Ask him whether he knows your father and will vouch for you."

I asked, in Spanish, whom was I speaking to.

"This is José," said the voice.

"José," I said. "Whoever you are, will you please tell the officer that you know my father, ex-ambassador Manguel?"

"Sure," said José.

I silently blessed the Argentinean sense of camaraderie and passed the phone back to the other officer.

"He'll tell you," I said.

The other officer listened to Jose's declaration in Spanish.

"I don't understand what you're saying. Can you try repeating it in English? Aha. Yes. And what is your position at the embassy, sir? I see. Thank you."

He put down the phone.

"I'm afraid that the janitor's vouching for you isn't sufficient," he said.

In the meantime, Peter was going through my rucksack with keen interest. He opened my tube of toothpaste, squeezed some out, and tasted it. He flicked through my copy of *Siddhartha*. He sniffed at my joss sticks. Finally he found my address book. He disappeared with it inside the office. When he reemerged, he had a smile on his face, like that of Lawrence after the capture of Khartoum.

"It seems that you failed to tell us you were sharing a house in London. One of your friends there told me that you work selling knickknacks on Carnaby Street. I assume you haven't got a work permit? Now why would the ambassador's son do that?"

I was taken to a small white room with a cot and told that I'd have to wait there until the first train back to Paris. All night long I thought about what I was about to lose: my room, the books I had collected, my artistic career, which had received the blessing of Mick Jagger. Ever since I had started to read, London had been in my mind a sort of Garden of Eden. The stories I liked best took place there; Chesterton and Dickens had made it familiar to me; it was what to others are the North Pole or Samarkand. And now, because of two pesky, prissy officials, it had become just as remote and unattainable. Bureaucracy, unfair immigration laws, power given to blue-eyed employees who are allowed to squeeze other people's toothpaste seemed to me then (and now) despicable abominations. France, on the other hand, was the land of Freedom, Fraternity, Equality, though perhaps not in that order. I thought fondly of Robespierre.

And that is how, in November 1970, I became a moderate anarchist.

Homage to Proteus

"Who in the world am I? Ah, *that's* the great puzzle!"

Alice's Adventures in Wonderland, Chapter 2

MY LIBRARY TELLS ME THAT the problem is an ancient one.

Legend has it that Proteus was not only king of Egypt but also a sea god, shepherd of the water flocks, capable of seeing the future and of constantly changing his appearance. Dante imagined this versatility as a punishment: in the eighth circle of his Hell, he dreamt that thieves and robbers, who during their mortal life lay hands on what doesn't belong to them, are condemned after death to not even being able to possess the shape of their earthly bodies and endlessly turn into something else, "never again being that which they once were."

All of us must one day be confronted with the terrible question that the Caterpillar asks Alice in Wonderland: "Who are *you?*" Indeed: Who are we? The answers that we try to give throughout our unfolding lives are never utterly convincing. We are the face in the mirror, the name and nationality given to us, the sex that our cultures steadfastly define, the reflection in the eye of those we look at, the fantasy of the one who loves us and the nightmare of the one who hates us, the incipient body in the cradle and the motionless body in the winding sheet. We are all these things, and also their contrary, our self in the shadows. We are the secret traits missing in our supposed faithful likeness, in the description of us meant to be exact. We are someone about to come into being, and also someone who has been, long ago. Our identity, and the time and place in which we exist, are fluid and transient, like water.

There is another scene in *Alice's Adventures in Wonderland* that perfectly illustrates the heroine's many identities, but also those of her readers, and it take place in one of the first chapters of the book. After falling down the rabbit hole, Alice feels she's no longer herself, and wonders who it is that has taken her place. Instead of despairing, she decides to wait until someone looks down to call her, saying: "Come up again, dear!" And then she'll ask: "Who am I, then? Tell me that first, and then, if I like being that person, I'll come up: if not, I'll stay down here till I'm somebody else."

The many faces (all our own) that await our inquisitorial eye in dreams and in books and in everyday life end up, alas, becoming real. At first their appearances may amuse us or befuddle us; after a time they cling like masks of flesh to our skin and bones. Proteus could change his shape but only until someone grabbed him and held him secure: then the god would allow himself to be seen as he really was, as a blending of all his metamorphoses. So it is with our myriad identities. They change and dissolve in our eye and the eyes of others, until the moment when we are suddenly able to pronounce the word *I*. Then they cease to be illusions, hallucinations, guesswork and become, with astonishing conviction, an epiphany.

PART TWO

The Lesson of the Master

"Come back!" the Caterpillar called after her.

"I've something important to say!"

Alice's Adventures in Wonderland, Chapter 5

Borges in Love

"'Tis so," said the Duchess: "and the moral of that is—
'Oh, 'tis love, 'tis love, that makes the world go round!'"

"Somebody said," Alice whispered, "that it's done by
everybody minding their own business!"

"Ah, well! It means much the same thing," said the
Duchess.

Alice's Adventures in Wonderland, Chapter 9

ONE AFTERNOON IN 1966, in Buenos Aires, I was asked to dinner at the flat
of the writer Estela Canto. A woman of about fifty, a little deaf, with wonderful, artificially red hair and large, intensely myopic eyes (she coquettishly refused to wear glasses in public), she stumbled through the small, grimy kitchen
putting together a meal of tinned peas and sausages, shouting bits of Keats and
Dante Gabriel Rossetti. To her, Borges had dedicated one of his finest short
stories, "The Aleph," and she would let no one forget it. Borges, however, did
not reciprocate the memory. At least when I mentioned her name and told him
I would be seeing her, he said nothing: someone told me later that for Borges,
silence was a form of courtesy.

By the time I met Canto, her books were no longer considered part of
the Argentinean literary scene. In the wake of the so-called Latin American
boom that had launched Manuel Puig's generation, editors no longer wanted
to publish her, and her novels now sold at remainder prices in stores as dusty
as her kitchen. Long ago, in the forties, she had written essays in the style of
William Hazlitt (whom she admired) for several of the literary periodicals of
the time, from the *Anales de Buenos Aires,* which Borges edited for a while, to
Sur. Her realistic stories, which echoed (she thought) Leonid Andreyev's, had
been published in the literary supplements of the newspapers *La Nación* and

La Prensa, and her novels, which hesitated between psychology and symbolism, had been well reviewed, if not read, by the Buenos Aires intelligentsia. According to Canto, her downfall was caused by her being too clever. With her brother Patricio Canto, an excellent translator who discreetly encouraged rumors of sibling incest, she devised a plan to win a literary contest juried by Borges, the novelist Eduardo Mallea, and the short-story writer and critic Carmen Gándara. The two Cantos would write a novel with something to please everyone: a quotation from Dante for Borges, a philosophical discussion on art, literature, and morals for Mallea, a line by Gándara for Gándara. They hid behind the name of a literary woman in whose loyalty they believed and submitted the manuscript under the title *Luz era su nombre* (Light Was Her Name), which was unanimously awarded the first prize. Unfortunately, artistic friendships being what they are, the literary woman betrayed them, the plot was revealed, and the conspiring siblings were ostracized from every literary salon in Buenos Aires. Partly out of spite and partly out of a misguided fondness for Russian literature, the Cantos joined the Argentinean Communist Party (which, Ernesto Sábato once said, was indistinguishable from the Conservative Party because most of its senile members attended its meetings asleep). Communism, to Borges, who in his regretted youth had written a book of poems in praise of the Bolshevik Revolution, was anathema.

During the dinner, Canto asked me if I would like to see the manuscript of "The Aleph" (which twenty years later she would sell at Sotheby's for more than twenty-seven thousand dollars). I said I would. From a grease-aureoled brown folder she pulled out seventeen pages meticulously composed "in the handwriting of a dwarf" (as Borges once described his minuscule, unattached letters), with a few minor corrections and alternative versions. She pointed to the dedication inscribed on the last page. Then she reached over the table, took my hand (I was eighteen and terrified), and put it to her cheek. "Feel these bones," she ordered. "You can tell I was beautiful then."

"Then" was 1944, the year Canto met Borges at the house of Adolfo Bioy Casares and his wife, Silvina Ocampo. Ocampo, a fine poet and better short-story writer, was the sister of Victoria Ocampo, the rich and aristocratic founder of the magazine *Sur.* Bioy, eight years younger than Silvina, was the heir to one of the largest dairy empires in Argentina. His mother's name, Marta, became the dairy trademark *La Martona;* Borges and Bioy's first collaboration had been a series of ads for *La Martona* yogurt.

Estela Canto's first encounter with Borges was, from her point of view, far from a *coup de foudre*. "And yet," she added with a nostalgic smile, "neither was Beatrice much impressed with Dante."

As if to justify her reaction, Canto's description of the forty-five-year-old Borges (later published in her memoir, *Borges a contraluz*) was deliberately unappealing. "He was plump, rather tall and straight-backed, with a pale and fleshy face, remarkably small feet and a hand that, when clasped, seemed boneless, limp, as if uncomfortable when having to bear the inevitable touch. The voice was shaky, it seemed to grope for words and seek permission." I once had occasion to hear Borges use the shakiness of his voice to great effect, when a journalist asked him what he admired most in General San Martín, Argentina's national hero, who had fought against the Spanish in the wars of independence. Borges answered, very slowly, "His bronze busts . . . that decorate . . . public offices . . . and school . . . playgrounds; his name . . . repeated . . . endlessly . . . in military . . . marches; his face . . . on the ten-peso . . . bill . . ." There was a long pause during which the journalist sat bewildered. Just as she was about to ask for an explanation of such a curious choice, Borges continued, ". . . have distanced me from the true image of the hero."

After the night of her first meeting with Borges, Canto often had dinner at the Bioys', dinners at which the conversation was lively, since Ocampo had the unsettling habit of springing questions on her guests, such as "How would you commit suicide, given the choice?" One summer evening, as he and Canto were, by chance, leaving together, Borges asked if he could walk her to the subway. At the station, Borges, stuttering, suggested that they might walk a little farther. An hour later they found themselves in a café on Avenida de Mayo. Obviously the talk turned to literature, and Canto mentioned her admiration for *Candida*, and quoted a section from the end of the play. Borges was enchanted and remarked that this was the first time he had met a woman who was fond of Bernard Shaw. Then, peering at Canto through his incipient blindness, he paid her a compliment in English: "A Gioconda smile and the movements of a chess knight." They left as the café was closing and walked until three-thirty in the morning. The next day Borges deposited at her house, without asking to see her, a copy of Conrad's *Youth*.

Borges's courting of Estela Canto lasted a couple of years, during which, she said, "he loved me and I was fond of him." They would go for long walks or for aimless tram rides across the southern neighborhoods of Buenos Aires. Borges was fond of trams: it was on the number 7 tram, on his way to and from his miserable job at a municipal library, that he taught himself Italian by reading a bilingual edition of Dante's *Commedia*. "I started Hell in English; by the time I had left Purgatory I was able to follow him in the original," he once said. When he wasn't with Canto, he wrote to her, incessantly, and his correspondence, which she later included in *Borges a contraluz*, is quietly moving. One undated letter, apologizing for having left town without letting her know, "out of fear or courtesy, through the sad conviction that I was for you, essentially, nothing but an inconvenience or a duty," goes on to confess: "Fate takes on shapes that keep repeating themselves, there are circling patterns; now this one appears again: again I'm in Mar del Plata, longing for you."

In the summer of 1945 he told her that he wanted to write a story about a place that would be "all places in the world," and that he wanted to dedicate the story to her. Two or three days later he brought to her house a small package which, he said, contained the Aleph. Canto opened it. Inside was a small kaleidoscope, which the maid's four-year-old son immediately broke.

The story of the Aleph progressed along with Borges's infatuation with Canto. He wrote to her, on a postcard, in English:

Thursday, about five.

I am in Buenos Aires. I shall see you tonight, I shall see you tomorrow, I know we shall be happy together (happy and drifting and sometimes speechless and most gloriously silly), and already I feel the bodily pang of being separated from you, torn asunder from you, by rivers, by cities, by tufts of grass, by circumstances, by days and nights.

These are, I promise, the last lines I shall allow myself in this strain; I shall abound no longer in self-pity. Dear love, I love you; I wish you all the happiness; a vast and complex and closewoven future of happiness lies ahead of us. I am writing like some horrible prose poet; I don't dare to reread this regrettable postcard. Estela, Estela Canto, when you read this I shall be finishing the story I promised you, the first of a long series.

Yours,
Georgie

"The story of the place that is all places" (as Borges calls it in another postcard) begins with the summer of the death of the beautiful Buenos

Aires aristocrat Beatriz Viterbo, with whom Borges, the narrator, is in love. Beatriz's cousin, the pedantic and bombastic poet Carlos Argentine Daneri (it was rumored that Borges based the character on his brother-in-law, the writer Guillermo de Torre, who faithfully subscribed to the vocabulary recommended by the Royal Spanish Academy of Letters), is composing a huge epic poem that will include everything on earth and in Heaven; his source of inspiration is the Aleph, a place in which all existence has been assembled. This place, Daneri tells Borges, is under the nineteenth step down to Beatriz's basement, and one must lie on the floor in a certain position in order to see it. Borges complies, and the Aleph is revealed to him. "The diameter of the Aleph would not have been more than two or three centimeters, but the entire cosmic space was there, undiminished in volume." Everything appears before his astonished eyes in a Whitmanesque enumeration: "I saw the populous sea, I saw the dawn and the evening, I saw the crowds of America, a silvery spider's web in the center of a black pyramid, I saw a broken labyrinth (it was London), I saw eyes very close to me, unending, observing their own reflection in me as if in a mirror . . ." The list continues for another page. Among the visions, Borges impossibly sees his own face and the faces of his readers—our faces—and "the atrocious remains of that which had deliciously been Beatriz Viterbo." Also, to his mortification, he sees a number of "obscene, incredible, precise letters" that the unattainable Beatriz had written to Daneri. "I was dazed and I wept," he concludes, "because my eyes had seen that secret and conjectural object whose name men usurp but that no man has ever seen: the inconceivable universe."

Once the story was finished, Borges published it in *Sur*, in the issue of September 1945. Shortly afterward, he and Estela Canto had dinner at the Hotel Las Delicias in Adrogué, on the outskirts of Buenos Aires. This was a place of great importance to Borges. Here, as a young man, he had spent a few happy summers with his family, reading; here, a desperately unhappy thirty-five-year-old man, he attempted suicide on 25 August 1934 (an attempt he commemorated in 1978, in a story set in the future called "25 August 1983"); here he set his metaphysical detective story, "Death and the Compass," transforming Las Delicias into the beautifully named villa Triste-le-Roy. In the evening he and Canto walked through the darkened streets, and Borges recited, in Italian, Beatrice's lines to Virgil, begging him to accompany Dante on his voyage through Hell. This is Dorothy L. Sayers's translation:

O courteous Mantuan soul, whose skill in song
Keeps green on earth a fame that shall not end
While motion rolls the turning sphere along!
A friend of mine, who is not Fortune's friend,
Is hard beset upon the shadowy coast.

Canto recalled the lines and told me that Borges had made fun of the flat-
tery Beatrice used to get what she wanted. "Then Borges turned to me," Canto
said, "though he could barely make me out under the misty street lamp, and
asked if I would marry him."

Half amused, half serious, she told him that she might. "But Georgie,
don't forget that I'm a disciple of Bernard Shaw. We can't get married unless
we go to bed first." To me, across the dinner table, she added, "I knew he'd
never dare."

Their relationship, such as it was, continued halfheartedly for another
year. According to Canto, their breakup came about through Borges's mother,
who, as her son's constant chaperone, had little regard for his women friends.
Later, in 1967, after his mother had apparently consented to his marriage to
Elsa Astete de Millán ("I think it will be all right for you to marry Elsa, because
she's a widow and she knows about life"), Canto commented, "She's found
him a replacement." The marriage was, however, a disaster. Elsa, jealous of
anyone for whom Borges felt affection, forbade him to visit his mother and
never invited her to their flat. Elsa shared none of Borges's literary interests.
She read very little. Borges enjoyed telling his dreams every morning over coffee and toast; Elsa didn't dream, or said she didn't dream, which Borges found
inconceivable. Instead she cared for the trappings that fame had brought
Borges and which he so emphatically despised: medals, cocktails, meetings
with celebrities. At Harvard, where Borges had been invited to lecture, she
insisted that he be paid a higher fee and that they be given more luxurious
accommodations. One night, one of the professors found Borges outside the
residence, in slippers and pajamas. "My wife locked me out," he explained,
deeply embarrassed. The professor took Borges in for the night and the next
morning confronted Elsa. "You're not the one who has to see him under the
sheets," she answered. Another time, in their flat in Buenos Aires, where I had
gone to visit him, Borges waited for Elsa to leave the room and then asked me,
in a whisper: "Tell me, is Beppo here?" Beppo was Borges's large white tomcat.
I told him that he was, asleep in one of the armchairs. "Thank God," Borges

said, in a scene straight out of Nabokov's *Laughter in the Dark*. "She told me he'd run away. But I could hear him and I thought I was losing my mind."

Borges's escape from Elsa was decidedly inglorious. Since divorce did not exist in Argentina, his only recourse was a legal separation. On 7 July 1970, his American translator, Norman Thomas di Giovanni, picked him up in a taxi at the National Library (where Borges had his office) and secretly accompanied him to the airport, where they caught a plane for Córdoba. In the meantime, instructed by Borges under di Giovanni's guidance, a lawyer and three removal men rang the doorbell at Elsa's flat with a legal writ and the order to take away Borges's books. The marriage had lasted just under four years.

Once again, Borges felt that it was not his destiny to be happy. Literature provided consolation, but never quite enough, since it also brought back memories of each loss or failure, as he knew when he wrote the last lines of the first sonnet in the diptych "1964":

No one loses (you repeat in vain)
Except that which he doesn't have and never
Had, but it isn't enough to be brave
To learn the art of oblivion.
A symbol, a rose tears you apart
And a guitar can kill you.

Throughout his almost centenary life, Borges fell in love with patient regularity, and with patient regularity his hopes came to nothing. He envied the literary alliances we encountered in our readings: the British soldier John Holden and Ameera, his Indian wife, in Kipling's "Without Benefit of Clergy" ("Since when hast thou been a slave, my queen?"), the chaste Sigurd and Brynhild from the *Völsunga Saga* (two lines of which are now engraved on his tombstone in Geneva), Stevenson and Fanny (whom Borges imagined happy), G. K. Chesterton and his wife (whom he imagined content). The long list of names of Borges's beloveds can be culled from the dedications to his stories and poems: Estela Canto, Haydée Lange, María Esther Vázquez, Ulrike von Kuhlmann, Silvina Bullrich, Beatriz Bibiloni Webster de Bullrich, Sara Diehl de Moreno Hueyo, Margot Guerrero, Cecilia Ingenieros — "all unique," as Bioy said, "and all irreplaceable."

One evening, over the usual colorless pasta at the restaurant of the Hotel Dora, he told me that he believed, with literary faith, in what he called "the mystery of women and the heroic destiny of men." He felt unable to re-create that mystery on the page: the few women in his short stories are cogs in the plot, not characters in their own right, except perhaps the avenging Emma Zunz, whose argument was given to him by a woman, Cecilia Ingenieros. The two rival women artists in "The Duel" (a story that properly acknowledges its debt to Henry James) are sexless except in name, and so is the old woman in "The Elderly Lady." The shared woman in "The Intruder" is little more than a thing the rival brothers have to kill in order to remain faithful to each other. The strangest of Borges's fictional women, Ulrica, in the eponymous story, is less a woman than a phantom: she, a young Norwegian student, gives herself to the elderly Colombian professor Javier Otarola, whom she calls Sigurd and who in turn calls her Brynhild. First she appears willing, then cold, and Otarola says to her, "Brynhild, you walk as if you wished a sword between the two of us." The story ends: "There was no sword between us. Time drifted away like sand. Love flowed, secular in the shadows, and I possessed for the first and last time the image of Ulrica."

Borges's men, on the other hand, fulfill their heroic destinies with stoic determination, hardly ever knowing whether they have achieved anything, a few times aware that they have failed. The dreaming magus of "The Circular Ruins," who realizes that he too is someone's dream; the laborious novelist Herbert Quain, who admits that his work belongs "not to art, but to the mere history of art"; the metaphysical detective Erik Lönrrot, who goes willingly to his own death; the bull-faced prisoner in the labyrinth waiting patiently for his redeemer to slay him; the playwright Jaromir Hladík, for whom God performs a secret miracle to allow him to complete a play before dying; the sedentary Juan Dahlmann, who, in "The South," is suddenly offered an epic death to crown his quiet life — all these were the men whose fate Borges felt he somehow shared. "Plato, who like all men, was unhappy . . ." began one of his lectures at the University of Buenos Aires. I think Borges felt this to be the inescapable truth.

Borges had wished for a simple, uncomplicated union; fate allotted him entanglements that seemed plotted by Henry James, whose arguments, though he much admired their invention, he found at times too psychologically convoluted. His last attempt at marriage, to María Kodama, apparently took place on 26 April 1986, less than two months before his death, through a license issued in absentia by the mayor of a small Paraguayan town. I say "apparently" because the procedures were shrouded in confusing secrecy, and since Borges's marriage to Elsa had never been annulled, it would seem that in marrying María he might have been guilty of bigamy. María had been one of his students in the Anglo-Saxon courses and later, in the sixties, had begun to accompany him on his travels. Her marriage to Borges surprised most people and angered many who felt that she had deliberately distanced the old man from his friends. The truth is that Borges's friends felt jealous of anyone for whom Borges showed affection or interest, and Borges, with the willfulness of Jehovah, allowed these jealousies to flourish.

Now, in his eighties, with María in charge, Borges no longer dined at the Bioys', no longer met with many of his old acquaintances: all this was blamed on María, never on Borges's mutability. No one recalled that over the years Borges had often erased a name from a poem's dedication and replaced it, in a childlike switch of affections, with that of another, more recent recipient: the new erasures were attributed to María. Even the fact of his dying in Geneva, far from his eternal Buenos Aires, was blamed on María's jealousy. A day or so before his death, Borges called Bioy from Geneva. Bioy said that he sounded infinitely sad. "What are you doing in Geneva? Come home," Bioy said to him. "I can't," Borges answered. "And anyway, any place is good enough to die in." Bioy said that in spite of their friendship, he felt, as a writer, hesitant to touch such a good exit line.

But there were those—Borges's editor at Gallimard, Héctor Bianciotti, for instance, and Cortázar's widow, Aurora Bernárdez—who saw María Kodama merely as a devoted and zealous companion. According to them, Borges had met at last his adamant, jealous, remote, protective Beatrice. To Bianciotti, Borges had said, "I'm dying of cancer of the liver, and I'd like to end my days in Japan. But I don't speak Japanese, or only a few words, and I would like to be able to talk my last hours away." From Geneva he asked Bianciotti to send him books never mentioned in his writings: the comedies of Molière, the poems of Lamartine, the works of Rémy de Gourmont. Then Bianciotti understood: they were the books Borges had told him he had read as an adolescent in Geneva. The last book he chose was Novalis's *Heinrich von Ofterdingen,* which he asked the German-speaking nurse to read to him throughout the long, painful wait. The day before he died, Bianciotti came to see him and sat by his bed throughout the night, holding the old man's hand, until the next morning.

Borges died on 14 June 1986. Ten years later, rereading "The Aleph" for his memory's sake, I wondered where it was that I'd come across the idea of the all-encompassing space in Borges's work—Thomas Hobbes's *nunc-stans* or *hic-stans* quoted as an epigraph to "The Aleph." I looked through my two shelves of Borges: the tattered original Emecé editions, cluttered with typos; the two fat volumes of the incomplete *Obras completas* and *Obras completas en colaboración*, no less typo-ridden; the glossy and somewhat more prolix Alianza editions; the erratic English translations; the superb French Pléiade edition of his *Oeuvres*, so lovingly edited by Jean-Pierre Bernès that in my mind it almost supersedes the original Spanish. (Borges might not have minded: he once said of the English version of William Beckford's *Vathek*, written in French, that "the original is unfaithful to the translation.")

Roger Caillois, responsible for making Borges known in France ("I'm an invention of Caillois," Borges said once), suggested that the master's central theme was the labyrinth; as if to confirm this supposition, the best-known collection of somewhat clumsily translated Borges pieces in English bears that title in the plural. Astonishingly (at least for me, who thought myself quite familiar with Borges's work), as I reread his books, I found that, far more than the labyrinth, it is the idea of an object, or a place or person or moment that is all objects, places, persons, and moments, that pervasively appears throughout his writing.

I made a list on the endpaper pages of my Pléiade volume, but I am sure it is far from exhaustive:

It is headed by the most obvious: "The Zahir," companion piece to "The Aleph." The *zahir*, which means "visible" in Arabic, is an object (a coin, but also a tiger, an astrolabe) that once seen cannot be forgotten. Quoting Tennyson's line about the flower in the crannied wall, Borges says that "perhaps he meant that there is no event, however humble, that does not imply the history of the world and its infinite concatenation of effects and causes." Then comes the celebrated Library of Babel, "which some call the Universe," and that universe abridged into a single book of infinitely thin pages, mentioned in a note to the story and expanded in the late "Book of Sand." The universal encyclopedia sought by the narrator in the long story "The Congress" is not impossible: it already exists and is the universe itself, like the map of the Nation of Cartographers (in *Dreamtigers*), which Lewis Carroll foresaw in *Sylvie and Bruno* and which, in Borges's short fable, coincides with the country it sets out to map.

Characters too can be, like places and objects in Borges's work, all-encompassing. Sir Thomas Browne, whom Borges loved, had said it for all time: "Every man is not only himself; there hath been many Diogenes, and as many Timons, though but few of that name: men are liv'd over again, the world is now as it was in Ages past; there was none then, but there hath been some one since that parallels him, and is, as it were, his revived self." Borges rejoiced in the paragraph and asked me to read it to him several times. He approved of Browne's seemingly naive "though but few of that name," which "makes him dear to us, eh?" and chuckled without really expecting an answer. One of the earliest of these "revived selves" is Tom Castro, the unlikely impostor from *A Universal History of Infamy,* who, though a semi-idiot, tries to pass himself off as the aristocratic Tichborne heir, following the dictum that one man is in fact all men. Other versions of this protean character are the unforgetting and unforgettable Funes (in "Funes the Memorious"), whose memory is a rubbish heap of everything seen throughout his short life; the Arab philosopher Averroës (in "The Search of Averroës"), who tries, across the centuries, to understand Aristotle, much like Borges himself in search of Averroës and the reader in search of Borges; the man who has been Homer (in "The Immortal") and who has also been a sampling of all men throughout our history and who created a man called Ulysses who calls himself Nobody: Pierre Menard who becomes Cervantes in order to write, once again but in our time, *Don Quixote.* In "Everything and Nothing" Shakespeare begs God to let him, who has been so many men, be one and himself. God confesses to Shakespeare that He too is nothing: "I dreamed the world [says God] as you dreamed your work, my Shakespeare, and among the forms of my dream are you who like Myself is many and no one." In "The Lottery of Babylon" every man has been a proconsul, every man has been a slave: that is to say, every man has been every man. My list also includes this note, with which Borges ends his review of Victor Fleming's film *Dr. Jekyll and Mr. Hyde:* "Beyond Stevenson's dualist parable and close to the *Assembly of the Birds* composed in the twelfth century of our era by Farid ud-din Attar, we can imagine a pantheistic film whose many characters, in the end, resolve themselves into One, which is everlasting." The idea became a script written with Bioy (*The Others*) and then a film directed by Hugo Santiago. Even in Borges's everyday talk, the theme of all-in-one was constantly present. When I saw him, briefly, after the Malvinas War had been declared, we talked, as usual, about literature and touched on the theme of the double. Borges said to me sadly, "Why do you think no one's noticed that General Galtieri and Mrs. Thatcher are one and the same person?"

But this multiplicity of beings and places, this invention of an eternal being and an eternal place, is not enough for happiness, which Borges considered a moral imperative. Four years before his death Borges published one more book, *Nine Essays on Dante,* composed of pieces written in the forties and fifties and revised much later. In the first paragraph of his introduction, Borges imagines an old engraving found in a fictional oriental library, in which everything in the world is arduously depicted. Borges suggests that Dante's poem is like that all-encompassing engraving, the *Commedia* as the Aleph.

The essays are written in Borges's slow, precise, asthmatic voice; as I turn the pages, I can hear his deliberate hesitations, the ironic questioning tone with which he liked to end his most original remarks, the solemn recitativo in which he would quote long passages from memory. His ninth essay on Dante, "Beatrice's Last Smile," begins with a statement that he would have made in conversation with disarming simplicity: "My purpose is to comment on the most moving verses ever achieved in literature. They are included in the thirty-first canto of *Paradiso* and, although they are famous, no one appears to have noticed the sorrow hidden in them, no one has heard them fully. It is true that the tragic substance they hold belongs less to the book than to the author of the book, less to Dante the protagonist than to Dante the writer or inventor."

Borges then goes on to tell the story. High on the peak of Mount Purgatory, Dante loses sight of Virgil. Led by Beatrice, whose beauty increases as they cross each new heaven, he reaches the Empyrean. In this infinite region, things far removed are no less clearly visible than those close by ("as in a Pre-Raphaelite canvas," Borges notes). Dante sees, high above, a river of light, flocks of angels, and the Rose made from the souls of the just, arranged in orderly rows. Dante turns to hear Beatrice speak of what he has seen, but his Lady has vanished. In her place, he sees the figure of a venerable old man. "And she? Where is she?" Dante cries. The old man instructs Dante to lift his eyes and there, crowned in glory, he sees her high above him, in one of the circles of the Rose, and offers her his prayer of thanks. The text then reads (in Barbara Reynolds's translation):

Such was my prayer and she, so distant fled,
It seemed, did smile and look on me once more,
Then to the eternal fountain turned her head.

Borges (always the craftsman) noted that "seemed" refers to the faraway distance but horribly contaminates Beatrice's smile as well.

How can we explain these verses, Borges asks. The allegorical annotators have seen Reason or the Intellect (Virgil) as an instrument for reaching faith, and Faith or Theology (Beatrice) as an instrument for reaching the divinity. Both disappear once the goal is reached. "This explanation," Borges adds, "as the reader will have noticed, is no less irreproachable than it is frigid; these verses were never born from such a miserable equation."

The critic Guido Vitali (whom Borges had read) suggested that Dante, creating Paradise, was moved by a desire to found a kingdom for his Lady. "But I'd go further," Borges says. "I suspect that Dante constructed literature's best book in order to insert a few meetings with the unrecapturable Beatrice. Or rather, the circles of punishment and the southern Purgatory and the nine concentric circles and Francesca and the Siren and the Gryphon and Bertrand de Born are inserts; a smile and a voice, which he knows are lost, are what is essential."

Then Borges allows us the ghost of a confession: "That an unhappy man should imagine happiness is in no way extraordinary; all of us do so every single day. Dante too does it as we do, but something, always, allows us to glimpse the horror behind these happy fictions." He continues, "The old man points to one of the circles of the lofty Rose. There, in a halo, is Beatrice; Beatrice whose eyes used to fill him with unbearable beatitude, Beatrice who used to dress in red gowns, Beatrice of whom he had thought so much that he was astonished to learn that certain pilgrims, whom he saw one morning in Florence, had never even heard of her, Beatrice who once cut him cold, Beatrice who died at the age of twenty-four, Beatrice de Folco Portinari who had married Bardi." Dante sees her and prays to her as he would pray to God, but also as he would pray to a desired woman.

> O thou in whom my hopes securely dwell,
> And who, to bring my soul to Paradise,
> Didst leave the imprint of thy steps in Hell.

Beatrice then casts her eyes on him for a single moment and smiles, and then turns forever towards the eternal fountain of light.

And Borges concludes, "Let us retain one indisputable fact, a single and humble fact: that this scene was imagined by Dante. For us, it is very real; for him, it was less so. (Reality, for him, was the fact that first life and then death had snatched Beatrice away). Absent for ever from Beatrice, alone and perhaps humiliated, he imagined the scene in order to imagine himself with her. Unfortunately for him, fortunately for the centuries that would read him, his knowledge that the encounter was imaginary deformed the vision. That is why the atrocious circumstances take place—so much more infernal, of course, because they take place in the highest heaven, the Empyrean: Beatrice's disappearance, the old man who takes her place, her sudden elevation to the Rose, the fleeting smile and glance, the everlasting turning away."

I am wary of seeing in one man's reading, however brilliant that reading might be, a reflection of his own self; as Borges would no doubt argue, in his defense of the reader's freedom to choose and to reject, not every book serves as a mirror for every one of its readers. But in the case of the *Nine Essays* I think the inference is justified, and Borges's reading of Dante's destiny helps me read that of Borges. In a short essay published in *La Prensa* in 1926, Borges himself had stated: "I've always said that the lasting aim of literature is to display our destinies."

Borges suggested that Dante wrote the *Commedia* in order to be, for a moment, with Beatrice. It is not impossible that in some way, in order to be with a woman, any woman of the many he desired, to be privy to her mystery, to be more than just a wordsmith, to be or to try to be a lover and be loved for his own sake and not for that of his inventions, Borges created the Aleph, again and again, throughout his work. In that imaginary all-encompassing place where everything possible and impossible is happening, or in the arms of the man who is all men, she, the unattainable, might be his, or if she still would not be his, she would at least not be his under circumstances less painful to bear because he himself had invented them.

But as Borges the master craftsman knew very well, the laws of invention won't bend any more easily than those of the world called real. Teodelina Villar in "The Zahir," Beatriz Viterbo in "The Aleph," do not love the intellectual narrator, Borges, who loves them. For the sake of the story, these women are unworthy Beatrices—Teodelina is a snob, a slave to fashion, "less preoccupied with beauty than with perfection"; Beatriz is a society belle obscenely infatuated with her obnoxious cousin—because, for the fiction to work, the miracle (the revelation of the Aleph, or of the memorable zahir) must take place among blind and unworthy mortals, the narrator included.

Borges once remarked that the destiny of the modern hero is not to reach Ithaca or obtain the Holy Grail. Perhaps his sorrow, in the end, came from realizing that instead of granting him the much longed-for and sublime erotic encounter, his craft demanded that he fail: Beatriz was not to be Beatrice, he was not to be Dante, he was to be only Borges, a fumbling dream-lover, still unable, even in his own imagination, to conjure up the one fulfilling and almost perfect woman of his waking dreams.

Borges and the
Longed-For Jew

"Well! *What* are you?" said the Pigeon. "I can see
you're trying to invent something!"
Alice's Adventures in Wonderland, Chapter 5

IN 1944, AGENTS OF HIMMLER'S secret service began arriving in Madrid to
set up an escape route out of Germany for the defeated Nazis. Two years later,
for reasons of security, the operation was moved to Buenos Aires, where it
established itself inside the Presidential Palace, with the accord of the recently
elected president, Juan Domingo Perón. Argentina had remained neutral during World War II, but most of its military had supported Hitler and Musso-
lini. The rich upper classes, noted for their antisemitism, though they opposed
Perón in almost everything else, remained silent about his pro-Nazi activities.
In the meantime, rumors of what was taking place began to circulate within the
Jewish community. In 1948, to stifle the incipient protests of the Argentinean
Jews, Perón decided to appoint an ambassador to the newly created state of
Israel and chose my father, Pablo Manguel, for the post. Because my father
was Jewish (the family had arrived from Europe and settled in one of Baron
Hirsch's colonies in the Argentinean interior), there was much opposition to
his nomination, especially from the Ministry of Foreign Affairs, traditionally
staffed by Catholic nationalists. A Vatican-approved candidate was proposed,
but Perón, who realized how much he needed the Jewish support, held firm.
In later years, and in spite of the (still) growing documentary evidence, Perón
would deny ever having helped the Nazi cause and held up my father's nomination as proof of his Jewish sympathies. Today we know that among Perón's
most notorious protégés were Adolf Eichmann and Josef Mengele.

In Perón's Argentina, Jorge Luis Borges was one of the few intellectuals to speak out against the Nazis. As early as April 1934, in answer to an accusation by the editors of the nationalist magazine *Crisol* (that he "maliciously hid his Jewish ancestry"), Borges published a short text, "I, a Jew," in which he acknowledged that he often delighted in imagining himself a Jew, but that, alas, he had not been able to trace a single Jewish ancestor in the past two hundred years of his family history. Though he had never felt it necessary to defend his belief in the importance and value of the Jewish culture which had fed his own literature (the stories of the Bible, the wisdom of the Talmud, the scholarship of Gershom Scholem, the nightmares of Gustav Meyrink and Kafka, the poetry of Heinrich Heine, the legend of the Golem, the mysteries of the Kabbalah), he mocked the antisemites who obsessively sought Jewish roots in all their enemies. "Statistically speaking," Borges mused, "the Jews were very few. What would we think of someone in the year 4000 who discovers everywhere descendants of the inhabitants of San Juan [one of the least populated of the Argentinean provinces]? Our inquisitors seek Hebrews, never Phoenicians, Numidians, Scythians, Babylonians, Huns, Vandals, Ostrogoths, Ethiopians, Illyrians, Paphlagonians, Sarmatians, Medes, Ottomans, Berbers, Britons, Libyans, Cyclops, or Lapiths. The nights of Alexandria, Babylon, Carthage, Memphis have never succeeded in giving birth to one single grandfather; it was only to the tribes of the bituminous Dead Sea that such a gift was granted."

Neither did he condemn German Kultur. In an article published on 24 March 1939 in *El Hogar* (a popular Argentinean family weekly), Borges reviewed a book by a certain Louis Golding, ominously called *The Jewish Problem*. Borges agreed with Golding's attack on antisemitism, but he disagreed with the author's tactics. Antisemites, Borges said, "seek (absurdly) to deny Jewish contributions to the culture of Germany; Golding seeks (absurdly) to limit the culture of Germany to Jewish contributions alone. He declares racism to be absurd, but, with an almost servile symmetry, he does nothing more than oppose Jewish racism to Nazi racism. He constantly moves from a necessary defense to an unnecessary onslaught. Unnecessary, because Israel's virtues do not require the demerits of Germany. Unnecessary and imprudent, because this is somehow equivalent to accepting the thesis of the enemy, that postulates a radical difference between a Jew and a non-Jew." A year later, shortly after Germany's invasion of Denmark, Borges transcribed a dialogue with an Argentinean Germanophile. For Borges, his interlocutor is a contradiction: rather than a lover of Germany (of whose culture he knows nothing), he is merely a hater of England. He is also an antisemite: that is to say, he wants to expel from Argentina the Slavo-Germanic community whose members boast names of German origin (Rosenblatt, Grünberg, Nierenstein) and speak a German dialect, Yiddish.

But beyond mockery, Borges thought that Jewish culture carried, metaphysically, a symbolic weight. He felt that Hitler was engaged in a purpose that was ultimately impossible — the annihilation of Jewish culture — because Jewish culture (Borges believed) stood essentially for the culture of humanity; if that were so, then Hitler's wish to eliminate the Jews was merely part of a cosmic machinery set up to prove *in aeternum* the Jews' survival. "Nazism suffers from unreality," he wrote in "A Comment of August 23, 1944," the day of the liberation of Paris. "It is uninhabitable; men can only die for it, lie for it, kill and wound for it. No one, in the intimate depths of his being, can wish it to triumph. I shall hazard this conjecture: Hitler wants to be defeated." Two years later, in the short story "Deutsches Requiem" (a sort of precursor to Jonathan Littell's *Les Bienveillants*), a Nazi officer attempts to explain himself and his deeds: "The world was dying of its Judaism and of that sickness of Judaism which is the faith of Jesus; we taught it violence and the faith of the sword. That sword will now kill us, and we are comparable to the sorcerer who weaves a maze in which he is forced to roam until the end of his days, or to David who pronounces judgment on a stranger and condemns him to death, and then hears the revelation: *You are that man*." At that point, the Nazi officer utters these powerful words of his own damnation: "If victory and injustice and happiness be not for Germany, let them be for other nations. Let Heaven exist, even if our place be Hell."

"Like the Druzes, like the moon, like death, like next week, the distant past forms part of those things that can be enriched by ignorance," Borges had written in "I, a Jew." In such a state, in which good and evil are swept away with the same indifference, the events of the past will be reinvented and a false memory will be set up as truth. This is what happens in one of his later stories, "Utopia of a Man Who Is Tired." Here Borges describes a nightmare set in the future, in which he is led by a guide who helpfully explains to him the brave new world. At one point Borges sees a domed tower. "That is the crematorium," his guide points out. "Inside is the lethal chamber. They say it was invented by a philanthropist whose name, I believe, was Adolf Hitler."

A dignified, self-effacing, intellectually honest man, Borges wished not to be remembered; he hoped that a few of his writings would survive, but to his own fame he was indifferent. He longed for personal oblivion ("to be forever but not to have been," he says in a poem) and yet feared the capricious memory of History, or, rather, the capriciousness with which we tend to rewrite the facts of History to suit our meanest, basest impulses. That is why he despised politics ("the vilest of all human activities") and believed in the truth of fiction and in our ability to tell true stories.

Faking It

"Please your Majesty," said the Knave. "I didn't write it, and they can't prove that I did: there's no name signed at the end."

"If you didn't sign it," said the King, "that only makes the matter worse. You *must* have meant some mischief, or else you'd have signed your name like an honest man."

Alice's Adventures in Wonderland, Chapter 12

ON 29 OCTOBER 1932, THE Buenos Aires newspaper *Crítica* printed the following announcement in the abominable style to which its readers were accustomed:

"*Crítica* will publish the most thrilling detective novel. Its plot is based on events that took place in Buenos Aires. From a real-life occurrence that some time ago deeply shook the public of this city, the author has constructed a moving story in which the mystery becomes denser and denser with every page of *El enigma de la calle Arcos* [The Riddle of Arcos Street]. Who killed the wife of Galván, the chess player? Or was it a strange form of suicide? How did the criminal vanish after committing the deed? How did the criminal leave the victim's room without forcing a single lock? The pilgrimage of a chestful of jewelry. Beginning tomorrow, Sunday, in all our editions."

The success of the serial, which appeared under the impossible name of Sauli Lostal, led to its publication in book form a year later. On 4 November 1933, an advertisement in the same paper announced that *El enigma de la calle Arcos* was now available for sale. "The first great Argentinean detective novel. It stands apart completely from the old models of the genre, grisly and lacking verisimilitude. Full of emotion and realism, of spine-tingling and interest, it is a true accomplishment. A thick volume with illustrations. And only 95 cents." The book, published by the Am-Bass press, numbered 245 pages. The illustrator was Pedro Rojas, whose style, to judge from the cover, matched that of the writing.

It is very difficult to give an English-speaking reader a sense of the atrocious style. Let me try:

> Moments later in the chamber adjacent to the guards' office, Oscar Lara and Suárez Lerma — the latter enjoying still a few sips of *mate* — were conversing about the motive that had led there, on such an unsettled night, the journalist. It did not take long for the assistant to convey to him the facts that the other was jotting down with special care. They had just finished this task when the tinkle of the telephone bell was heard. The assistant Lara approached the instrument, unhooked the receiver, pressed it against his ear and between the police official and the person who had called there commenced the following dialogue, later reconstructed by the speakers themselves.

Thirty years after the appearance of the novel, in the magazine *Filología*, the critic Enrique Anderson Imbert published an article titled "A New Contribution to the Study of Borges's Sources." In it, Anderson Imbert suggested that Borges had used *El enigma de la calle Arcos* as the model for his "El acercamiento a Almotásim" (The Approach to al-Mu'tasim"), a fiction that purports to be the review of a detective novel of that name, written by the Indian lawyer Mir Bahadur Ali. According to Borges, the illustrated original was published in Bombay in 1932 and reprinted by Victor Gollancz in London two years later, with an introduction by Dorothy L. Sayers and the omission ("perhaps charitable" says Borges) of the illustrations.

Borges's "El acercamiento a Almotásim" appeared for the first time not in a periodical (as did most of his pieces) but in a collection of essays, *Historia de la eternidad* (History of Eternity, 1936). The fact that it was published in a volume of nonfiction, in an appendix that carried the sober title "Two Notes" (the second "note" being an essay on "the art of insulting"), suggested to its first readers that Mir Bahadur Ali was a real person and that his book (under the respectable imprint of Gollancz) was available for purchase. Intrigued by Borges's enthusiastic review, his friend Adolfo Bioy Casares ordered a copy from London. Unsuccessfully.

Borges's text was to undergo at least two more incarnations. In 1941, he included "El acercamiento a Almotásim," this time obviously as a fiction, in his collection of short stories *El jardín de senderos que se bifurcan* (The Garden of Forking Paths). Three years later he included the whole of *El jardín* as the first section of what is perhaps his most famous volume, *Ficciones;* the second was called "Artificios" and comprised half a dozen new stories. Just to complicate things, in recent editions of Borges's books (the Alianza edition, for instance), "El acercamiento a Almotásim" was excised from *Ficciones* and returned to its place in *Historia de la eternidad*.

On 13 July 1997, in an article published in the literary section of *La Nación* of Buenos Aires, the Argentinean short-story writer Juan Jacobo Bajarlía attempted to better Anderson Imbert's guesswork and suggested that not only was *El enigma de la calle Arcos* known to Borges but that the master himself had written it. According to Bajarlía, the writer Ulises Petit de Murat (a friend of Borges's in his youth) had revealed to him, in confidence, that Borges was the author of that forgotten detective novel, which, Murat told Bajarlía, Borges "had composed directly on the typewriter, allotting to it a couple of hours a day."

One month later (17 August), the novelist Fernando Sorrentino published, also in *La Nación*, an answer to Bajarlía. Courteously, implacably, definitively, Sorrentino demonstrates the impossibility of such authorship. Offering factual, mechanical, ethical, and stylistic reasons, Sorrentino demolishes Bajarlía's arguments. First, Borges never learned to type. Second, Borges never wrote a novel, a genre he many times dismissed, at least as far as his own talents were concerned. ("To imagine the plot of a novel is delectable," he once said. "To actually write it out is an exaggeration.") Third (and this is perhaps Sorrentino's strongest point), the novel's turgid style and infamous use of the Spanish language is so far removed from Borges's careful prose styles (whether the intricate voice of his baroque period in the twenties and thirties or the sparer voice of later years) that it is impossible to imagine one man capable of both. "I believe that no one can write utterly in a style that is not his own," Sorrentino reasonably argues. "Even someone proposing the most outrageous parody will end up, sooner or later, showing his own style between the paragraphs he concocts." And he reminds us that, even on those rare occasions when Borges introduces an alien voice in his writing (as when he attributes an atrocious poem to his rival in the short story "The Aleph"), Borges's own intelligence, humor, and subtle vocabulary shine through the execrable verses. For Sorrentino, there is no such thing as the perfect literary disguise.

Here we could add that Borges had an uncanny ear for ugly prose, and he mocked it mercilessly. Because of his prodigious memory, he could recite long snatches of horrible verse by writers famous and little known, and he parodied their speech (as Sorrentino points out) in several of his writings. One comic story, written with Bioy, "El Testigo" (The Witness), in which the two authors parody the worst of Argentinean speech, has as its epigraph Isaiah 6:5, without spelling out the quotation. I looked it up. It says, "Then said I, Woe is me! for I am undone; because I am a man of unclean lips, and dwell in the midst of a people of unclean lips." Such literary consciousness is never present in *El enigma de la calle Arcos*.

Sorrentino ends with one final fact, devastating for Bajarlía's argument: the identity of the obviously pseudonymous "Sauli Lostal." On 27 February 1997, a certain Tomás E. Giordano published a letter in the newspaper *Clarín* of Buenos Aires, stating that after seeing an advertisement for a new edition of *El enigma de la calle Arcos* "by an author whose real identity remains unknown," he felt compelled to clarify the mystery. According to Giordano, Sauli Lostal was the anagram of Luis Stallo, a gentleman with whom his father had established a brief commercial acquaintance, and who was not a man of letters but a businessman, a fairly cultured Italian who had settled in Argentina after traveling the world. "His restless spirit," wrote Giordano, "strengthened by a relentless dedication to reading, compelled him to take part in 1933 in a contest organized by the then popular evening paper *Crítica*, in which readers were asked to find a more ingenious outcome for the novel *Le Mystère de la chambre jaune* [The Mystery of the Yellow Chamber] by Gaston Leroux, whose ending the newspaper found somewhat disappointing." The result was *El enigma de la calle Arcos*. An investigation of the Buenos Aires phonebooks for 1928, 1930, 1931, and 1932 revealed the existence of a Luis A. Stallo living in the city during those years. In spite of these incontrovertible facts, the attribution of *El enigma de la calle Arcos* to Borges persists. Even Nicolás Heft's otherwise impeccable *Bibliografía completa* of Borges, published in 1997 by Fondo de Cultura Económica, retains the attribution in its later editions.

El enigma de la calle Arcos is the most notorious but certainly not the only execrable text attributed to Borges. In 1984, for instance, the prestigious Italian magazine *Nuovi argomenti*, edited by Alberto Moravia, Leonardo Sciascia, and Enzo Siciliano (three of the most distinguished names of the Italian literary scene), published a story, "El misterio de la cruz" (The Mystery of the Cross), attributed to Borges. The accompanying letter said that the story had been written in 1934 and translated by the superb writer and translator Franco

Lucentini, and that permission had been granted to publish it by Borges himself and by one of his Italian publishers, Franco María Ricci. In an open letter to the newspaper *La Stampa* of Turin, Lucentini denied ever translating the story, which, he said, not only does not resemble anything by Borges but also "seems to have been written by a semi-illiterate person."

In 1989, the Mexican magazine *Plural*, founded by the poet Octavio Paz, published a poem entitled "Instantes" (Moments) supposedly written by Borges the year of his death. It was preceded by an unctuous commentary by a certain Mauricio Ciechanower, who noted that the piece was "pregnant with a masterly power of synthesis." The poem is an idiotic feel-good meditation that would not be out of place on a Hallmark greeting card. It reads (in a literal and, in my mind, generous translation):

> If I could live my life over again
> I would try to make more mistakes in the next one.
> I would not try to be so perfect, I'd relax more.
> I'd be more of a fool than I've been, in fact
> I'd take very few things seriously.
> I'd be less hygienic.
> I'd run more risks, I'd travel more, I'd watch
> More sunsets, I'd climb more mountains, I'd swim more rivers.
> I'd go to more places where I've never been, I'd eat
> More ice cream and less beans, I'd have more real problems
> And fewer imaginary ones.
> I was one of those people who lived sensibly and prolifically
> Every moment of his life; of course I had moments of happiness.
> But if I could go back I'd try to have
> Only good moments.
> In case you don't know, that is what life is made of, only moments;
> Don't miss out on the present moment.
> I was one of those who never go anywhere without a thermometer,
> A hot-water bottle, an umbrella and a parachute;
> If I could live again, I'd travel lighter.
> If I could live again, I'd start to walk barefoot at the beginning
> Of spring and carry on like that until autumn.
> I'd take more rides on the merry-go-round, I'd watch more sunsets

And I'd play with more children, if I had another life in front of me.
But I'm 85 years old and I know I'm dying.

Three years later, a new translation of these verses, by Alastair Reid, who had previously made excellent translations of several pieces by Borges, appeared in the *Queen's Quarterly*. No one objected.

Then, on 9 May 1999, the critic Francisco Peregil published in the newspaper *El País* of Madrid the following revelation: "The real author of the apocryphal poem is an unknown American writer called Nadine Stair who published it in 1978, eight years before Borges died in Geneva, when she was 86." The text (as a piece of turgid poetic prose) appeared in the periodical *Family Circus* of Louisville, Kentucky, on 27 March 1978 and has since appeared, in a number of different versions, in all sorts of different places, from the *Reader's Digest* to printed T-shirts.

No doubt since the beginnings of literature, all manner of writings have been attributed to famous writers for a variety of reasons: as an honest intent to restore the paternity of a text, as a dishonest intent to lend it prestige, as a sly device to lend fame to the text's attributor. Borges himself, in one of his most celebrated stories, "Pierre Menard, autor del *Quijote*," adds (ironically, of course) a further possibility to this list of intentions: to lend new life to a text, that is to say, a fresh reading, by considering it in a different and unexpected context. "To attribute *The Imitation of Christ* to Louis-Ferdinand Céline or to James Joyce," Borges asks at the conclusion of the story, "is that not enough of a renewal for these tenuous spiritual admonitions?"

I am not certain that this is what the false attributors had in mind when they decided to blame Borges for *El enigma de la calle Arcos* or Nadine Stair's poem. In any case, whatever his accusers' intentions, Borges's suggestion merits exploration, since it may lend to the notion of "fake" a positive connotation that we usually deny it.

On Christmas Eve 1938, Borges left his house to fetch his friend Emma Risso Platero. He had invited her to dinner and was bringing her a present, no doubt a book. Since the elevator was not working, he ran up the stairs, not noticing that one of the freshly painted casement windows had been left open. He felt something graze his forehead, but didn't stop to investigate. When Rissa Platero opened the door, Borges realized, because of the look of horror on her face, that something was seriously wrong. He touched his forehead: it was bathed in blood. In spite of first-aid treatment, the wound became infected, and for a week he lay in bed, suffering from hallucinations and high fever. One night, he found he wasn't able to speak: he was rushed to the hospital for an immediate operation, but septicemia had set in. For a month, the doctors thought that he might die. In his autobiography, dictated in English, Borges himself described the events, which later served as the basis for a short story, "The South." He writes: "When I began to recover, I feared for my mental integrity. I remember that my mother wanted to read to me from a book that I had just ordered, C. S. Lewis' *Out of the Silent Planet*, but for two or three nights I kept putting her off. At last, she prevailed, and after hearing a page or two I fell to crying. My mother asked me why the tears. 'I'm crying because I understand,' I said. A bit later, I wondered whether I could ever write again. I had previously written quite a few poems and dozens of short reviews. I thought that if I tried to write a review now and failed, I'd be all through intellectually but that if I tried something I had never really done before and failed at that it wouldn't be so bad and might even prepare me for the final revelation. I decided I would write a story. The result was "Pierre Menard, Author of *Don Quixote*."

"Pierre Menard, Author of *Don Quixote*" appeared in the issue of the magazine *Sur* of September 1939. In this story, which appeared in the guise of a memoir contributed to a Pierre Menard Festschrift of sorts, Borges describes the apocryphal Menard's attempt to write *Don Quixote* again: not to copy it, not to effect a pastiche. "His admirable ambition," Borges writes, "was to produce a few pages that would coincide — word by word and line by line — with those of Miguel de Cervantes." The story was hugely successful. One literary gentleman friend congratulated him but remarked that the effort was somewhat useless, since any truly cultivated reader would know all those facts about Menard.

Borges's strategy is double-edged. On the one hand, he suggests (playfully, no doubt) that authorship is a casual, haphazard thing and that, given the right time and place, any writer might be the author of any text. The epigraph of his first book of poems, *Fervor de Buenos Aires*, written when he was not quite twenty-four years old, already announces: "If the pages of this book design to consent one happy verse, may the reader forgive me the discourtesy of having been the first to claim it. Our nothings barely differ; it is a trivial and fortuitous circumstance that you are the reader of these exercises, and I their writer."

On the other hand, Borges suggests, it is the reader who determines the nature of a text through, among other things, attribution. The same text read as penned by one writer changes when read as penned by another. *Don Quixote* written by Cervantes (cultured seventeenth-century scholar) is not that same *Don Quixote* written by Menard (contemporary of William James). *El enigma de la calle Arcos* attributed to Sauli Lostal is not *El enigma de la calle Arcos* attributed to Borges. No book is entirely innocent of connotations, and every reader reads not only the words on the page but the endless contextual waves that accompany his or her very existence. From such a point of view there are no "fakes," merely different books which happen to share an identical text.

Borges's own writings are full of such redemptive fakes. Among them, there are:

• Writers such as the already mentioned Mir Bahadur Ali and Pierre Menard, and others, such as the English eccentric Herbert Quain, author of infinite fictional variations of one ur-novel.

• Adulterated versions of scholarly sources, as in the "translations" collected in various volumes under Borges's name. Here it may be useful to note that Borges's first attempts at fiction were imitations of Marcel Schwob's *Imaginary Lives*, brief biographies which he wrote for the *Revista multicolor de los sábados* from 1933 on, and then collected two years later as *A Universal History of Infamy*. In these short texts, both sources and quotations used by Borges were transformed by him through interpretation and in translation. When the unspeakable Andrew Hurley translated *A Universal History of Infamy* in the abominable Viking edition of 1998, he attempted to "restore" the texts with ridiculous results. "I have used the English of the original source," says Hurley. "Thus, the New York gangsters in 'Monk Eastman'" (one of the stories) "speak as Asbury quotes them, not as I might have translated Borges' Spanish into English had I been translating in the usual sense of the word; back-translating Borges' translation did not seem to make much sense." Thus runs Hurley's confession of ineptitude. Hurley obviously ignores that Borges called these stories "exercises in narrative prose."

• Imaginary books carefully annotated, as in various sources given in his stories and essays, or quoted from, such as the unforgettable Chinese encyclopedia which imperturbably divides animals into "(a) those that belong to the Emperor, (b) embalmed, (c) those that are domesticated, (d) suckling pigs, (e) mermaids, (f) fabulous beasts, (k) those drawn with a very fine camel's hair brush, (l) others, (m) those that have just broken a vase, (n) those that from a distance look like flies." And, of course, such mythical fake creations as the parallel universe of Tlön Uqbar, Orbis Tertius, and the Library of Babel.

And yet, all these fictions are never gratuitous: they are necessary inventions, filling in gaps that the history of literature neglected to fill. The Chinese encyclopedia quotation provided Michel Foucault with the starting point for *Les Mots et les choses*. "The Library of Babel" (and Borges himself, under the name Juan de Burgos) needed to exist before Umberto Eco was able to write *The Name of the Rose*. Herbert Quain is the required precedent for OULIPO. Menard is the obvious link between Laurence Sterne and James Joyce, and it is not Borges's fault that France forgot to give him birth. We should be thankful to Borges for remedying such acts of carelessness.

Fake, then, in Borges's universe, is not a sin against creation. It is implied in the act of creation itself and, whether openly recognized or adroitly concealed, it takes place every time a suspension of disbelief is demanded. "In the beginning was the Word" asks us to believe not only that "the Word was with God" but that "the Word was God," that *Don Quixote* is not only the words read by Menard, but that he is also their author.

Life, which so many times provides us with fake representations, provided Borges himself with a perfect simulacrum of a Borgesian fictional device in which the reader imbues a certain text with the required perfection of an all-encompassing answer.

In April 1976, the second world convention of Shakespearean scholars met in Washington, D.C. The high point of the congress was to be a lecture on Shakespeare by Jorge Luis Borges entitled "The Riddle of Shakespeare," and thousands of scholars fought like rock-band groupies for the privilege of occupying one of the seats in the largest hall available at the Hilton Hotel. Among the attendants was the theater director Jan Kott, who, like the others, struggled to get a seat from which to hear the master reveal the answer to the riddle. Two men helped Borges to the podium and positioned him in front of the microphone. Kott describes the scene in *The Essence of Theatre:*

Everyone in the hall stood up, the ovation lasted many minutes. Borges did not move. Finally the clapping stopped. Borges started moving his lips. Only a vague humming noise was heard from the speakers. From this monotonous humming one could distinguish only with the greatest pains a single word which kept returning like a repeated cry from a faraway ship, drowned out by the sea: "Shakespeare, Shakespeare, Shakespeare . . ." The microphone was placed too high. But no one in the room had the courage to walk up and lower the microphone in front of the old blind writer. Borges spoke for an hour, and for an hour only this one repeated word — Shakespeare — would reach the listeners. During this hour no one got up or left the room. After Borges finished, everyone got up and it seemed that this final ovation would never end.

No doubt Kott, like the other listeners, lent the inaudible text his own reading and heard in the repeated word — "Shakespeare, Shakespeare, Shakespeare" — the answer to the riddle. Perhaps there was nothing else to say. With a little help from ailing technology, the master faker had achieved his purpose. He had turned his own text into a resonant fake composed by an audience full of Pierre Menards.

PART THREE

Memoranda

"The horror of that moment," the King went on, "I shall never, *never* forget!"

"You will, though," the Queen said, "if you don't make a memorandum of it."

Through the Looking-Glass, Chapter I

The Death of Che Guevara

"Supposing it couldn't find any?" she suggested.

"Then it would die, of course."

"But that must happen very often," Alice remarked thoughtfully.

"It always happens," said the Gnat.

Through the Looking-Glass, Chapter 3

CAN WE READ POLITICS AS literature? Perhaps, sometimes, in certain cases. For example: on 8 October 1967, a small battalion of Bolivian army rangers trapped a group of guerrilleros in a scrubby gully in the wilderness east of Sucre, near the village of La Higuera. Two were captured alive: a Bolivian fighter, known simply as Willy, and Ernesto "Che" Guevara, hero of the Cuban Revolution, leader of what Bolivia's president, General René Barrientos, called "the foreign invasion of agents of Castro-Communism." Lieutenant Colonel Andrés Selich, hearing the news, scrambled into a helicopter and flew to La Higuera. In the ramshackle schoolhouse, Selich held a forty-five-minute dialogue with his captive. Until the late 1990s, little was known of Che's last hours; after a silence of twenty-nine years, Selich's widow finally allowed the American journalist Jon Lee Anderson to consult Selich's notes of that extraordinary conversation. Beyond their importance as a historical document, there is something poignant about the fact that a man's last words were respectfully recorded by his enemy.

"Comandante, I find you somewhat depressed," Selich said. "Can you explain the reasons why I get this impression?"

"I've failed," Che replied. "It's all over, and that's the reason why you see me in this state."

"Are you Cuban or Argentinean?" asked Selich.

"I am Cuban, Argentinean, Bolivian, Peruvian, Ecuadorian, etc. . . . You understand."

"What made you decide to operate in our country?"

"Can't you see the state in which the peasants live?" asked Che. "They are almost like savages, living in a state of poverty that depresses the heart, having only one room in which to sleep and cook and no clothing to wear, abandoned like animals . . ."

"But the same thing happens in Cuba," retorted Selich.

"No, that's not true" Che fired back. "I don't deny that in Cuba poverty exists, but [at least] the peasants there have an illusion of progress, whereas the Bolivian lives without hope. Just as he is born, he dies, without ever seeing improvements in his human condition."

The CIA wanted Che alive, but perhaps their orders never reached the Cuban-born CIA agent Félix Rodríguez, in charge of supervising the operation. Che was executed the next day. To make it appear that their captive had been killed in battle, the executioner fired at his arms and legs. Then, as Che was writhing on the ground, "apparently biting one of his wrists in an effort to avoid crying out," one last bullet entered his chest and filled his lungs with blood. Che's body was flown to Vallegrande, where it lay on view for a couple of days, observed by officials, journalists, and townspeople. Selich and other officers stood at the head, posing for the photographer, before having the corpse "disappear" into a secret grave near the Vallegrande airstrip. The photographs of the dead Che, with their inevitable echo of the dead Christ (the half-naked lean body, the bearded, suffering face), became one of the essential icons of my generation, a generation that was barely ten years old when the Cuban Revolution took place in 1959.

The news of the death of Che Guevara reached me towards the end of my first and only year of university in Buenos Aires. It was a warm October (summer had started early in 1967), and my friends and I were making plans to travel south and camp in the Patagonian Andes. It was an area we knew well. We had trekked in Patagonia most summers throughout high school, led by enthusiastic left-wing monitors whose political credos ran from conservatist Stalinism to free-thinking anarchism, from melancholic Trotskyism to the Argentinean-style socialism of Alfredo Palacios, and whose book bags, which we rifled as we sat around the campfire, included the poems of Mao Tse-tung (in the old-fashioned spelling), of Blas de Otero and Pablo Neruda, the stories of Saki and Juan Rulfo, the novels of Alejo Carpentier and Robert Louis Stevenson. A story by Julio Cortázar that had as its epigraph a line from Che's diaries led us to discuss the ideals of the Cuban Revolution. We sang songs from the Spanish Civil War and the Italian Resistance, the rousing "Dirge of the Volga Boatmen" and the scabrous rumba "My Puchunguita Has Ample Thighs," various tangos, and numerous Argentinean zambas. We were nothing if not eclectic.

Camping down south was not just an exercise in tourism. Our Patagonia was not Bruce Chatwin's. With youthful fervor, our monitors wanted to show us the hidden side of Argentinean society — a side that we, from our comfortable Buenos Aires homes, never got to see. We had a vague idea of the slums that surrounded our prosperous neighborhoods — *villas miseria* as we called them, or "misery villages" — but we knew nothing of the slavelike conditions, such as those described by Che to Selich, that still existed for many of the peasants on our country's vast estates, nor of the systematic genocide of the native people that had been officially conducted by the military until well into the thirties. With more or less earnest intentions, our monitors wanted us to see "the real Argentina."

One afternoon, near the town of Esquel, our monitors led us into a high and rocky canyon. We walked in single file, wondering where this dusty, unappealing stone corridor would lead us, when up in the canyon's walls we began to see openings, like the entrances to caves, and in the openings the gaunt, sickly faces of men, women, and children. The monitors walked us through the canyon and back, never saying a word, but when we set up camp for the night they told us something of the lives of the people we had seen, who made their home in the rocks like animals, eking out a living as occasional farmhands, and whose children rarely lived beyond the age of seven. Next morning, two of my classmates asked their monitor how they could join the Communist Party. Others took a less sedate path. Several became fighters in the seventies war against the military dictatorship; one, Mario Firmenich, became the bloodthirsty capo of the Montoneros guerrilla movement and for years held the dubious celebrity of heading the military's most-wanted list.

The news of Che's death felt colossal and yet almost expected. For my generation, Che had incarnated the heroic social being most of us knew we could never become. The curious mix of resoluteness and recklessness that appealed so strongly to my generation, and even to the one that followed, found in Che the perfect incarnation. In our eyes he was in life already a legendary figure, whose heroism we were certain would somehow survive beyond the grave. It did not surprise us to learn that after Che's death, Rodríguez, the treacherous CIA agent, suddenly began to suffer from asthma, as if he had inherited the dead man's malady.

Che had seen what we had seen, he had felt, as we had felt, outrage at the fundamental injustices of "the human condition," but unlike us, he had done something about it. That his methods were dubious, his political philosophy superficial, his morality ruthless, his ultimate success impossible seemed (perhaps still seems) less important than the fact that he had taken upon himself to fight against what he believed was wrong even though he was never quite certain what in its stead would be right.

Ernesto Guevara de la Serna (to give him his full name before fame reduced it to a simple "Che") was born in the city of Rosario, in Argentina, on 14 May 1928, though the birth certificate stated "June" to hide the reason for his parents' hasty marriage. His father, whose ancestors first arrived in Argentina with the conquistadores, owned a plantation in the subtropical province of Misiones. Because of Ernesto's asthma, which plagued him throughout his life, the family moved to the more salubrious climate of Córdoba and later, in 1947, to Buenos Aires. There Ernesto studied at the faculty of medicine and, armed with a doctor's title, set off to explore the Latin American continent "in all its terrible wonder." He was enthralled by what he saw and found it hard to give up the wandering life: from Ecuador he wrote to his mother announcing that he had become "a 100 percent adventurer."

Among the many people he met on this Grand Tour, one in particular seemed to haunt him: an old Marxist refugee from Stalin's pogroms whom Ernesto came across in Guatemala. "You will die with the fist clenched and the jaw tense," said this far-flung Tiresias, "in perfect demonstration of hate and of combat, because you are not a symbol, you are an authentic member of a society that is crumbling: the spirit of the beehive speaks through your mouth and moves in your actions; you are as useful as I, but you don't know the usefulness of the help you give to the society that sacrifices you." Ernesto could not have known that the old man had given him his epitaph.

In Guatemala, Ernesto became acutely aware of political strife and identified for the first time with the revolutionary cause. There, and in Mexico soon afterward, he became acquainted with the Cuban émigrés who were leading the struggle against the dictator Fulgencio Batista, whose corrupt regime had so fascinated and repelled Ernest Hemingway and Graham Greene. With a canny nose for troublemakers, the CIA agent David Atlee Phillips, appointed

at the time to Central America, opened a file on the young Argentinean doctor—a file that over the years was to become one of the thickest in the CIA's
records. In July 1955 the first meeting between Ernesto Guevara and Fidel
Castro took place in Mexico. Castro, who as far back as 1948, as a twenty-
one-year-old law student, had begun plotting against Batista's regime, took an
immediate liking to the Argentinean whom the other Cubans had started calling "Che" after the Argentinean colloquial address. "I think there is a mutual
sympathy between us," wrote Che in his diaries. He was right.

After the triumph of the Cuban Revolution in 1959, Che sought an ambitious sequel. We do not know whether he would have lent his support, out
of loyalty to the revolution, to the tyrannical measures Castro was to take in
the years to come in order to protect his regime. Che's sights were far in the
future. After the war in Cuba, Che believed, the revolutionaries would spread
to neighboring nations (Bolivia was the first chosen). Here they would wage
war against the oligarchy and their imperialist bosses, wars that would finally
force the arch-enemy, the United States, to step into the fray. As a result, Latin
America would unite against "the foreign invader" and defeat imperialism on
the continent. Che's battle was not against all forms of power, nor was it even
against the notion of a tiered society. He was certainly not an anarchist: he
believed in the need for organized leadership and he imagined a pan-American
state under a strong-handed but moral government. In a small book on the
Greek idea of liberty, *La Grèce antique à la découverte de la liberté*, the French
historian Jacqueline de Romilly pointed out that Antigone's revolt stemmed
not from a rejection of authority itself but, on the contrary, from obedience to
a moral law rather than to an arbitrary edict. Che too felt compelled to obey
such moral laws, and it was for them that he was willing to sacrifice everything and everyone, including, of course, himself. As we know, events never
proceeded beyond the Bolivian campaign. Whether Che ever learned what the
usefulness of his sacrifice was is a question that remains unanswered.

And yet something of Che's ideal survives beyond the political defeat,
even in these days when greed has almost acquired the quality of a virtue
and corporate ambition overrides mere social (let alone socialist) considerations. In part, he has become another colorful Latin American figure, like
Emiliano Zapata or Pancho Villa, used to decorate T-shirts and shopping bags:
in Bolivia, the National Tourist Board now conducts tours to the site of Che's
final campaign and the hospital where his body was displayed. But that is not
all that remains. The face of Che—alive with his starred beret, or dead, staring

as if his eyes could see into a point beyond our shoulder—still seems to encompass a vast and heroic view of men and women's role in the world, a role that may seem to us today utterly beyond our capabilities or our interest.

No doubt he had the *physique du rôle*. Epic literature requires an iconography. Zorro and Robin Hood (via Douglas Fairbanks and Errol Flynn) lent the live Che their features, and in the popular imagination he was a younger Don Quixote, a Latin American Garibaldi. Dead, as the nuns at the Vallegrande hospital noted when they surreptitiously snipped off locks of his hair to keep inside reliquaries, he resembled the deposed Christ, dark uniformed men surrounding him like Roman soldiers in modern costume. Up to a point, the dead face superseded the live one. A notorious passage in Fernando Solanas's four-hour documentary *The Hour of the Furnaces* (1968), which brilliantly chronicles Argentinean history from its earliest days to the death of Che, held the camera for several minutes on that lifeless face, forcing the audience to pay visual homage to the man who carried for us our urge for action in the face of injustice, who bore for us our bothersome *agenbite of inwit*. We stare at that face and wonder, At what point did he pass from lamenting the sorrows of this world, pitying the fate of the poor, and conversationally condemning the ruthless greed of those in power, to doing something about it, taking action against the unjust tide?

Perhaps it is possible to point to the moment in which the passage took place. On 22 January 1957, Che Guevara killed his first man. Che and his comrades were in the Cuban bush; it was midday. A soldier started shooting at them from a hut barely 70 feet from where they stood. Che fired two shots. At the second shot, the man fell. Until that moment, the earnest indignation at universal injustice had expressed itself in Byronic gestures, bad verse that Che wrote with echoes of nineteenth-century bombast, and the sort of academic prose known in Latin America as revolutionary, littered with the vocabulary of inaugural speeches and purple metaphors. After that first death something changed. Che, the ardent but conventional intellectual, became irrevocably a man of action, a destiny that had perhaps been his all along, even though everything in him seemed to conspire against his fulfilling it. Racked by asthma that made him stumble through long speeches, let alone long marches, conscious of the paradox of having been born into the class that benefited from the unfair system he had set out to challenge, moved suddenly to act rather than to reflect on the precise goals of his actions, Che assumed, with stubborn determination, the role of the romantic fighter-hero and became the figure whom my generation required in order to ease our conscience.

Thoreau declared that "action from principle, the perception and the performance of right, changes things and relations; it is essentially revolutionary, and does not consist wholly with anything which was. It not only divides states and churches, it divides families; ay, it divides the individual, separating the diabolical in him from the divine." Che (who, like all Argentinean intellectuals of his time, must have read "Civil Disobedience") would have agreed with this paraphrase of Matthew 10:34–35.

The Blind Bookkeeper

I told them once, I told them twice:

They would not listen to advice.

Through the Looking-Glass, Chapter 6

SOMETIME IN THE SPRING OF 1943, Northrop Frye wrote a paper which, a holograph note on the typescript tells us, was intended for an Emmanuel College publication "that never came off." Its title is "The Present Condition of the World" and its thrust the problem of steering "a middle course between platitude and paradox," between "Olympian detachment and Bacchic outcries" when discussing this condition, which, Frye reminds us, is one of universal warfare. With his habitual clarity, Frye warns us against judging that war reaps any benefits. "A corrupt tree can only bring forth corrupt fruit, and the notion that some good may be salvaged from this evil and monstrous horror is, however pathetic and wistful, a pernicious illusion." And Frye concludes: "And that such benefits will be 'worth' the blood and misery and destruction of the war is nonsense, unless posterity are insanely cynical bookkeepers."

Much of Frye's paper is concerned with the deistic society whose goal, he reminds us, is war. This is a truth very much worth recalling in our third millennium. It is of the essence, and we can only lament that Frye left his paper incomplete. But like all of Frye's writings, it is rich with tempting asides. One in particular, that of a certain actor in this warmongering society, may prove useful to explore. I refer to the bookkeeper, the person in charge of tallying the sum of our follies.

Bookkeeping is an excellent word. Its present meaning is fully justified. In the brightest of our mornings, when writing was invented, the first human to scratch a readable sign on a piece of clay was not a poet but an accountant. The earliest examples of writing we have, now probably destroyed in the looting of the Iraq National Museum in Baghdad, are two small tablets that record a

certain number of goats or sheep: the receipts, in fact, for a commercial trans-
action. Our first books were ledgers, and it should not surprise us that poets
later retained the two essential characteristics of their accountant elders: the
delight in making lists and the responsibility of keeping records.

Two of our founding books, the *Iliad* and the *Odyssey*, excel in both. Their
author agreed with Frye on the sterility of war and would never have suggested that the fruit of war is peace. Homer loathed war. "Atrocious," "scourge
of men," "lying, two-faced," are the terms he uses to describe it. In Homer's
poems, pity and mourning are never far from the battlefields, and it is not by
chance that pleas for compassion begin and end the *Iliad*. The debits and cred-
its in Homer's books are not those of our politicians. Homer the bookkeeper is
never insanely cynical.

Who then are these sane and merciful bookkeepers who, like Homer, set
our accounts in order? What characteristics must they have, or, rather, what
characteristics do we imagine them to have so that they can perform their
work efficiently? Why have we brought into being a Homer to father our two
primordial stories?

The history of writing, of which the history of reading is its first and last
chapter, has among its many fantastical creations one that seems to me peculiar among all: that of the authorless text for which an author must be invented.
Anonymity has its attraction, and Anonymous is one of the major figures of
every one of our literatures. But sometimes, perhaps when the depth and re-
verberations of a text seem almost too universal to belong on an individual
reader's bookshelf, we have tried to imagine for that text a poet of flesh and
blood, capable of being Everyman. It is as if, in recognizing in a work the expression in words of a private, wordless experience hidden deep within us, we
wished to satisfy ourselves in the belief that this too was the creation of human
hands and a human mind, that a man or woman like us was once able to tell
for us that which we, younger siblings, merely glimpse or intuit. In order to
achieve this, the critical sciences come to our aid and do their detective work
to rescue from discretion the nebulous author behind the *Epic of Gilgamesh*
or *La Vie devant soi*, but their labors are merely confirmation. In the minds of
their readers, the secret authors have already acquired a congenial familiarity,
an almost physical presence, lacking nothing except a name.

Homer begins long after the composition of his poems, a parent adopted,
as it were, by his children. Long centuries of literary criticism lent him features
both concrete and emblematic, first through apocryphal biographies, later as

an allegory, an idea, as the identity of a nation, and even as the embodiment of poetry itself. In every case, however, it was the readers who had first to conceive of an author for the poem to be conceivable.

This history of conceived authorship is, in some sense, a parallel history of literature. For the Greeks he was the beginning of all things Greek, of Greek civilization and history. For Virgil he was a Roman in all but birth. For the poets of Byzantium, he was a historian whose knowledge of humanity was great but whose knowledge of history was shaky. For Dante, a famous but retired craftsman. Thomas de Quincey, towards 1850, asked whether Homer (a name absent otherwise in Greek literature) might not be a deformation of the Semitic "Omar" and imagined him as a brother of the *Arabian Nights'* storytellers. The much-derided Heinrich Schliemann, following the diva-gations of the historian Karl Blind, suggested that Homer, like his Trojans, was Aryan, blue-eyed, red-haired, martial, musically gifted and philosophi-cal. Alexander Pope likened Homer to an English gentleman. Goethe saw in Homer a self-portrait: perhaps for that reason in 1805 he chose to listen to the famous Homeric lectures of Friedrich August Wolf hidden behind a curtain, embarrassed at the description of a poet whose German reincarnation he felt himself to be. Samuel Butler argued, ironically, that Homer was a woman. For Rudyard Kipling, for Ezra Pound, for James Joyce, for Derek Walcott, and for Jorge Luis Borges, Homer was everyone and no one. The linguists Milman Parry and Albert B. Lord twinned Homer with the *guzlars,* the epic Serbian singers who still chant their verses from village to village. In 2008, the German poet Raoul Schrott argued that Homer was inspired by the archaic songs of Sumer and suggested that he was a transplanted Middle Eastern poet who had learned his craft in Babylon or Ur. This Babylonian influence does not seem incongruous: the *Epic of Gilgamesh* has indeed an atmosphere not unlike that of the *Odyssey,* and the adventures of two men, Gilgamesh and Enkidu, whom the reader feels as one, are similar to those of a single man who calls himself Nobody and whom the reader sees as many.

A diversity of occupations, a diversity of influences, a diversity of ethni-cities mark the long history of the man we call Homer. What no one, neither Aristotle nor Joyce, appeared to have doubted was that the main physical fea-ture of Homer, real or imagined, singular or plural, must have been his blind-ness. Already the *Hymn to Apollo,* from about the seventh century B.C., tells the maidens of Delos that when a stranger asks them, "Who is the sweetest man of all the singers who comes here to you," they should answer, "The blind

man who lives in rocky Chios; all his songs will be the best, now and in the
time to come."

But what reason might there be for always depicting our bookkeeper as
blind? Homer's blindness is an unvarying trait in the numerous "Lives" of
Homer that were produced from the fifth century B.C. on. The best known of
these is a *Life of Homer* written in the fourth or fifth century B.C. and once attributed to Herodotus, in which it is stated that Homer was not born blind but
contracted an eye illness while visiting Ithaca, the city where he also learned
the story of Odysseus, which he would one day immortalize in his verse. The
citizens of Ithaca were pleased with the synchronicity: the moment and place
in which the poet was given his story were also those in which he was given
his blindness, as if illumination within required the lack of light without.

But Ithaca's presumption did not go unchallenged. Where exactly Homer
became blind held such obvious importance for his readers that the pseudo-
Herodotus (whom we know to have been Ionian) went on to deny Ithaca's
claim and argued instead that it was in Ionian Colophon that blindness had
struck him. "All Colophonians agree with me on this," he added with assurance in his book. Other places could boast of having lent Homer family roots
or a deathbed, and seven cities disputed his birthplace, but the site in which
blindness overtook him was, in literary terms, of the essence.

Always, according to the pseudo-Herodotus, it was the poet's blindness
that gave him the name by which we know him today. As a child, the future
author of the *Odyssey* was given the name Melesigenes, after the river Meles;
he acquired the name Homer much later, in Cimmeris, where the wandering
poet had proposed to the local senate that in exchange for bed and board, he
might make the town famous with his songs. The senators (in the tradition
of most government bodies) refused, arguing that if they set this dangerous
precedent, Cimmeris would soon be overrun with blind beggars (*homers* in
Cimmerian) in search of handouts. To shame them, the poet adopted the name
Homer.

Emblematically, blindness has a double and contradictory meaning. It is
said to be vision-inspiring, supposed to open the inner eye, but it is also the
reverse of sight, and stands for the quality of misguided judgment personi-
fied by the goddess Ate, the deity who causes mortals to make wrong deci-
sions and become victims of undiscriminating Nemesis. The double quality
of blindness is apparent in Homer's poems: at King Alcinous's court, where
Odysseus is received incognito, the blind bard Demodocus perceives in his

darkness what others cannot see or know. Seer of the truth, blind Demodocus sings of Odysseus himself, whom no one else in the court has recognized, and tells of Odysseus's quarrel with Achilles and the ploy of the Wooden Horse, causing the secret wanderer to weep at the memory of a past now distant. And yet Odysseus, however much he might admire Demodocus for his gift, knows that darkness is also the lot of the dead whose kingdom no light reaches and who bemoan their imposed blindness. Furthermore, Odysseus knows that blindness can be a punishment, a death-in-life, which he inflicts on the cannibal Cyclops who has imprisoned him and his companions. Blindness is also the punishment inflicted by the Muses on the bard Thamyris for having boasted that he could surpass them in song.

This Greek ambiguity survived in Judeo-Christian times. According to the Old Testament, blindness disqualified the descendants of Aaron from performing sacrifices to God; it was also a punishment sent to the men of Sodom for their lack of kindness towards strangers. But at the same time, the blind were protected by God's covenant: it is forbidden in Leviticus to place stumbling blocks in their way, and, according to Deuteronomy, anyone who misleads a blind person is eternally cursed. Blind Bartimaeus (Mark 10:46–52) recognizes Jesus as the Son of David and asks to "receive" (not "have restored" as some translations have it) his sight; his blindness from birth has allowed him to see the truth, and he now wishes for his eyes to be truly opened. Milton (*Paradise Lost*, 3.35–42) laments that for him, as for "Blind *Thamyris* and blind *Maeonides*," "Seasons return, but not to me returns / Day, or the sweet approach of Ev'n or Morn," and yet he rejoices in the fact that his blind eyes "feed on thoughts, that voluntary move / Harmonious numbers; as the wakeful Bird / Sings darkling, and in the shadiest Covert hid / Tunes her nocturnal Note."

As the millennial tradition has it, Homer is both a poor blind man and an enlightened seer; this double quality provides the justification for our multiple readings of his poems. Our invention of a blind Homer excuses a ritual understanding of the *Iliad* and the *Odyssey* as metaphors of life, life as battle and life as voyage; at the same time, these readings imply his existence as primordial author, the mythical Father of Poetry, and thereby guarantee the poems' prestige. Whether we conceive of Homer as the creator of the *Iliad* and the *Odyssey* or we conceive the two as giving rise to their colossal creator—that is to say, whether we believe, as Nietzsche suggested, that a person had been made out of a *Begriff* (a concept) or a *Begriff* out of a person—this circular process defines our relationship to the poetic act itself, an act which exists between an endless sequence of interpretations, each owing its vocabulary and perspective to a particular vision of the world, and also our relationship to an all-encompassing creative genius from the farthest regions of time — someone whom it is impossible to antecede, a man indifferent to all deluding worldly sights, capable, because of his blindness, of seeing beyond them into the truth.

The concept of blindness builds upon itself. To be blind is not to see the outer reality; implicit in this observation is the suspicion that the inner reality is perceived more clearly if not encumbered by any other. If the world of color and form is no longer grasped (that is to say, limited, as Blake says, by our senses), then the poet is free to apprehend the universe in its fullness, the past through his story's past and the future through the future of his characters. He can become both our seer and our bookkeeper in the fullest sense. When Hector says to Andromache in the *Iliad:*

There will be a day when holy Troy will perish.
And Priam, and the people of Priam of the fine ash-spear

the reader knows of what fate he is speaking and that it isn't only Priam's own that lies open to the poet.

I have mentioned the pragmatic source of the invention of writing in Mesopotamia. But technologies are often, always perhaps, diverted from their original intentions. Soon the recording of buying and selling transactions was joined by the story of those transactions, and the buyers and sellers who until then were headings on either column acquired individual features and personal narratives. Writing became, to a large extent, the place that not only recorded our world but also created it, and the words that until then were spoken to render memory present and to name experience and desire were set down in clay to keep the stories available to generation after generation of readers. The bookkeeper, who in order to account for a trading of sheep or goats needed both his eyes, now, symbolically at least, was best thought to be blind, because readers realized that the stories that mattered were not those copied from nature but those that distilled and translated the natural and social world into the language of myth. Frye, in his notes at the end of his unfinished paper, remarks that the prophet's role is to preach the Word of revealed, not natural, religion. If we take the etymological meaning of the term *religion* ("to bind again" or "to bind more strongly"), we have something akin to the definition of poetry.

On this etymological level, the opposition between natural and revealed rebinding acquires a startling meaning. On the one hand, we are creatures bound to the earth and to the things of this earth. We are not different from any other living thing or even, from a molecular point of view, from other inanimate things. The old image of humans as stardust is scientifically true: our atoms belonged long ago to exploded stars. But as Darwinism has taught us, each species has evolved different methods to adapt to this material world, and our species acquired along the way the ability of self-consciousness, to know not only that we are on this earth but that *we* are on this earth. And through this self-consciousness, or simultaneously with this self-consciousness, we acquired the gift of imagination. Not imagination regarded as some flimsy, immaterial quality like that of the fantastical phlogiston which our great-grandparents thought to cause combustion, but as a biological human function such as eating or breathing. This function enables us to learn by creating in the mind situations that do not materially exist in order to study them and overcome any difficulties they may present, to be used later when such situations arise in real life. Battles are fought in the mind and strange landscapes explored before we ever have to take up arms or set upon our travels; the *Iliad* and the *Odyssey* are our preparation for every struggle and every displacement. Poetry—literature—binds us again to the world, more strongly this time, because it helps us become conscious of it and of ourselves.

The state of universal warfare that Frye saw as the state of the world in the last years of World War II is, to some degree, that of the world today. In 1943, Frye described the United States as the "archetypal country" (according to a holograph note in the margin of the typescript). And this is still the case today, even though there are signs that the archetype is shifting. The battlefields have changed ground, the soldiers wear different uniforms, but the weapons are just as deadly and the madness just as keen. Samson killing the Philistines by killing himself was metamorphosed into the Japanese kamikaze pilots, who in turn metamorphosed into the suicide terrorists whose carnage we suffer now every day somewhere in the world.

And on either side, we continue to create our enemies. We require these enemies to keep the industry of war going but also to keep our sense of self cocooned. We are fearful of the stories we don't know, and we are afraid that those who tell them will impose on us their versions of the world, and that we shall no longer know who we are. We don't want to change the plots we know for plots that we may not understand, or that may not move us if we do, or may move us in mysterious ways. We want the comfort of a familiar face by the bed. We hold to the conviction that our stories are better than anyone else's. We distrust foreign tongues, and we don't encourage translation. The balance sheet that the writers of the twentieth century drew of the deathly experience of war was meant to be a cautionary one, summed up as "Never Again." It didn't stick, as daily experience has since proven. All the chronicles, all accounts factual and fictional, all the symbols and fables woven from the debris left by the slaughter and the destruction somehow failed to build for us a peaceful, or even a more humanly acceptable, world. If there is a God who reads us, then His patience or indifference is certainly remarkable.

Heinrich Heine, in the eighth chapter of *Atta Troll*, imagined that for bears, the Creator would have a bearish aspect whose fur was divinely "spotless and white as snow." Closer to the time of the *Iliad*, Xenophanes of Colophon (that same island of Colophon that claimed the honor of having blinded Homer) argued that if cows, horses, and lions had fingers and could paint and sculpt like men, the cows would create gods like cows, the horses gods like horses, and "so on with all the others." We imagine our gods as we imagine our authors, much as we imagine ourselves to be. Perhaps we imagine that our authors and gods have failed because we know that we ourselves are fallible.

The perceived failure of our storytelling is not, therefore, one-sided. Literature is a collaborative effort, not as editors and writing schools will have it, but as readers and writers have known from the very first line of verse ever set down in clay. A poet fashions out of words something that ends with the last full stop and comes to life again with its first reader's eye. But that eye must be a particular eye, an eye not distracted by baubles and mirrors, concentrated instead on the bodily assimilation of the words, reading both to digest a book and to be digested by it. "Books," Frye once noted, "are to be lived in."

As the Homer we invented for ourselves understood, the poet alone, even gifted with blindness, cannot alone create a new world. Demodocus's song requires that Odysseus listen and weep, and that he understand for the first time the battles he has fought and the travels he has endured. Odysseus must, for the sake of poem, become blind as well, blind as Demodocus, blind through his tears if necessary, in order to be able to draw his eyes away from the ambitions of Agamemnon and the foul moods of Achilles, from the beauty of Circe and the terrors of the Cyclops, and look at something darker and lovelier and deeper within himself.

Perhaps in the same way, the reader too must acquire a positive blindness. Not blindness to the things of the world, certainly not to the world itself, nor to the quotidian glimpses it offers of bliss and horror. But blind to the superficial glitter and glamour of what lies all around us, as we stand erect in our selfish point of observation, a point that, because we stand in it, remains invisible to us and makes us believe that we are the center of the world, and that everything is ours for the taking. With greedy eyes we want everything to be made to our measure, even the stories we demand to be told. They should not be stories larger than ourselves, or stories of such minuteness that they take us inward, into our unacknowledged being, but merely adventures that are skin deep, easily perused and quick to grasp without causing the merest ripple. We are given to read neatly packaged books alike in size and color, which the industry tells us will entertain us without worry and lend us thoughts without reflection, offering us simple, ready-made models, ambitious, egotistical, and thin, to which we can aspire without giving up anything. We want our poets to be like the tyrant described in W. H. Auden's epitaph:

> Perfection, of a kind, was what he was after,
> And the poetry he invented was easy to understand;
> He knew human folly like the back of his hand,
> And was greatly interested in armies and fleets;
> When he laughed, respectable senators burst with laughter,
> And when he cried the little children died in the streets.

The blind bard is a universal paradigm. Our Homer, creator of the mythical world on a human scale, required the one feature that prevents our senses from misleading us, from being distracted by a conventional reality, from being "programmed" (as we'd say today) by preconceived patterns of thought. But we too, the readers, on the other side of the page, require such a gift to keep us, as Rupert Brooke more accurately put it, from "being blinded by our eyes." Such a gift, as Northrop Frye taught us, lies at the core of the true craft of reading.

The Perseverance of Truth

"I've a right to think," said Alice sharply, for she
was beginning to feel a little worried.

"Just about as much right," said the Duchess,
"as pigs have to fly . . ."

Alice's Adventures in Wonderland, Chapter 9

ON 19 JANUARY 2007, I READ that that the Turkish-Armenian journalist Hrant Dink had been murdered in Istanbul by a seventeen-year-old Turkish nationalist for having criticized the government's denial of the Armenian genocide. The murder of journalists who attempt to tell the truth is a time-honored custom, and the justifications advanced for such crimes enjoy an equally long tradition (I use the terms *honored* and *enjoy* advisedly.) From John the Baptist and Seneca to Rodolfo Walsh and Anna Politkovskaya, truth-tellers and their executioners inhabit a surprisingly vast literary shelf.

A little over twenty-four centuries ago, in the year 399 B.C., three Athenian citizens brought a public action against the philosopher Socrates for being a menace to society. After the trial, in which both the prosecution and the defendant presented their case, the majority of the jury of representative Athenian citizens found Socrates guilty and, with peculiar severity, condemned him to death. Plato, the disciple who perhaps loved Socrates best, wrote some time afterwards a record of his defense, which has come down to us under the title of the *Apology*. In it, Plato has Socrates discuss many subjects: the notion of impiety, the character of his accusers, the charges of heresy, of corrupting the young, and of insulting the Athenian democratic identity: this latter charge carries for us today a curious familiar ring. And like a luminous thread running through the entire allocution, Socrates discusses the question of a citizen's responsibilities in a just society.

Halfway through the speech, Socrates considers the risks a man will run who is willing to tell the truth in the world of politics. "No man on earth who conscientiously," says Socrates, "prevents a great many wrongs and illegalities from taking place in the state to which he belongs, can possibly escape with his life. The true champion of justice, if he intends to survive even for a short time, must necessarily confine himself to private life and leave politics alone."

Indeed. A long roll-call of truth-sayers, dating back to the first prophets, have paid with their lives for this human vocation, and every year Amnesty International publishes a bulky reminder of how many of them are kept today in prison, all around the world, for no other reason than that of speaking out. Hans Christian Andersen, in "The Emperor's New Clothes," forgot to tell us what happened to the little boy who pointed out that the Emperor had in fact no clothes on. Surely we would not be surprised to learn that his fate was not a happy one.

Socrates explains to the court that he is well aware of the risks of telling the truth. The person who opposes wrongs and illegalities, says Socrates, pays for telling the truth about these wrongs and illegalities with his own life. So much is clear. But then, Socrates—Socrates, for whom the pursuit of truth is, as it should be for everyone, the primary purpose in life—Socrates goes on to say that, if a person wants to save his skin "even for a short time," this pursuit must be restricted to his private circle and not be allowed to overflow into the vaster circles of society itself.

But how is such a thing possible?

Unless Socrates is being dangerously ironic, he of all people must know that every pursuit of the truth, every questioning of a lie, every attempt to bring into the light fraud, imposture, and deceit, every pointing out that the Emperor is in fact naked must, necessarily, spill over into the common ground, into the world we share with our fellow citizens. At either end of our life we are alone, in the womb and in the grave, but the space in between is a common realm in which rights and responsibilities are defined by each of our neighbors' rights and responsibilities, and every perjury, every falsehood, every attempt to conceal the truth damages everyone in that realm—including, in the final account, the liar himself. After Socrates was forced to put an end to his life, the Athenians repented, closed the wrestling yards and the gymnasia in a sign of mourning, and banished two of the accusers from Athens while condemning the third one to death.

As Socrates knew well, every society defines itself in two ways: through what it allows and through what it forbids—through that which it includes and recognizes as its own image and through that which it excludes, ignores, and denies. And every citizen living within the walls of a society has a double obligation: an obligation to obey those common inclusions and exclusions (that is to say, society's laws) and an obligation to his or her own self. A living society must have, within its fabric, the means to allow every citizen the performance of this double duty: both to obey and to question, both to comply and to change society's laws. A society in which citizens are allowed one but not the other (a dictatorship or an anarchic state) is a society that does not trust its own tenets and is therefore threatened with extinction. Human beings require the common protection of the law, together with the freedom to voice their thoughts and testimonies and doubts, as much as they need the freedom to breathe. This is of the essence.

Perhaps it may be easier to understand Socrates' words if we listen for their echo in a distant and strange disciple of his, a certain gentleman of La Mancha who, obsessed by his reading of novels of chivalry, sets out one day to be a knight errant and to carry out the precepts of valor, honor, and righteousness "for the increase of his honor and as a service to his society." Like Socrates, Don Quixote knows of the risks of attempting to prevent "a great many wrongs and illegalities from taking place in the state to which he belongs." And for this, Don Quixote is deemed a madman.

But what precisely is his madness? Don Quixote sees windmills as giants and sheep as warriors, and has faith in enchanters and flying horses, but in the midst of all this fantasy, he believes in something as solid as the earth he treads: the obligatory need for justice. Don Quixote's storybook visions are circumstantial imaginations, ways of coping with the drabness of reality. But his driving passion, his unshakable conviction, is that orphans must be helped and widows rescued—even if, as a consequence of his actions, both the savior's and the victim's fates become worse. This is the great paradox that Cervantes wants us to face: justice is necessary even if the world remains unjust. Evil deeds must not be allowed to go unchallenged even if other deeds, of greater evil perhaps, will follow. Jorge Luis Borges put it this way, in the mouth of one of his most fearful characters: "Let Heaven exist, even if our place be Hell."

In this pursuit of justice (which is the human way of seeking out truth) Don Quixote acts individually. Never, in his many adventures, does he lust for a position of power, a seat of government, a role in the world of politics. It is Sancho, his squire, who is offered (in the tradition of the novels of chivalry) the lordship of a realm as reward for his efforts. And it is Sancho to whom Don Quixote offers advice about public affairs: dress the part, know something of both arms and letters, show humility, avoid passion in judgment. Between irony and wisdom, Don Quixote's recommendations define the role of the head of state — a role to which, clearly, he himself does not aspire.

Towards the end of all the adventures, returning home with Sancho after having been tortured and mocked by dukes and duchesses, Don Quixote has this to say to his native village: "Open your arms and welcome your son, Don Quixote, who though vanquished by a stranger's hand, returns the victor of himself; and that, as has often been told, is the greatest victory that can be desired." And here is perhaps part of the answer to my question. Maybe this is what Socrates meant when he said that "the true champion of justice, if he intends to survive even for a short time, must necessarily confine himself to private life and leave politics alone." Not to seek public victory or praise but merely a private victory over oneself, an honorable role in the intimate sphere, vanquishing the cowardly impulse to close one's eyes to injustice and to remain silent about society's wrongdoings.

This is Don Quixote's underlying concern: not to ignore society's atrocities, not to allow those in power to bear false witness, and, above all, to chronicle the things that happen. And if, to get to the truth, Don Quixote must retell reality in his own literary vocabulary, so be it. Better to see windmills as giants than to deny the existence of windmills absolutely. Fiction, in Cervantes's case, is the way of telling the truth when Spain had decided to rebuild its own history on a lie, the lie of a pure, uncontaminated Christian kingdom, barely a century after the expulsion of the Jews and the Arabs, and at the time of the banishment of all Arab and Jewish converts. For that reason, in order to denounce the fictional reality, Cervantes invents an honest fiction and tells the reader that he is not the father but merely the stepfather of *Don Quixote*, that the real author is a certain Cide Hamete Benegeli, an Arab scholar, one of the supposedly disappeared people, so that credulous readers will believe that the book they hold in their hands is merely a translation from a tongue long banned in the realm. Fiction, Cervantes implies, must reveal the deceit of an identity in which Spanish history attempts to clothe itself, an identity cleansed of any Jewish or Arab influence, an identity that need not question or take itself to task because it is supposed to be cloaked in Christian purity. Innocent as the boy in Andersen's tale, Don Quixote points his sword at that identity and shouts: "But it is naked!"

For Cervantes, history, the faithful account of what has happened, can be "translated" in many ways in order to be better told. It can be revealed in a novel, it can purport to be the words of a mysterious Arab author, it can be told as a story of magic and violence and wonder. But however put into words, it must, in the deepest sense, be true. History, Don Quixote tells Sancho early in the book, is the mother of truth, "rival of time, storehouse of deeds, witness of the past, example and pattern of the present, a warning to all future ages." And Spain is only now learning the lesson Cervantes tried to teach it four centuries ago — though even today it is unwilling to recognize its full import. Although the existence of a Jewish and Arab Spain is, these days, for the most part acknowledged, the question of a fake national identity has come up once again in Spain's refusal to recognize the crimes of the Franco era. Unconscionably, Judge Baltazar Garzón has been denied the request to have Franco's mass graves opened and an inquiry set up into the atrocities committed by both sides, Nationalists and Republicans. But like the invention of Spain's identity in Cervantes's time, this too may perhaps one day be deemed worthy of a story.

Like Spain then and now, collectively, we find it difficult to acknowledge murky moments in our society's history. Through cowardice, through ignorance, through arrogance, and, in fewer cases, through shame, most societies have at times denied or attempted to change certain culpable events in their past. In the first half of the second millennium B.C., the priests of the Temple of Shamash in Mesopotamia faked the date on one of their newly erected monuments in order to lend it eight more centuries of existence, thus managing to increase the royal allowance to their venerable institution. The Chinese emperor Shi Huangdi, in 213 B.C., commanded that all the books in his realm be destroyed so that history could begin with his accession. During the Third Reich, to prove that no Jewish inspiration had ever contributed to German Kultur, the propaganda minister, Paul Joseph Goebbels, proclaimed that Heinrich Heine's celebrated poem "Die Lorelei" was an ancient German ballad of anonymous authorship. Joseph Stalin ordered that party members who had fallen from grace be deleted from official photographs so that no record of their political existence remain for future historians. Closer to our time, the Chinese Communist Party refused to acknowledge that the massacre at Tiananmen Square had ever taken place. The examples, alas, are endless.

Sometimes, the event denied concerns one single individual wished into oblivion; sometimes millions of men, women, and children deliberately and systematically murdered. In every case, the denial is a society's attempt to do the impossible, to do that which medieval theologians concluded was impossible even for God: to alter the past. Alice, in *Through the Looking-Glass*, explaining her intention to climb to the top of a hill, is interrupted by the Red Queen, who says that she could show her hills "in comparison with which you'd call that a valley." "No, I shouldn't," Alice answers bravely. "A hill *can't* be a valley. That would be nonsense —." Indeed, that would be nonsense. Over and over again, our societies insist on such nonsense, arguing that hills are valleys and that whatever has evidently and painfully taken place never really happened.

In the thirteenth century, the Armenian poet Hovhannès d'Erzenga, known as Blouz, wrote that "only the true sun gives light: let us distinguish it from the untrue one." This obvious injunction is not easy to carry out. Not because, in a few cases, it is hard to distinguish truth from falsehood, the true sun from the untrue one, but because to do so would imply that a public fault has been committed, an unjustifiable deed performed, and most societies have a limited vocabulary of apology and repentance.

Perhaps because of this, because of the difficulty of uttering a collective self-reproach to purge our troubled souls, most religions have ritualized the act of contrition. The Catholic *mea culpa* repeated three times during mass, the Jewish Day of Atonement in which forgiveness is asked from your friends and neighbors, the request for God's pardon uttered in the five daily Muslim prayers are all attempts to recognize human frailty in our societies, and the terrible acts of which we are capable. These rituals pay homage to the victims, of course, but above all they offer the victimizers, if not oblivion for their sins, never oblivion, at least the chance to redeem themselves by acknowledging that they have done wrong. Words can be misused, can be forced to tell lies, to whitewash the guilty, to invent a nonexistent past in which we are told we must believe. But words can also have a curative, creative power. By allowing the misdeed to take shape first in the mouth of the victimizer and then in the ear of the victim, by transporting it from what happened to what is acknowledged to have happened, words effectively allow history to be, as Don Quixote proposed, the mother of truth.

So as not to permit unspeakable events to remain unspoken, so-called democratic societies, as secular organizations, sometimes raise monuments to commemorate their victims and to bear witness to past atrocities. However, the danger with monuments is that unless they are somehow transformed into a living, shared experience, they become the mute carriers of those memories, enabling the society to discharge itself of the burden of remembrance and allow the unspeakable events to become silent once more. What has been called "the duty of memory" in a society must be an active duty, one of forceful remembering, so that the terrible acts will not be repeated, or, if they are, so that they cannot be repeated claiming ignorance of their import and of how future society will judge them. In 2009, in the *New York Times*, the Nobel Prize winner Paul Krugman maintained that unless Barack Obama orders an inquest into what happened during the Bush administration (and we expect that he won't), those who hold power will believe that they are above the law "because they don't face any consequences if they abuse their power." As Don Quixote would argue, most acts of injustice are committed because those responsible know that they will not be made to face the consequences. Under such circumstances (and here we return to Socrates), it is every citizen's duty "conscientiously" to try to prevent "a great many wrongs and illegalities from taking place in the state to which he belongs." And that duty includes the *active* duty of memory, a secular ritual of atonement in which the guilty acts of the past are put into words for all to hear.

But memory can betray us. Sometime in the 1960s, psychologists identified a phenomenon in our psyche which they called the "perseverance of memory." Often when we learn of a fact that later proves to be untrue, the force with which that information was first received can be so great that it overrides the knowledge that the "fact" is untruth, and we continue to remember the "fact" as true in spite of being told otherwise. That is to say, the memory of a known falsehood assimilated as true perseveres in our mind and prevents the corrected information from replacing it. If this is so, if we can "remember" as true what we positively know to be false, then it should not surprise us that, on a collective level, the duty of memory can become distorted and a revisionist version of the past can supplant that which historians have factually proven. In the Athenian court, Socrates can be shown to have done what he demonstrably has not done and be condemned to death for it, and the Bush administration may, in future years, be remembered "for bringing peace to the Middle East" (as Condoleezza Rice has pronounced). History may be the mother of truth, but it can also give birth to illegitimate children.

However, if governments can sometimes rely on this social perseverance of memory to misinform and misconstruct, they must also take into account another equally powerful perseverance: what I would call the "perseverance of truth." There is an old English saying, "Truth will out." Beyond our fantasies and our logic, beyond our invention of social realms and fairy tales about the universe, lies the implacable reality of what is and of what has happened, and it will always eventually appear from under the innumerable layers of deceit. We can, with practice, as the White Queen says to Alice, believe "six impossible things before breakfast," but this feat of irrationality will ultimately change nothing in the relentless course of the world.

Adolf Hitler, who had much practice in such things, asked his military cabinet, shortly before the invasion of Poland in 1939: "Who, after all, speaks today of the annihilation of the Armenians?" Hitler's rhetorical question has thousands of answers because, ever since the terrible decade in which over a million and a half Armenians were massacred by order of the Ottoman Turkish government, Don Quixotes around the world have been repeating, "Here is an unforgivable atrocity, here is an evil deed that cannot be forgotten, here is a terrible act of great injustice. You may want to believe the impossible, that the great crime never took place. But it did. And nothing you can say can undo the tragic event." From the anonymous protesters in America who in 1915 collected over a million dollars for the Armenian cause to individual brave voices such as that of Hrant Dink, Hitler's question is not allowed to go unanswered.

And yet those thousands of voices are not enough. Since Hitler's time, the world has condemned, and continues to condemn, the atrocities of the Third Reich, and Germany itself has recognized, and continues to recognize, those atrocities. "Yes," the Germans say, "this happened. And we repent in the name of our forefathers. And we beg forgiveness, if such a thing is possible. And we will not forget nor allow anyone to forget what happened here, on our soil. And we will not allow this to happen again." And every time a neo-Nazi group tries to reinvent the historical past, Germany and the majority of Germans say "No." This is what I mean by the perseverance of truth.

But Turkey, or at least the Turkish government, unfortunately has not yet reached that stage of recognition. In spite of those thousands of acknowledging voices around the world, a large section of Turkish society, as if attempting to lend strength to Hitler's question with an accomplice silence, still refuses to admit the historical facts: that the entire population of Anatolia, the oldest extant population in the region at the time, over a million and a half men, women, and children, was exterminated between 1909 and 1918 in what the poet Carolyn Forché has called "the first modern genocide."

Hrant Dink wanted nothing more than that which every serious journalist, every honest intellectual, every self-respecting citizen wants: that the truth be recognized. His murder confirms Socrates' assertion with which I began this essay, that "no man on earth who conscientiously prevents a great many wrongs and illegalities from taking place in the state to which he belongs, can possibly escape with his life." Hrant Dink must have known this, and also Socrates' corollary, that "the true champion of justice, if he intends to survive even for a short time, must necessarily confine himself to private life and leave politics alone." Such a confinement, as Dink understood and as Socrates himself knew, is impossible, because everything we do, every decision we make, every opinion we give as private citizens has political consequences. Politics is, by definition, a collective activity in which a few occupy the seats of power and the rest of us the remaining myriad roles. No citizen is dispensable, no voice useless in the continuing struggle to render our societies less false in their pretences and more true to themselves. "My only weapon was my sincerity," Dink wrote in his last published article. As Socrates knew all too well, sincerity is a weapon that is deadly in more ways than one. This was Dink's final lesson: that even though the seeker of truth may be silenced, his sincerity (from the Latin *sincerus*, meaning "clean" or "pure") will eventually do away with the lie.

AIDS and the Poet

"I think I should understand that better," Alice said
very politely, "if I had it written down."
Alice's Adventures in Wonderland, Chapter 9

IN THE LATE 1990S, THE PAPERS announced that the government of South
Africa was going to set up a program to import and produce low-cost drugs
to treat patients with AIDS. Almost four years after the announcement, the
Association of Pharmaceutical Industries, representing several of the largest
laboratories in Europe and North America, filed a suit in the High Court of
Pretoria, claiming that the South African law which allowed for such a program—a law signed by Nelson Mandela—contravened the international
copyright and patent agreement meant to protect the rights of scientists, artists, and writers.

In South Africa today there are millions people infected with the HIV
virus, close to 10 percent of the population, perhaps the highest percentage
in the world. They cannot be treated, purely for economic reasons. A year
of AIDS drugs for one person costs, in Europe or North America, between
twenty and thirty thousand American dollars. This in Africa (and in most of
Asia and in South America) is far beyond a common mortal's dreams. Local
pharmaceutical companies, however, have managed to produce generic drugs
(that is to say, the same drugs as their costly European and American counter-
parts without the designer labels) at a tiny fraction of the price, about four
hundred dollars for a year's treatment. In answer to this, the largest of all pharmaceutical companies, GlaxoSmithKline (born from the fusion of two British
giants, Glaxo-Wellcome and SmithKline-Beecham), solemnly declared that
"the patent system must be maintained at all costs." At all costs.

It will be said that without the monetary investment of these companies,
scientific research would be impossible. To allow for new discoveries, those

with the money must be coaxed into investing in research and, in order to get people with money to invest in anything, they must be convinced that their money will make a profit. Not just a profit, but a large profit. And a guaranteed profit. And what greater guarantee can be found on this earth than sickness leading unto death, and the human desire to overcome it? Therefore the temptation for setting up a pharmaceutical company in our time is clearly strong. The motives behind such companies are not what one would call philanthropic: the call for healing is not foremost in their mandate. There is an illumination in the sixteenth-century French manuscript *Chants royaux du Puy de Rouen* that depicts Christ as an apothecary, dispensing (at cost, I'm sure) the drugs of eternal life to Adam and Eve. I do not believe that this image is known to the trustees of GlaxoSmithKline.

A few years later, because of international pressure, thirty-nine of the biggest companies dropped their suit in South Africa. The protests and letter campaigns of Doctors Without Borders and other organizations created what one of the pharmaceutical companies called "exceedingly adverse publicity"; carefully balancing profit gained from usury and profit lost from a tainted image, the advertisement-savvy companies chose to negotiate. However, the question of the legitimacy of these gargantuan profits remains unanswered.

How can we (I mean our societies) tempt these companies into investing in scientific research without giving them in exchange the lives of millions of human beings? I leave the practical problem of funds, trusts, rates, and taxes to faith-healing economists, and choose to concentrate instead on the other factor in this equation: the moral context which allows these practices to thrive.

Is it possible for a society to pose convincingly such moral imperatives while addressing effectively the practical demands of the scientific industry? Is it possible for a society to consider, at the same time, the urgencies of science and the context within which that science develops? "Erst kommt das Fressen, dan kommt die Moral," sniggered Bertolt Brecht some time ago. "First comes the fodder, then the morals." Is it possible for a society to lend equal importance to both morals and fodder, to the ethos and the business of a society simultaneously? This ancient question keeps cropping up, again and again, in all ages and under all skies. It was asked when Agamemnon sacrificed his daughter Iphigenia for the sake of fair winds that would allow the Greeks to sail to Troy. It was illustrated by George Bernard Shaw in *Major Barbara*. It was imagined by Mary Shelley in *Frankenstein* and by H. G. Wells in *The Island of Dr. Moreau.* Its true essence was put into a story by Oscar Wilde, when the Young King, who refuses to be crowned in jewels crafted by suffering, asks whether the rich man and the poor man are not brothers and receives the answer, "Aye, and the name of the rich brother is Cain."

This unanswerable question is all-important. Literature, as we know all too well, does not offer solutions, but poses good conundrums. It is capable, in telling a story, of laying out the infinite convolutions and the intimate simplicity of a moral problem, and of leaving us with the conviction of possessing a certain clarity with which to perceive not a universal but a personal understanding of the world. "What in the world is this emotion?" asks Rebecca West after reading *King Lear.* "What is the bearing of supremely great works of art on my life that makes me feel so glad?" I know that I have come across that emotion in all kinds of literature, supremely great and supremely small, in a line here and there, a paragraph, and sometimes, not often, a whole book, for no obviously discernible reason, when something that is being told about a particular character or situation suddenly acquires for me, its reader, enormous private importance.

Are Don Quixote's quixotic gestures commendable when, after he has threatened a farmer for viciously beating his young apprentice, the farmer redoubles his punishment once Don Quixote is safely out of sight? Is Hercule Poirot, at the end of his long life, justified in murdering a murderer in order to prevent others from being murdered? Is it excusable for Aeneas to abandon to her tears the welcoming Dido for the sake of the glory of the future Roman Empire? Should Monsieur Homais have received the *croix d'honneur* after the death of the miserable Bovarys? Is Lady Macbeth a monster or a victim, and should we pity her or fear her, or (this is much more difficult) fear and pity her at precisely the same time?

Reality deals in specifics under the guise of generalities. Literature does the contrary, so that *A Hundred Years of Solitude* can help us understand the fate of Carthage, and Goneril's arguments can assist us in translating the dubious ethical dilemma of General Paul Aussaresses, the torturer of Algiers. I am tempted to say that perhaps this is *all* that literature really does. I am tempted to say that every book that allows a reader to engage with it asks a moral question. Or rather: that if a reader is able to delve beyond the surface of a given text, such a reader can bring back from its depths a moral question, even if that question has not been put by the writer in so many words, but its implicit presence elicits nevertheless a bare emotion from the reader, a foreboding or simply a memory of something we knew, long ago. Through this alchemy, every literary text becomes, in some sense, metaphoric.

Literature handbooks since the Middle Ages have arduously distinguished between metaphor and image, image and simile, simile and symbol, symbol and emblem. Essentially, of course, the intellectual insight that conjures up these devices is the same: an associative intuition intent on apprehending the reality of experience not directly but once removed, as Perseus did in order to see the face of the Gorgon, or Moses the face of God. Reality, the place in which we stand, cannot be seen as long as we are in it. It is the process of "once removed" (through imagery, through allusion, through plot) that allows us to see where and who we are. Metaphor, in the widest sense, is our means of grasping (and sometimes *almost* understanding) the world and our bewildering selves. It may be that all literature can be understood as metaphor.

Metaphor, of course, breeds metaphor. The number of stories we have to tell is limited, and the number of images that echo stories meaningfully in every mind is small. When Wallace Stevens tells us that

> In that November off Tehuantepec
> The slopping of the sea grew still one night,

he is seeing once more the sea (the same sea) that Stéphane Mallarmé longed for so lovingly, after telling us that "all flesh is sad" and that he has "read all the books." It is the same terrifying sea that Paul Celan hears, "umbellet von der haiblauen See," "barking in the shark-blue sea." It is the wave that breaks three times for the tongue-tied Tennyson on "cold grey stones"—the same "tremulous cadence" that moves Matthew Arnold on Dover Beach and makes him think of Sophocles "who long ago / Heard it on the Aegean, and it brought / Into his mind the turbid ebb and flow, / Of human misery." Mallarmé, Celan, Tennyson, Arnold, Sophocles are all present in Stevens when, far away on a distant shore, he sees the metallic water shine and grow still. And what does the reader find in that sight, in that sound? Arnold says it exactly: we find "in the sound a thought." A thought, we can add, that translates itself through the power of metaphor into a question and into the vaporous ghost of an answer.

Every act of writing, every creation of a metaphor is a translation in at least two senses: in the sense that it recasts an outer experience or an imagining into something that elicits in the reader a further experience or imagining; and in the sense that it transports something from one place to a different one — the sense in which the word was employed in the Middle Ages to describe the moving of the pilfered remains of saints from one shrine to another, an activity generously known as *furta sacra*, "holy thefts." Something in the act of writing, and then once more in the act of reading, pilfers, enshrines, and changes Arnold's essential literary thought from writer to writer and reader to reader, building on the experience of creation, renewing and redefining our experience of the world.

A few years after Kafka's death, Milena Jesenskà, the woman he had loved so dearly, was taken away by the Nazis and sent to a concentration camp. Suddenly life seemed to have become its reverse: not death, which is a conclusion, but a mad and meaningless state of brutal suffering, brought on through no visible fault and serving no visible end. To attempt to survive this nightmare, a friend of Milena's devised a method: she would resort to the books she had read, stored in her memory. Among the texts she forced herself to remember was a short story by Maxim Gorky, "A Man Is Born."

The story tells how the narrator, a young boy, strolling one day somewhere along the shores of the Black Sea, comes upon a peasant woman shrieking in pain. The woman is pregnant; she has fled the famine of her birthplace and now, terrified and alone, she is about to give birth. In spite of her protests, the boy assists her. He bathes the newborn child in the sea, makes a fire, and prepares tea. At the end of the story, the boy and the peasant woman follow a group of other peasants: with one arm, the boy supports the mother; in the other he carries the baby.

Gorky's story became, for Milena's friend, a paradise, a small safe place into which she could retreat from the daily horror. It did not lend meaning to her plight, it did not explain or justify it; it did not even offer her hope for the future. It simply existed as a point of balance, reminding her of the light at a time of dark catastrophe.

Catastrophe: a sudden and violent change, something terrible and incomprehensible. When the Roman hordes, following Cato's dictum, razed the city of Carthage and plowed the land with salt; when the Vandals sacked Rome in 455, leaving the great metropolis in ruins; when the first Christian Crusaders entered the cities of North Africa and after slaughtering the men, women, and children set fire to the libraries; when the Catholic kings of Spain expelled from their territories the cultures of the Arabs and the Jews, and the Rabbi of

Toledo threw up to Heaven the keys of the Ark for safekeeping until a happier time; when Pizarro executed the welcoming Atahualpa and effectively destroyed the Inca civilization; when the first slave was sold on the American continent; when large numbers of Native Americans were deliberately contaminated with smallpox-infected blankets by the European settlers (in what must count as the world's first biological warfare); when the soldiers in the trenches of World War I drowned in mud and toxic gases in their attempt to obey impossible orders; when the inhabitants of Hiroshima saw their skin fly off their bodies under the great yellow cloud up in the sky; when the Kurdish population was attacked with toxic weapons; when thousands of men and women were hunted down with machetes in Rwanda; and when the suicide planes struck the twin towers of Manhattan, leaving New York to join the mourning cities of Madrid, Belfast, Jerusalem, Bogotá, and countless others, all victims of terrorist attacks — in all these catastrophes, the survivors may have sought in a book, as did Milena's friend, some respite from grief and some reassurance of sanity.

For a reader, this may be the essential, perhaps the only justification for literature: that the madness of the world will not take us over completely though it invades our cellars (the metaphor belongs to Machado de Assis) and then softly takes over the dining room, the living room, the whole house. Joseph Brodsky, prisoner in Siberia, found it in the verse of W. H. Auden. For Reinaldo Arenas, locked away in Castro's prisons, it was in the *Aeneid;* for Oscar Wilde, at Reading Gaol, in the words of Christ; for Haroldo Conti, tortured by the Argentinean military, in the novels of Dickens. When the world becomes incomprehensible, when acts of terror and terrifying responses to that terror fill our days and our nights, when we feel unguided and bewildered, we seek a place in which comprehension (or faith in comprehension) has been set down in words.

Every act of terror protests its own justification. It is said that before ordering each new atrocity, Robespierre would ask, "In the name of what?" But every human being knows, intimately, that no act of terror is possibly justified. The constant cruelty of the world and, in spite of everything, its daily miracles of beauty, kindness, and compassion bewilder us because they spring up with no justification, like the miracle of rain (as God explains to Job) falling "where no man is." The primordial quality of the universe seems to be absolute gratuity.

Of all this we are aware, as we also aware the old trusims: that violence breeds violence, that all power is abusive, that fanaticism of any kind is the enemy of reason, that propaganda is propaganda even when it purports to rally us against iniquity, that war is never glorious except in the eyes of the victors, who believe that God is on the side of large armies. This is why we read, and why in moments of darkness we return to books: to find words and metaphors for what we already know.

Metaphor builds on metaphor and quotation on quotation. For some, the words of others are a vocabulary of quotations in which they express their own thoughts. For others those foreign words *are* their own thoughts, and the very act of putting them on paper transforms those words imagined by others into something new, reimagined through a different intonation or context. Without this continuity, this purloining, this translation, there is no literature. And through these dealings, literature remains immutable, like the tired waves, while the world around it changes.

During a staging of Eugène Ionesco's *Rhinoceros* in Algiers, at the height of the War of Independence, after the hero, Béranger, had pronounced the play's last brave words, "Je ne capitule pas!" the entire audience, Algerian *independantistes* and French colonials, burst out in cheers. For the Algerians, Béranger's cry echoed their own, intent on not giving up their struggle for freedom; for the French, the cry was theirs, intent on not surrendering the land their fathers had conquered. Ionesco's words are, of course, the same. The sense (the reading) is different.

It may be useful here to look at the practical side of this question of intellectual ownership, that is to say, at the notion of literary copyright. What it sets out to do is not protect the right of, say, Homer, to put himself forward as sole inventor of the expression "the wine-dark sea" but rather to regulate the exploitation of that expression by, say, Ezra Pound and the Greek Tourist Board. While Martial brags about his poems being read by even the centurions posted at the empire's farthest borders, he also complains about publishers who sell those poems to those far-flung centurions without paying him, the author, for the privilege. It was in order to make sure that Martial got his sestertium that on 4 August 1789 the Revolutionary Assembly in Paris abolished all privileges of individuals, cities, provinces, and organizations and replaced them with the notion of rights. Authors as well as publishers, printers, and booksellers were granted particular rights regarding a text, and would from then on share in the profits of what the author had written, the publisher published, the printer printed, and the bookseller sold. Two essential points were made. The first, that "the work is deemed created, independently of its being rendered public, by the very fact of its having been conceived by the author, even if left unfinished." The second, that "intellectual property is independent of the property of the material object itself." That is to say, *Rhinoceros* belongs to Ionesco even before the first production, independent of the fact that Algerians and French may each have appropriated the play through their individual readings. The "value" of *Rhinoceros* belongs to Ionesco.

What is this value? This is the best answer I know: "Value does not carry whatever it is written on its forehead. Instead, it transforms each of the fruits of labor into a hieroglyph. In time, man seeks to decipher the meaning of the hieroglyph, to penetrate the secrets of the social creation to which he contributes, and this transformation of useful objects into objects of value is one society's creations, just like language itself." The author of this splendid discovery is the sadly ill-reputed Karl Marx. Value as meaning: anyone interested in literature can grasp the common sense of this notion, akin to Keats's Beauty as Truth and Truth as Beauty. "What imagination seizes as beauty must be Truth—whether it existed there or not," Keats wrote to a friend. Value then is a metaphor, as are Truth and Beauty. They stand as conceptual realities, things that we know are there, in our flesh and blood, but that, like the thrill of *King Lear,* cannot be defined more precisely.

A company, an aptly called Anonymous Society, a Multinational, or an Umbrella Organization, is a thing invisible and incorporeal, except in its effects. It has no face, no soul. The "value" of its labors, the meaning of its metaphors is falsely advertised, and it is society's dull obligation to read its pronouncements closely, over and over again, in order to be aware of their potential harm in which we are, as citizens, implicated.

In March 2000, Paul Stewart, one of the directors of the German pharmaceutical company Boehringer Ingelheim, was touring an AIDS clinic in the township of Khayelitsha, outside Cape Town. Boehringer is the maker of Nevirapine, a drug used to treat certain AIDS-related illnesses, and Stewart, according to an article by Jon Jeter in the *Washington Post* (20 April 2001), was in South Africa to prevent the production of a generic version of the drug. At a certain point in the tour, Stewart came upon an emaciated seven-year-old boy alone in a crowded waiting room. The boy was too weak to lift his head, and his chest was covered in raw blisters. Stewart grew pale. "I would like to pay for his treatment, personally," he blurted out. Wisely, the clinic's director told Stewart that it was too late for such private emotional responses. Stewart had to do more than address one single heartbreaking case. He had to confront the vastness of the problem, the large moral question, the horror of which the seven-year-old boy was the visible reality, a horror in which Stewart's company played an intricate part, a horror which Stewart could not change by the expiatory gesture of digging into his pockets.

I am not certain that a piece of writing, any writing, however brilliant and moving, can affect the reality of South Africa's AIDS sufferers, or any other reality. There may be no poem, however powerful, that can remove one ounce of pain or transform a single moment of injustice. But there may be no poem, however poorly written, that may not contain, for its secret and elected reader, a consolation, a call to arms, a glimmer of happiness, an epiphany. Something there is in the modest page that, mysteriously and unexpectedly, allows us, not wisdom, but the possibility of wisdom, caught between the experience of everyday life and the experience of literary reality.

There is perhaps a metaphor that may conjure up this space between our imagining of the world and the page (from the point of view of the writer) or the space between the solid page and our imagining the world (from the point of view of the reader). In the seventh canto of the *Inferno*, Dante describes the punishment of thieves who in the looking-glass universe of sin and retribution are condemned to losing even their own human forms and are endlessly transformed into creature after monstrous creature. These transformations happen in staggered stages, gradually, so that at no one time is the agonized soul a single self-possessed shape. And Dante says (this, in Richard Wilbur's translation):

> Just so, when paper burns, there runs before
> the creeping flame a stain of darkish hue
> that, though not black as yet, is white no more.

Between the blankness of the page and the authoritarian letters in black, there is a space, a moment, a color in which, ever-changing, the writer and the reader both may find illumination just before the meaning is consumed by the flames.

PART FOUR

Wordplay

"The question is," said Alice, "whether you *can* make words mean so many different things."

"The question is," said Humpty Dumpty, "which is to be master — that's all."

Through the Looking-Glass, Chapter 6

The Full Stop

"Begin at the beginning," the King said, very gravely, "and go
on till you come to the end: then stop."
Alice's Adventures in Wonderland, Chapter 12

DIMINUTIVE AS A MOTE OF DUST, a mere peck of the pen, a crumb on
the keyboard, the full stop is the unsung legislator of our writing systems.
Without it, there would be no end to the sorrows of young Werther, and the
travels of the Hobbit would have never been completed. Its absence allowed
James Joyce to weave *Finnegans Wake* into a perfect circle, and its presence
made Henri Michaux compare our essential being to this dot, "a dot that death
devours." It crowns the fulfillment of thought, gives the illusion of conclu-
siveness, possesses a certain haughtiness that stems, like Napoleon's, from its
minuscule size. Anxious to get going, we require nothing to signal our beginnings, but we need to know when to stop: this tiny memento mori reminds
us that everything, ourselves included, must one day come to a halt. As an
anonymous English teacher suggested in the 1680 *Treatise of stops, Points or
Pauses*, a full stop is "a Note of perfect Sense, and of a perfect Sentence."

The need to indicate the end of a written phrase is probably as old as
writing itself, but the solution, brief and wonderful, was not set down until
the Italian Renaissance. For ages, punctuation had been a desperately erratic
affair. Already in the first century A.D., the Spanish author Quintilian (who
had not read Henry James) had argued that a sentence, as well as expressing
a complete idea, had to be capable of being delivered in a single breath. How
that sentence should be ended was a matter of personal taste, and for a long
time scribes punctuated their texts with all manner of signs and symbols, from
a simple blank space to a variety of dots and slashes. In the early fifth century,
Saint Jerome, translator of the Bible, devised a system, known as *per cola et
commata*, in which each unity of sense would be signaled by a letter jutting

out of the margin, as if beginning a new paragraph. Three centuries later, the *punctus*, or dot, was used to indicate both a pause within the sentence and the sentence's conclusion. Following such muddled conventions, authors could hardly expect their public to read a text in the sense they had intended.

Then, in 1566, Aldus Manutius the Younger, grandson of the great Venetian printer to whom we owe the invention of the pocket book, defined the full stop in his punctuation handbook, the *Interpungendi ratio*. Here, in clear and unequivocal Latin, Manutius described for the first time its ultimate role and aspect. He thought that he was offering a manual for typographers; he couldn't know that he was granting us, future readers, the gifts of sense and music in all the literature to come: Hemingway and his staccatos, Beckett and his recitativos, Proust and his largo sostenuto.

"No iron," wrote Isaac Babel, "can stab the heart with such force as a full stop put just at the right place." As an acknowledgement of both the power and the helplessness of the word, nothing else has served us better than this faithful and final speck.

In Praise of Words

"Speak English!" said the Eaglet. "I don't know the meaning of half those long words, and, what's more, I don't believe you do either."
Alice's Adventures in Wonderland, Chapter 3

RENÉ DESCARTES BELIEVED THAT monkeys could speak but preferred to remain silent in order not to be forced to work. The intellectual process of granting reality to an invention and then applying to that invention the rigid rules of reality is nowhere more splendidly demonstrated than in our relationship to language. Long ago in a faraway desert, a man of whom we know nothing decided that the words he had scratched onto clay were not conventional accounting signs numbering legal decrees or heads of cattle but the terrible manifestations of a willful god, and that therefore the very order of these words, the number of letters they contained, and even their physical appearance must have a sense and a meaning, since the utterance of a god cannot hold anything superfluous or arbitrary. The Kabbalists took this faith in the literary act even further. Since (as the book of Genesis recorded) God had said "Let there be light" and there was light, they argued that the very word *light* possessed creative powers, and that if they knew the mot juste and its true intonation, they too would be able to become as creative as their Creator. The history of literature is, in some sense, the history of this hope.

Less interested in imitating the Almighty, less confident in the magical powers of the word, but equally concerned with discovering the secret rules that govern a system of signs and symbols, wordplay enthusiasts, like the ancient Kabbalists, permutate, count, rearrange, divide, and reassemble letters for the sheer delight of drawing order out of chaos. Behind the passion of crossword-puzzle solvers, punsters, anagrammatists, palindrome makers, dictionary scourers, Scrabble players, and code breakers lies a kind of mad faith in the ultimate rationality of language.

Word games are very ancient. There are examples of acrostics among the Mesopotamians, anagrams among the Hebrews, pangrams among the Greeks, palindromes among the Romans. Puns (which reveal behind their at times doubtful humor the weblike coherence of the cosmos) are, of course, universal. At least according to Saint Jerome's translation of the Bible, the founding of the Catholic Church was based upon a pun made by Jesus when he said, pointing to Peter (*Petrus* in Latin), "Upon this rock (*petram*) I will build my church."

Word games are myriad: texts that eschew one or several letters of the alphabet (such as Georges Perec's novel *La Disparition*, brilliantly translated into English by Gilbert Adair, which excludes in both languages the letter *e*); texts that avoid all vowels except one ("I'm living nigh grim civic blight; / I find its victims, sick with fright"); tautonyms, or words made up of two identical parts (such as *murmur*), which in turn develop into the highly sophisticated "charade sentence" ("Flamingo pale, scenting a latent shark / Flaming opalescent in gala tents — hark!"); transposal words obtained by rearranging the letters of another word (*carol* to *coral*); three-way homonyms, the scourge of foreigners learning English (*idol, idle,* and *idyll*); "undominated" words in which an alphabetic sequence can be found containing all the letters in that sequence, when no word exists with a longer sequence of those same letters (as in *deft*).

The fact that many of these classifications are also hugely entertaining should not lead anyone to question their seriousness. Poets, for instance, have long used them, from Lasus of Hermione, who in the sixth century B.C. excluded sigma from his "Ode to the Centaurs," to Cervantes, who included in his preface to *Don Quixote* a few "truncated" sonnets (in which not the final but the penultimate syllable of each line carries the rhyme), and from Gerald Manley Hopkins with his fondness for charade sentences ("Resign them, sign them") to the anonymous bard who penned, "Time wounds all heels." Poetry, in fact, is proof of our innate confidence in the meaningfulness of wordplay. That we should trust rhyme to lend meaning or alliteration to express a thought is not too far from the spirit of the Renaissance necromancers who believed that the secret name of Rome was *Roma* spelled backwards. (What hope is there for Vancouver, which magically reads *Revuocnav* — "Revue of Knaves" in the Evenki tongue, or Toronto, which reveals itself as Otnorot, "The Rot of Otno" in Esperanto?)

Martin Gardner observed that much of today's wordplay "would not have been made without the help of computers" but adds that he does not want to "give the impression that computers are required for making new discoveries." Indeed. Though computers can tell us (for instance) that there are 3,276 ways in which three letters can be chosen from the alphabet with repetition allowed, such mechanical methods provide, I believe, scant entertainment to either seasoned lexicophiles or inveterate Kabbalists. At the dawn of the computer age, Arthur C. Clarke penned a warning. In a short story called "The Nine Billion Names of God," a Tibetan lamasery engages the services of Western computer experts to run through all possible combinations of letters in order to come up with one that is the hidden name of God—a task which, these Tibetans believe, lends a reason to the existence of the universe. The experts install the computer, and over several months it spews out countless jumbles of names. At last, the final combination is produced. As the experts pack up to leave, one of them casually looks up at the sky. Overhead, without any fuss, the stars are going out.

A Brief History of the Page

The Fish-Footman began by producing from under his
arm a great letter, nearly as large as himself.
Alice's Adventures in Wonderland, Chapter 6

THE PAGE LEADS AN UNDERHAND existence. Lost among its brethren within the covers of a book, or singled out to carry, all on its own, a limited piece of scribbling; turned, torn, numbered, dog-eared; lost or recalled, lit up or deleted, skimmed or scrutinized the page comes into our reader's consciousness only as a frame or container of what we mean to read. Its brittle being, barely corporeal in its two dimensions, is dimly perceived by our eyes as they follow the track of the words. Like a skeleton supporting the skin of a text, the page disappears in its very function, and in that unprepossessing nature lies its strength. The page is the reader's space; it is also the reader's time. Like the changing numbers of an electronic clock, the pages mark the numbered hours, a doom to which we, the readers, are called to submit. We can slow down or speed up our reading, but whatever we do as readers, the passing of time will always be clocked by the turning of a page. The page limits, cuts, extends, censors, reshapes, translates, stresses, defuses, bridges, and separates our reading, which we arduously attempt to reclaim. In this sense, the act of reading is a power struggle between reader and page over the dominion of the text. Usually, it is the page that wins.

But what exactly is a page?

According to Jorge Luis Borges, the infinite Library of Babel which he imagined containing all the books in the universe (not only all those that have already been written but all those that may or may not be one day written) could be reduced to no more than one book. In a footnote to the story, Borges suggests that the vast library is useless: one single volume would suffice, if that volume were made up of an infinite number of infinitely thin pages. The handling of this volume would, of course, be painfully cumbersome: each apparent page would unfold into other pages, and the inconceivable middle page would have no verso.

Here we have, in one nightmarish moment, the page in all its glory and all its horror: as an object that allows or demands a frame for the text it contains so that we, the readers, can address it piecemeal and inquire into its meaning; and also as an object that restricts the text to fit its frame, cutting it down to size, separating it from its whole, changing or circumscribing its sense. Every page is of this double nature.

If we define *page* as the single spatial unit within which a portion of text is contained, then the Sumerian clay tablets and large granite slabs of 5000 to 2000 B.C. count as pages. For practical reasons, the Sumerian page appears to have been considered mainly as a setter of limits. Any given text must fit the space allotted to it: if the text runs on, it must divide itself in units of self-contained sense. The Sumerian tablet doesn't break off in mid-sentence and continue on another tablet. The space of the tablet and the space of the text coincide.

Both the Sumerian stone slabs and clay tablets were conceived as two-sided. The slabs stood as high as monuments, bearing inscriptions on one or both sides. The tablets, like those used by students, for instance, in order to learn how to write in the scribe schools, carried on the recto the teacher's text and on the verso the student's attempt at reproducing that text. The learning system required that the student learn literally to bear in mind the teacher's writing until he reached the tablet's other side.

This dual notion ceased almost entirely with the creation of the scroll around the sixth century B.C. Most scrolls were written on one side only, on which the fibers ran horizontally, but there were also scrolls written on both sides—such a scroll was known as *opisthograph*, and was fairly uncommon. In the scroll, both the idea of frame and the idea of recto-verso seem to disappear. The sheets of papyrus used to form most scrolls were no larger than fifteen inches high by nine inches wide and did not break the text up into something akin to our individual, separate pages. Though the scrolls had margins and were divided into columns, with no space between words, it was the scroll itself that determined the extension of the text (in Greece they were generally twenty to thirty feet long). An ordinary scroll could contain one book of Thucydides or two or three books of the *Iliad*.

The scroll granted both writer and reader apparent freedom: no truncated lines, except from column to column; no cumulative sense of progression, except as the scroll unfurled and rolled up again; no imposed unit of text, except as the scrolling allowed only one section to be viewed at a time. Trying to demonstrate the paradoxical quality of this freedom, many centuries later, the Spanish writer Juan Benet composed a novel, *Una meditación* (1969), on a single roll of paper attached to his typewriter, which an elaborate mechanism prevented him from reversing—that is to say, whatever he wrote became the final draft, without the guidance or division of pages.

The appearance of the codex lends a new meaning to the concept of page. It has been suggested that the invention of the codex stemmed from the need to produce a more portable container for the text, and that a folded sheet was obviously more easily transportable than a scroll. Clay was cumbersome, papyrus was brittle, so parchment and vellum became the preferred materials for codex-making in Europe until the first paper mills were installed in Italy in the twelfth century. Other materials had been used in other parts of the world: fanlike wooden books in Korea and Egypt, block-printed books on paper in China, cloth books in other parts of Asia. Whatever the material—vellum, parchment, cloth, paper, or wood—all these pages quietly imposed their limits on the text.

But once the limiting qualities of the page were recognized by readers and writers, those very qualities called for disruption. Whether through shape, interior space, marginalia, or reshuffling, the page's characteristics were to be constantly altered. In the struggle over the supremacy of the text, the writer and the reader decidedly wanted to be in control.

The first shape of the page was perhaps dictated by the measurements of the human hand. The Sumerian clay tablet fit the hand of a child (the student scribe) or the hand of an adult (that first remote accountant to whom we owe the art of writing). The vagaries of social needs and political propaganda blew the amiable tablet to gigantic proportions: a code of laws from Ashur, for instance, from the twelfth century B.C., measured more than six and a half square feet. But periodically, the page reverted to its manufactured origins: the codex that Julius Caesar is supposed to have created by folding a scroll into pages to send dispatches to his troops; the medieval books of hours, meant for private devotions; Aldus Manutius's pocket classics; the standard-size books decreed by François I in 1527; the paperbacks of the twentieth century. In our time, the French publisher Hubert Nyssen created the elongated format that distinguishes the Actes Sud publications by measuring vertically the distance between the metacarpal bone and the tip of his index finger and horizontally from the root of his thumb to the far edge of his palm.

All these pocket-size pages give the illusion of being contained in the hand, but that illusion does not carry far. On the page the strings of words are cut off by the blank space of the margins and trail away in order to resurface on the next page, thereby forcing the reader to hold the text's meaning in constant suspense. Widows, hanging lines, irritants to the eye, have caused printers to suggest to the author changes (especially in journalism), so that the text itself is altered to fit the demands of the page's tyranny.

Partly to subvert these special demands, writer and readers created odd-shaped books: round, horizontally elongated "à l'italienne," heart shaped, in-folded, and accordion-style, which then in turn imposed their own individual limitations. In our time, the so-called artists' books routinely interfere with the classic shape: they enlarge the text to cross over the gutter, or reduce it to fit in its entirety a given space, or work the text into shapes that overwhelm the shape of the page itself. The shape of a page seems to cry out for counter-action.

When not changing the format or shape, the writer can change the text the page contains, so that the subversion becomes internalized. Laurence Sterne, composing his *Tristram Shandy* in the 1760s, introduced blank pages, pages filled with ellipses, and even a page printed completely in black. Lewis Carroll, in order to provide a limitless map for his Snark-hunters, designed a page that was completely white. And Guillaume Apollinaire with his *Calligrammes*, poems written in the physical shape of their subject, and concrete poets such as the Brazilian Haroldo do Campos, imposed a new shape to the page from inside, drawing the reader's attention away from the straight margins into new and startling textual designs.

This interior restructuring is of course quite ancient. Many are the medieval manuscripts that play with acrostics and crossword-puzzle-like grids, multiplying the use of a page many times. As the broadening of restrictions became apparent, the text began to breed its own commentary. The page metamorphosed into a series of concentric spaces. as when Scripture, for instance, written in a narrow central panel of the page, was carefully surrounded by a gloss, which was in turn surrounded by further annotations, which then received the reader's scribbles on the margins. These spaces are not in themselves protectionist: the comments of the third space, for example, may annotate either the central text or the gloss; the scribbles may refer to the notes, the gloss, or the central text. To take just one among thousands of possible examples: one of the manuscripts of Aristotle's *Parva naturalia*, now in the British Library (MS Royal 12 G.ii), from the second half of the thirteenth century. The text itself occupies the center top right; it is framed by glosses derived from Averroës and written presumably by a certain Henry de Renham of Kent. In turn, there are interlinear commentaries on both Aristotle and Averroës that look a little like our own proofreader's notes and are written in a smaller hand, filling the spaces left by the glosses. Dante's proposed four possible levels of reading—literal, allegorical, analogical, and anagogical—acquire physical reality on Henry de Renham's page, as text, gloss and commentary on text, and gloss quadruplicate the space allotted by the page to the text.

Sometimes the tyranny of the page is subverted on one level only, but that in a way that is powerfully intimate and personal. Montaigne, whose scribbling habits amounted to a conversation, would continue the dialogue at the back of the book he was reading, including the date on which he had finished it in order to better recall the circumstances of the event. Though Montaigne's books were in various languages, his marginal notes were always in French ("no matter what language is spoken by my books," he tells us, "I speak to them in my own"), and in French he extended the text and its notes through his own critical comments. For Montaigne this reading method was necessary for what he called his "quest for truth": not the story as given by the words within the confines of the page but the reflection of that story, mused upon and retold by the reader Montaigne in spaces reclaimed, there where the page left itself vulnerable to encroachment.

These blank spaces, left after the writer has tried to vanquish what Stéphane Mallarmé called "the terrifying whiteness of the page," are the very spaces in which the readers can exercise their power, in those gaps that were for Roland Barthes the essence of the erotic thrill, the interstices in the text (but we can apply this to the physical text on the page as well), which he described as "there where the clothes gape." In those openings between the edge of the paper and the edge of the ink, the reader (let us stretch this image as far as it will go) can cause a quiet revolution and establish a new society in which the creative tension is established no longer between page and text but between text and reader.

This is the distinction made by Jewish medieval scholars regarding the Torah. According to the Midrash, the Torah that God gave Moses on Mount Sinai was both a written text and an oral commentary. During the day, when it was light, Moses read the text God had written, and in the darkness of the night he studied the commentary God had spoken. The first action submits the reader to the authority of the page; the second forgoes the page and submits the text to the authority of the reader.

Conscious of the danger of the page's supremacy, the great eighteenth-century Hasidic master Rabbi Levi Yitzhak of Berdichev attempted to explain why the first page of each of the treatises of the Babylonian Talmud was missing, obliging the reader to begin on page 2. "Because however many pages the studious man reads, he must never forget that he has not yet reached the very first page." That is to say, the commentary of the Word of God has no foreseeable beginning, neither on paper nor in the reader's mind. By the elimination of the first page, no page could be said to force the Word of God into an explanation.

Since the page defines the text it contains by marking its beginning, middle, and end, eliminating the first page can be seen as an act of defiance. The nineteenth-century moralist Joseph Joubert went further. According to Chateaubriand, Joubert's library contained only the texts that Joubert was truly fond of. "When he read," says Chateaubriand, "he would tear out of his books the pages he didn't like, thereby achieving a library entirely to his taste, composed of hollowed-out books bound inside covers that were too large for them."

Joubert did not in fact destroy the sequence of pages; he merely interrupted it with moments of silence. In our time, Raymond Queneau tried to destroy the order imposed by the numbered pages by dividing each page into dozens of strips, each carrying a line of text. In this way, readers could construct their own pages by composing (as in the child's game book of mix and match) a near infinity of new texts. Queneau called his book *A Hundred Thousand Billion Poems*. Julio Cortázar, in a better-known example, proposed a book, the novel *Hopscotch,* that had the appearance of submitting to the given sequence of pages but then destroyed that semblance of order by suggesting first that the reader should follow a sequence of chapters other than the one set out in the table of contents and then that the reader allow either chance or personal choice to dictate the order in which the chapters were to be read. Here the reader claims supremacy over both the space and time of the reading.

Flaubert, as he was writing *Madame Bovary,* read certain sections of the novel to his friend Louis Bouilhet, but confessed that as he did the narrative time of those pages (113 pages, from page 139 to page 251) became not his own but something dictated by the flicking of the pages itself. "This afternoon," he wrote to Louise Colet, "I ended up abandoning my corrections; I no longer understood anything; immersed in my work, it became overwhelming; what seemed now like a mistake, five minutes later no longer seemed like one; it's all a series of corrections and corrections of corrections that are endless." And earlier he had written, "The middle pages of all long books are always awful."

Is our lot, in this electronic age, at all different? Electronic reading alters certain parameters. Reading on the screen precludes (up to a point) the time-restricting quality of reading on paper. The scrolling text (like that of the Roman or Greek scrolls) unfurls at a pace that is not dictated by the dimensions of the page and its margins. In fact, on the screen, each page shifts shape endlessly, remaining the same in size but altering its content, since the first and last line keep changing as we scroll, always within the fixed frame of the screen. Though reading a long text on the screen is thoroughly inconvenient (for physiological reasons that may, no doubt, change as we evolve), it does free us (if we want to be freed) from the very temporal realization of progress illustrated by the thickening bulk of pages held in the left hand and the diminishing bulk of pages held by the right.

In fact, Borges's imaginary book finds its incarnation in the not-quite-infinite pages of the e-book. The e-book page exceeds the nightmarish quality of Borges's book since none of its pages has a verso. Since text can always be added to the "volume," the e-book has no middle. The e-book page is the frame applied by the reader to what is essentially Borges's borderless text. Like every other literary creation, the e-book was foreseen in Borges's Library.

For the common reader, the notion of page becomes confused with the notion of leaf or folio, and the dictionary defines *page* as both "the leaf of a book" and "one side of it." In this sense, a short poem by Goethe on the infolded leaf of the gingko tree perhaps best describes the dual nature of the page. The gingko tree is called a living fossil, since it is the only modern representative of a species long vanished and, like the page of a book, does not exist in the wild. Each of its leathery leaves, though born from a single stem, seems double, and this ambiguity led Goethe to write his poem:

> This small leaf that traveled eastward
> And now in my garden lies,
> offers rich and secret meanings
> That bear wisdom to the wise.

Is it one green living creature
Split in two and yet left whole?
Are they two that fused together
To become a single soul?

The right answer to these questions
Can be found by everyone.
Can't you tell from my own verses
That I'm also two and one?

The Voice That Says "I"

"We, indeed!" cried the Mouse, who was trembling down to the
end of its tail. "As if *I* would talk on such a subject!"
Alice's Adventures in Wonderland, Chapter 2

IT WAS WHILE READING Stevenson's *Treasure Island* when I was eight or
nine that I was suddenly struck by the question of who I really was. My edition had an introduction titled "How This Book Came to Be Written" that
explained how Stevenson, one rainy afternoon, had started telling the story
to his stepson by drawing for him the island's map. A picture of the map was
faithfully reproduced as the frontispiece.

    Treasure Island begins with a confession: "I take up my pen in the year of
grace 17—, and go back to the time when my father kept the 'Admiral Ben-
bow' inn . . ." The appearance at the inn of the wicked Old Sea Dog afraid of
a certain "seafaring man with one leg" had begun to fill me with delightful
terror when, twenty-odd pages into the book, I noticed that the narrator was
suddenly addressed as "Jim." "Jim": I leafed again through the introduction.
There was no doubt about it. The author, I read, was someone whose Christian
names were "Robert Louis." And yet here, on the printed page, his name was
given as "Jim." I couldn't understand how that was possible. Was the narrator
not the person whose name appeared on the cover? It obviously was not a
mistake since "I take up my pen . . ." was clearly written in the first paragraph.
Therefore the "I" who had begun to tell me his story was not "Robert Louis,"
the book's announced author, but someone who called himself "Jim" and who,
conjured out of nowhere, had mysteriously usurped Robert Louis's position in
my book. Was then the story untrue? Could the author have *lied?*

    To say "I" and tell a story implied, for me, at the age of eight, a promise
of truth, the presence of a real-life narrator who was about to reveal to me, his
reader, something that had happened to him across the seas in another century.

With this switch from "Robert Louis" to "Jim," my confidence in storytelling was suddenly shaken. I realized that "I" could be not "I," the author, but someone the author only pretended to be, a trickster playacting on the page, a deceiver taking on the voice and gestures of someone else. And if this were so (the notion was unclear to me, since I was too young to put it into words) then the "You" whom the "I" addressed, that "You" whom I'd assumed magically to mean "Me," might also be a lie. From that moment on, I had to agree to comply with rules that I had until then ignored and to act out my role in a story I had still to discover. On that terrible afternoon, reading became, not a voyage of exploration guided by a trusted author, but a game in which the author only played the part of the author and the reader the part of the reader. Later on, as all readers must, I realized that my performance was the leading one, and that the existence of the story depended on my willingness and creative interpretation. But all those years ago in that first, essential moment of revelation, I felt the appearance of the imaginary "I" as a loss and a betrayal.

But why?

The "I" in *Treasure Island* is obviously the "I" of a made-up character, whether in Jim's narrative or, later on in the book, in the narrative of Dr. Livesey, and every reader, even the eight-year-old reader that I was, quickly accepts the device and allows him- or herself to believe in its fictional reality. We the readers accept the fact that "I" becomes someone who tells us to call him Ishmael, or Marcel, or Robinson; just as we accept the fact that these "I"s can truly speak to us, on intimate terms, across seas and centuries. The reader's faith not only moves mountains but allows their very stones to speak.

Sometimes, however, such faith seems hardly necessary. In certain cases, the rules of the game tell us that the "I" who speaks is, indeed, the "I" who writes. Under these circumstances, how are we to respond as readers to the "I" that carries the same name as the author, the author disguised not as a fictitious character but as himself, speaking from behind a mask that has the features of his own face? How are we to establish a dialogue with the writer who shamelessly crosses fully dressed into his own creation and forgoes his reality as author for the sake of the reality of a creature made out of words in his own image?

A writer much older than Stevenson may help us towards an answer.

Throughout the whole of Dante's *Commedia* runs the subject of identity, echoed in the repeated question of the shades: *"Who are you?"* The first lines of the poem, too well known to be quoted, conjure up from the very beginning the slender figure of the poet's first person singular. But who is this *"my-self"* who finds himself in the dark wood midway on the path of life, whose initialed sins are gradually wiped off his forehead as he ascends the laborious Mount Purgatory, who flies through the circular heavens with lightning speed towards the essential, ineffable Face? Are we, his readers, supposed to recognize, as we open the book, this frightened man who recalls for us in fragments particular scenes of his life, harping on the intangible Beatrice, on nebulous ancestors, and on his beloved and hated Florence? Who is it that stands there in the *"myself,"* between the collective *"our"* that qualifies *"life"* and the almost anonymous infinitive of *"to say"?* Who is it that tells us he *"returned,"* made anew like a budding plant after reaching the starlit mountain top? Whose *"desire and will"* turn to love at the end of the journey?

Halfway through his descent into Hell, Dante meets souls who have committed violence against nature, where, for reasons not entirely clear from a theological point of view but perfectly understandable for anyone with any experience of the world, artists and politicians don't mix. Here he meets a trio of distinguished Florentine Guelfs who praise Dante's inspired *"speech"* and, like so many other condemned souls, ask him to speak of them when he is back in the world of the living. Earthly fame continues to have its attractions, even for those who are no more.

> "Therefore, if you escape these dismal haunts
> and return to see again the lovely stars,
> mind that you speak of us to living men
> when you rejoice in telling them 'I was there.'"
> [*Inferno*, 16.82–85, trans. Richard Howard]

"I was" is how they sum up Dante's journey, his time spent in the other world: the act of being in the first person singular that asserts Dante's existence both as witness and as protagonist. Not "I was there," as Richard Howard's translation has it, in the sense of having trodden the unthinkable and everlasting place, but "I existed," in order to assert the action that Hamlet would later have in mind for his famous question. The voice, Dante's voice, that might grant them posthumous memory must have not only the experience of place but also that of time, and enjoy existence in the deepest, most essential sense, as a living body and an immortal soul. The poet who is to tell future gen-

erations the truth cannot be merely emblematic, cannot depend only on the reader's will to believe in him; he must be able to say *"I was"* and must acknowledge a factual biography, a specific mind, a physical body. Anonymous literature makes us uncomfortable: even the muddle of different books we call the Bible must have, we say, an Author whose floating beard lends him literary venerability. To avoid the discomfort of anonymity, early readers invented for the *Iliad* and the *Odyssey* a blind poet called Homer who knew about seafare and warfare, and who recited his verses on the island of Chios. Dante, more prudently, does not rely on posterity and has his own creations attribute these traits to himself. Everywhere on his otherworldly journey, Dante tells his readers how he meets people he knows well (a catalogue of social notables that caused Lamartine to brand the *Commedia* "a Florentine *Who's Who*"); the corollary to this is that they, in turn, must know Dante, and either greet him with rapture or curse him. Here then, admits the reader, are trustworthy witnesses, since they can recognize Dante in his own story; ergo, Dante must be real. Gradually, in the reader's eye, Dante (not the author of the poem but its protagonist, Dante the poet) begins to exist. But for what purpose?

Somewhere in the vast *Summa Theologica*, Saint Thomas Aquinas, Dante's teacher, invented a literary conceit called *quem auctor intendit,* "what the author intended," which has since become a strand in every literary tapestry, as much a part of any book as the plot or the protagonist. To the reader's implicit question, "Why are you telling me this?" Dante provides implicit answers: "Because I want you to know how I was lost and how love saved me; because I want you to learn from my visionary experience; because I want to defend my belief in a society in which State and Church fulfill their separate obligations." Dante's threefold intention can be read (as far as we can read anything) as political, moral, and personal: first, to oppose the legendary Donation of Constantine that granted the Church temporal power, and to follow Christ's precept in Matthew 22:21, rendering "unto Caesar the things that are Caesar's, and unto God the things that are God's"; second, to "teach by the example," according to scholastic methods, by means of his poetic model of the world; third, to fulfill the promise of his encounters with Beatrice and make them meaningful. Above all (but perhaps this is what we, as readers, want Dante's intention to be), the third purpose, the reasons of love. Falling in love is unreasonable and ineffable: Dante attempts to lend it logic and translate it into words. To follow Dante on this triple path and not abandon the story midway, we need to believe in the existence of the man whose words echo in our ear, as if he were ourselves. To be able to enter a fiction and take part in its reality, "I," in our mind, has to become "You."

The dialogue a writer establishes with the reader is one of artifice and deceit. To tell the truth, the writer must lie in a number of clever and convincing ways; the instrument for doing this is language—unreliable, manipulated and manipulative, officially sacrosanct in that it purports to say what the dictionary says it says, but in practice subjective and circumstantial. The narrative voice is always a fiction behind which the reader assumes (or is asked to assume) a truth. The author, the leading character, appears to the reader out of nowhere, almost but not quite a creature of flesh and blood, made present by his own words, like the Beckettian voice that spoke to Moses from the burning bush, saying, "I am what I am." This is the absolute, godlike, self-defining, circular identity that every writer grants himself in the first person singular. An identity to which the readers are asked to respond: "If we, often across miles and centuries, can hear the voice saying 'I' on the page, then 'I' must exist and 'We' must be forced to believe in it."

To say "I" is to place before the reader seemingly irrefutable proof of a speaker whose words can tell the truth or lie, but whose presence, vouched for by his voice, must not be doubted. To say "I" is to draw a circle in which writer and reader share a common existence within the margins of the page, where reality and unreality rub off each other, where words and what the words name contaminate each other. If that is the case, and if the characters we meet on Dante's long way from the dark forest to the Empyrean have the quality of dreams, then what of those others whom the evidence of our senses tells us are alive: we, the constant readers? "I'll tell you a story," says Dante, and in that preliminary utterance both he and his audience are trapped until the last word is reached—and also beyond it. "You, reader, exist," says the poet, "as the witness and receiver of my book, and therefore I, whom you can vouch for, since you see and hear my words, must exist too. And also, since they occupy the same linguistic space as you and I, you can vouch for the creatures of my story, the characters of my plot. At least within the circle of our relationship, bound by words, we must believe in one another and in one another's honesty, knowing that the lie that binds us holds the truth. Within that circle, can you, reader, decide in absolute terms that I exist but the Minotaur does not? That Beatrice and Saint Bernard and Virgil and Gianni Schicchi are real because history tells us that they once lived, but that the Angel who guards the Pass of Pardon does not except in faith, and that Charon is nothing but the stuff of ancient stories?" Dante, like every poet, repeats the words of the Unicorn to Alice through the Looking-Glass: "If you'll believe in me, I'll believe in you. Is that a bargain?" Seven centuries of readers have willingly entered into this Mephistophelian bargain.

But literary faith is never absolute: it exists between the skepticism that forbids enjoyment of the imagination and the madness that denies the world tangible reality. The historical Dante, the one who perhaps resembled the famous Giotto portrait, the Dante who underwent like every man the common pains and pleasures of the human lot, becomes inextricably entwined with the other, the Dante who said "I" in Paradise and whose singed beard, people said, came from having walked too close to the flames of Hell. For Dante, for the Dante we come to know, the *Commedia* is not a fiction: it is the enactment in words of a truth, that of salvation from the suffering of the world. If anything, it is the chronicle of a voyage, a piece of travel writing in foreign lands, with its geographical descriptions, dialogues with the inhabitants, notes of local history and politics, personal misadventures, and passion for lists: a guide for readers who may later have to undertake a similar journey.

The reading prescriptions set out by Dante in his famous letter to Can Grande della Scala explaining how his *Commedia* was to be understood are too constringent. They argue for a divided or graded reading (literal, allegorical, analogical, anagogical), when in fact, as Dante no doubt knew, no reader proceeds in such an orderly fashion. All or none of these levels takes priority in the act of reading. By saying or implying "I," the first words of a text already draw the reader into a murky place in which nothing is absolute, neither dream nor reality, and in which everything told is at once what it purports to be and something else, and also the mere words that make it up. The Earthly Paradise at the end of *Purgatorio* is the stage that Dante reaches after all seven initials of sin have been wiped from his forehead, and also the garden in which we lost our innocence, and also the grove from which Proserpine was taken, and also the starting place of our ascent to Heaven, and also the lighted counterpart of the dark wood of the beginning of Dante's voyage, and also the musical words "*humming / a continuo under their rhyming*" (*Purgatorio*, 28.17–18, trans. W. S. Merwin). But the Earthly Paradise is also the solid pine forest of Chiassi near Ravenna where Dante wrote the last cantos of *Purgatorio* when the sea still came up to its borders, and also the threadbare plantation that now stands far inland, a few steps from the church of San Apollinare.

To help the reader agree to believe and play the game of exchanged pretences, the writer offers his *excusatio propia infirmitatis,* the confession of his own weakness, a rhetorical device common in the literature of the Middle Ages. Over and over, Dante tells us that words do not suffice, that memory cannot translate experience into speech, that even memory cannot at times hold the unspoken act, and that the knowledge of certain experiences can only be granted by grace, *"for these whom grace hath better proof in store."*

> Words may not tell of that transhuman change;
> And therefore let the example serve, though weak,
> For these whom grace hath better proof in store.
> [*Paradiso* 1.70–72, trans. H. F. Cary]

Not only what is "transhuman" and lies beyond the human realm: all attempt at communication, all literature born from the dialogue between writer and reader, every artifact made of words suffers from this essential poverty. And by declaring language's inability to convey experience, the poet forces the reader, who shares language's shortcomings, to acknowledge not only the honesty of the writer's declaration but also, implicitly, the truth of what the writer confesses *cannot* be said. All means are valid to try and sharpen the imprecision of words.

> "Take note of my words just as I say them,
> and teach them to those who are living,"
> [*Purgatorio,* 33.52–53, trans. W. S. Merwin]

says Beatrice to Dante, and later, seeing that Dante's mind is tough as stone, she concedes:

> "I would also have you carry it away
> within you, painted even if not written."
> [*Purgatorio,* 33.76–77, trans. W. S. Merwin]

Images, though lesser tools than words, sometimes must serve where words fail, and even the divine Beatrice must, on occasion, fall back on images. One example should suffice. At the beginning of *Paradiso,* in order to explain to Dante why God's brilliance is equally distributed in the heavenly bodies,

Beatrice asks him to imagine an experiment involving three mirrors and a common source of light. Two of the mirrors are set at an equal distance from the viewer and the third farther away: even though the light appears smaller in this third mirror, the brilliance of all three reflections is the same. In this way, concrete experience becomes a metaphor for the otherwise ineffable: if what is seen or felt cannot at times be put into words, the impossible words can at times be put into action, for the reader to see and feel what cannot be told.

As Dante repeatedly tells us, truth (the experience of truth) recedes from human expression and understanding, plunges beyond language, beyond remembrance into an essential depth where things are known unto themselves, in their pure untranslatable essence, as that which is carried untouched from language to language in the act of translation.

Dante wants us to admit that it is he, the story's "I," who has journeyed through the three terrible realms, but the reader knows that Dante's experience is not entirely that of the "I" on the page nor that of the "I" who put him there: that it belongs to yet another "I" whom the reader must rescue from the page, pronouncing the word and yet understanding that it is speaking for somebody else. The reader knows that the voice that says "I" names itself and at the same time several others, since the writer creates by mirroring his creations. Into this game of mirrors, the reader must step in, in order to get to know the reality of words and to pronounce this "I" that he is not. Through the reader's goodwill, Dante can visit Hell and Purgatory and Heaven so that the reader can say at last, "I too was there."

The shock I received on first discovering that literature invents and that the world peopled by words is not that which the bureaucratic world of fact proclaimed has not entirely passed, more than half a century later. I'm still bewildered by the realization that if the writer who invented an adventurous narrator for the enjoyment of his stepson was not (or only partially) that narrator, and if the poet who conjured up the traveler in the realms to come was not (or not entirely) that traveler, then I, their diligent reader, was not the boy, am not the man on the other side of the page. At least not entirely, at least only partially. I don't know whether to rejoice or despair at this conclusion.

More than five centuries after Dante, on 15 May 1871, another traveler in Hell drafted the following report:

"If the old fools hadn't uncovered only the false meaning of 'I' we'd not have to sweep away those millions of skeletons that, since time everlasting, have accumulated the fruits of their one-eyed intellect, claiming to be its authors!" So wrote the seventeen-year-old Arthur Rimbaud to his friend Paul Demeny, two years before composing *Une Saison en enfer,* beginning the letter with the inevitable conclusion: "Car JE est un autre" — "Because *I* is someone else."

This is the truth that the reader must always bear in mind.

Final Answers

"May it please your Majesty," said Two, in a very humble tone,
going down on one knee as he spoke, "we were trying—"
Alice's Adventures in Wonderland, Chapter 8

A la mémoire de Simone Vauthier

ON 19 APRIL 1616, THE DAY after having been given extreme unction, Miguel de Cervantes Saavedra penned a dedication of his last book, *The Labors of Persiles and Segismunda*, to Don Pedro Fernández de Castro, Count of Lemos, a novel which, in his opinion, "dares to compete with Heliodorus." Heliodorus was a Greek novelist, once famous and now forgotten, whose *Aethiopica* Cervantes much admired. Three or four days later (historians remain undecided) Cervantes died, leaving his widow in charge of publishing the *Persiles*. His *Quixote*, if we can credit at least in part the modest disclaimer placed at the beginning of the first volume, was for Cervantes something lamentably minor. "What could this barren and ill-cultivated spirit of mine produce but the story of a dry, wizened son, whimsical and full of all manner of notions never before conceived?" he asks the reader. On his deathbed, intent on judging his own labors, Cervantes concludes that the *Persiles*, or perhaps his long, poetic unfinished *Galatea*, is to be his literary testament. Readers have decided otherwise, and it is *Don Quixote* that lives on as our contemporary, while the rest of Cervantes's work has largely become fodder for scholars. *Don Quixote* now stands for the whole of Cervantes's work, and perhaps for Cervantes himself.

Like Cervantes, we are mostly unaware of our destiny. Cursed with consciousness, we understand that we are on this earth on a journey that, like all journeys, must have had a beginning and will no doubt reach an end, but when was the first step taken and which will be the last, where are we meant to be

137

traveling to and why, and in expectation of what results, are questions that remain implacably unanswered. We can console ourselves, like Don Quixote himself, with the conviction that our goodwill and noble suffering mysteriously justify our being alive, and that through our actions we play a role that holds the secret universe together. But consolation is not reassurance.

Jews believe that thirty-six righteous men, the Lamed Wufniks, justify the world before God. No man knows that he is a Lamed Wufnik, nor does he know the identity of the other thirty-five, but, for reasons clear only to God, his existence prevents this world from crumbling into dust. Perhaps there is no act, however minuscule or trite, that does not accomplish a similar purpose. Perhaps each of our lives (and that of every insect, every tree, every cloud) stands like a letter in a text whose meaning depends on a certain sequence of appearing and disappearing letters, in a story whose beginning we ignore and whose end we will not read. If the letter L in this paragraph had consciousness, it might then ask itself the same questions in and, unable to follow the page on which it is written, equally receive no answers.

Not knowing what they are meant to do but feeling that they must know when they have done it: this paradox haunts artists from the beginning of time. Artists have always been aware that they engage (or have been recruited for) a task whose ultimate purport must escape them. They may realize, sometimes, that they have achieved something without understanding exactly what or how, or may guess that they are on the verge of achieving something that will, however, escape them, or that they have been allotted a task defined by the very impossibility of being achieved. Countless unfinished monuments, paintings, symphonies, and novels testify to their artistic hubris; a few others bravely proclaim that accomplishment is (though rarely) also within the human scope.

Somewhere halfway through Proust's *La Prisonnière*, Marcel learns that the writer Bergotte has died after a visit to the museum to see Vermeer's *View of Delft*. A critic had commented on "a small patch of yellow wall" so perfectly painted that, if seen on its own, it appeared to possess "a self-sufficient beauty." Bergotte, who thinks he knows the painting well, painfully undertakes the journey to fix his gaze on the little patch, in spite of being told by his doctor to stay in bed. "This is how I should have written," he laments, before collapsing. Bergotte has recognized in a tiny section of one of Vermeer's paintings an achievement such as he himself has never attained and, with this atrocious realization, he dies. The scene depicted by Proust is cautionary. The contemplation of success, of a work of art that in and of itself suffices, offers a reference against which an artist can measure his own work and learn his own fate, not in absolute terms, of course, but in the particular situation in which that other work has affected him. Now he knows what he means by reaching (or not reaching) a sort of perfection, and whether to continue or to stop.

In this sense, not all interruption is lack of success. When Kafka abandons his *Castle* before the formal conclusion of the story, when Gaudí dies before completing the church of the Sagrada Familia, when Mahler jots down only the first parts of his *Tenth Symphony*, when Michelangelo refuses to work further on his Florence *Pietà*, it is we, the audience, not the artist, who might consider the labors half-done. For the creator the result might be sketchy indeed, truncated yes, but not insufficient, like Vermeer's little patch of yellow isolated in the viewer's eye.

Rimbaud interrupted his poetic career at the age of nineteen; J. D. Salinger wrote no more stories after 1963; the Argentinean poet Enrique Banchs brought out his last book in 1911 and then lived on for another fifty-seven years without publishing a single new collection of verse. We don't know whether these artists felt, at a certain moment, the epiphany that they had achieved what they were meant to achieve and could therefore retire from the scene on which they felt they had no further business. Certainly from our distance as readers, their work seems self-sufficient, mature, perfect. But did the artists see it as such? Few are the artists who recognize their own genius without hyperbole or constricting modesty. The paradigm is Dante, who, in writing his great poem knows that it is great and tells the reader it is so. For most others, however, the learning of the craft never ceases, and no resulting work is fully achieved. Witness the following confession:

"From the age of six I felt the compulsion to draw the shape of things. In my fifties, I showed a collection of drawings, but nothing accomplished before I turned seventy satisfies me. Only at seventy-three was I able to intuit, even approximately, the true form and nature of birds, fish, and plants. Therefore, by the age of eighty I will have made great progress; at ninety I will have penetrated the essence of all things; at a hundred, I will no doubt have ascended to a higher state, indescribable, and if I live to be a hundred and ten years old, everything, every dot and every line, will live. I invite those who will live as long as I to hold me to my promise. Written in my seventy-fifth year by myself, formerly known as Hokusai, now called Huakivo-Royi, the old man maddened by drawing."

Whether the artist has abandoned his creative career or pursued it until his last breath has been drawn, whether he feels that something of what he has done will survive his dust and ashes, or whether he is certain that his work is, as Ecclesiastes warns us, nothing but "vanity and vexation of spirit," it is we, the audience, who continue to seek in what has been created and set before us a certain order of merit, an aesthetic, moral, or philosophical hierarchy. We think we know better.

Our arrogance, however, makes an assumption that is perhaps not tenable: that there is one among the works of Corot, of Shakespeare, of Verdi, that sublimates all others, a work for which all the rest must seem as preparations or drafts, a culminating work, a crowning achievement. In one of his short stories, Henry James put forward the notion that there is indeed a theme, a subject, a signature that runs through any artist's work like the repeated yet hidden figure in a carpet. The notion of a "testamentary" work that encapsulates the artist's summation and legacy is like James's "figure in the carpet," but without the carpet.

Just before she died, Gertrude Stein was heard to ask, "What is the answer?" As no answer came, she laughed and said, "In that case, what is the question?" Then she died. Stein understood that because our knowledge of the world is fragmentary, we believe the world to be fragmentary. We assume that the bits and pieces we encounter and collect (of experience, pleasure, sorrow, revelation) exist in splendid isolation like each of the motes in a cloud of stardust. We forget the all-encompassing cloud, we forget that in the beginning there was a star. *Don Quixote* or *Hamlet* might be the testamentary works of Cervantes and of Shakespeare, Picasso could have put away his brushes after *Guernica* and Rembrandt after *The Night Watch,* Mozart could have died happily having composed *The Magic Flute* and Verdi *Falstaff,* but we would be missing something. We would be missing the approximations, the tentative versions, the variations, the changes of tone and perspective, the circuitous itineraries, the circumventions, the dealings in the shadows, the rest of their creative universe. We would be missing the errors, the stillbirths, the censored snapshots, the trimmings, the lesser inspired creations. Since we are not immortal, we have to content ourselves with a sampling, and therefore the choice of testamentary works is fully justified. As long as we remember that under the pomp and circumstance there is a rustle and a stirring, a vast, dark, rich forest full of fallen or discarded leaves.

What Song the Sirens Sang

"Have you guessed the riddle yet?" the Hatter said,
turning to Alice again.

"No, I give up," Alice replied. "What's the answer?"
Alice's Adventures in Wonderland, Chapter 7

THE *ODYSSEY* IS A POEM OF false beginnings and false endings. In spite of
the initial invocation to the Muse, in which the poet begs her to sing (in Robert
Fagles's translation) of "the man of twists and turns / driven time and again
off course, once he had plundered / the hallowed heights of Troy," the reader
feels that these verses are not the start but the conclusion of the story, that the
Muse has now ended her task and that everything has already been told.

The first book of the poem closes the seafaring narrative. It tells us that
Odysseus left Troy a long time ago, that he suffered many misfortunes, and that
neither his wife nor his son know his whereabouts. The last book opens the
narrative to future undertakings, leaving the reader in suspense in the middle
of a battle interrupted by Athena. But not only do the start and the conclusion
of the poem explicitly assume the reader's foreknowledge. Every one of Odysseus's adventures carries the assumption of its own outcome and of the poem's
beginning and end. Every new episode assumes the entire *Odyssey* with a different and never-to-be-accomplished resolution: leading the life of a slave in
the arms of the lovely Calypso, becoming guilty of infidelity with Princess
Nausicaa, forgetting the world among the Lotus-Eaters, being ignominiously
devoured by the cannibal Cyclops, falling victim to the wrath of King Aeolus's
winds, suffering a hideous fate between Scylla and Charybdis, dying under the
swords of his wife's suitors. Tempted by endless endings, Odysseus's return is
an eternal one.

One of these possible fates is prophesized to Odysseus by the ghost of the
seer Tiresias in the Underworld: that after the story's conclusion, once Odys-

seus has reached his Ithaca again, he will "go forth once more" and come upon "a race of people who know nothing of the sea" and here, among strangers, meet his true end. Dante, who had not read Homer, magically intuited the prophecy and made it come poetically true. In the circle of Hell where liars and cheats are punished, Ulysses (as Odysseus was renamed by the Romans) tells Dante that he did indeed undertake this further voyage, urging his aged companions to set sail once again. The famous passage was rendered by Tennyson in equally famous lines:

> Tho' much is taken, much abides; and tho'
> We are not now that strength which in old days
> Moved earth and heaven, that which we are, we are;
> One equal temper of heroic hearts,
> Made weak by time and fate, but strong in will
> To strive, to seek, to find, and not to yield.

Dante's Ulysses sets off with his old crew, travels westward beyond the horizon, sees a mountain rise from the sea, rejoices but immediately despairs as a storm descends upon the ship and a whirlpool appears in its path and, "as Another willed," it sinks into the unknown waters. Here ends Dante's version of the *Odyssey*'s conclusion. Other than the implicit warning, that Ulysses' account may not necessarily be the true one since he was condemned to Hell for deceiving, Dante tells us nothing about the old king's intentions, about his will "to strive, to seek, to find" — what?

Homer, who offered Dante this coda to the story, also suggested (had Dante been able to read him) an answer to the question. The scene takes place in book 12 of the *Odyssey*, when Odysseus and his companions face the temptation of the Sirens. The enchantress Circe, after being ordered by the gods to release Odysseus from her charms, warns him of the dangers he will encounter as he sets forth (yet another retelling of the story). Among these dangers are the Sirens, capable of seducing mortals with their song. In Homer's version they are only two, perched on a mountain of skeletons and putrid flesh that rises in the middle of a green meadow, waiting for passing ships. Whoever hears them sing, Circe tells Odysseus, will not return home again, will never be embraced by his wife or see his children's smile, will be condemned to death and oblivion. To escape their wiles, Circe advises him to fill his men's ears with wax and have himself tied to the mast. Then, though unable to approach

them, Odysseus will nevertheless be able to hear the Sirens' mysterious song.
In Robert Fagles's translation:

> "Come closer, famous Odysseus — Achaea's pride and glory —
> moor your ship on our coast so you can hear our song!
> Never has any sailor passed our shores in his black craft
> until he has heard the honeyed voices pouring from our lips,
> and once he hears to his heart's content sails on, a wiser man.
> We know all the pains that the Achaeans and Trojans once endured
> on the spreading plain of Troy when the gods willed it so —
> all that comes to pass on the fertile earth, we know it all!"

Hearing them, Odysseus feels something within himself urging him to go
towards them and gestures to his men to set him free, but they, obeying his
first orders, tighten the rope that secures him to the mast. At last the ship sails
past the danger and the Sirens vanish on the horizon. Odysseus and his companions have avoided yet another ending. Odysseus is now the only man on
earth to have heard the Sirens' song and survived.

Who are these Sirens? Homer does not tell us what they looked like. Ancient Greek decorations, not as old as the poem itself, show them as women
with large wings or as birds with women's faces. In the third century B.C.,
Apollonius of Rhodes, taking his inspiration from Homer, has his heroes,
Jason and his crew, also meet the Sirens, and describes them as winged beings,
half birds and half women, daughters of a river god and of one of the nine
Muses. Apollonius says that the Sirens had served as Persephone's hand-
maidens, entertaining her with their singing. A later legend adds that, after
Persephone was kidnapped by the king of the Underworld, her mother, Deme-
ter, punished them for not protecting her daughter, giving them wings and
saying, "Now fly through the world and bring me back my child!" Another
legend has it that it was Aphrodite who punished the Sirens for refusing to
offer their maidenhead to either mortals or gods. Yet another tells that, in spite
of having wings, the Sirens were unable to fly because the nine Muses (their
mother and aunts), after defeating them in a singing contest, ripped off their
feathers to make themselves garlands. Of the Sirens' death there exist at least
two versions. One says that they were killed by Hercules, whose sixth task was
to eliminate the monstrous birds with beaks, wings, and claws of bronze who
fed on human flesh in the Stymphalian swamps. The other, that after being

snubbed by Odysseus, they plunged into the sea and drowned. It was perhaps this watery death that led in Latin tongues to the confusion between winged and fishlike creatures, calling both by the same name, unlike the distinction made in English between Sirens and mermaids, or in German between *Sirene* and *Nixe.*

Horrible as harpies or beautiful as nymphs, all Sirens are distinguished by their song. In the last book of Plato's *Republic,* eight Sirens sing each a different note that together constitute the Pythagorean harmony of the celestial spheres, dear to ancient astronomers until the time of Galileo. For Plato, the Sirens' song is less a deadly temptation than a necessary device for the correct working of the heavens. On the Sirens' song depends the balance of the universe itself.

But can we know the nature of such a song? According to Suetonius, the emperor Tiberius, whenever he met professors of Greek literature, enjoyed asking them three impossible questions of which the third was: "What song did the Sirens sing?" Fifteen centuries later, Sir Thomas Browne observed that, though puzzling, the question was "not beyond all conjecture." Indeed.

Several characteristics of the song are known to us. The first is its danger, since in its very attraction it makes us forget the world and our responsibilities in it. The second is its revelatory nature, since it tells of what has taken place and of what will take place in the future, of what we already know and of what we cannot discern. Finally, it is a song that can be understood by all, whatever their tongue or birthplace, since almost all men travel the sea and anyone might encounter the fearful Sirens.

These features lead on to further questions. First: where exactly lies the danger of their song? In the melody or in the words? That is to say, in the sound or in the meaning? Second: if their song reveals all, do the Sirens know their own tragic destiny or, like self-reflecting Cassandras, are they alone insensible to their own prophesizing music? And third: what is this language deemed to be universal?

If we suppose with Plato that their song is composed not of words but of musical notes, something in those sounds suffices to lend them sense. Something that the Sirens' voices transmit (and that cannot be reduced to pure rhythm or intelligence) calls on those who hear them like a rutting animal, emitting a sound untranslatable except as an echo of itself. The Church of the Middle Ages saw in the Sirens an allegory of the temptations that beset the soul in search of God, and in their voices the beastly noises that lure us away from the divine. But it is perhaps for that same reason that the sense of the Sirens' song, unlike the sense of God's will, is "not beyond all conjecture." The problem, I believe, touches upon certain aspects of the essential conundrum of language.

The tongues developed in the Homeric and pre-Homeric world, under the influence of migrations and conquests, for the purpose of both commercial and artistic communication, were "translated" tongues. That is to say, tongues that for reasons of war or trade served to establish connections between Greeks and "barbarians," between those who called themselves civilized and the others, the speakers of babble. The passage of one vocabulary to another, the translation (in physical terms) of one perception of meaning to another perception of that same meaning is one of the essential mysteries of the intellectual act. Because if a semantic communication, oral or written, colloquial or literary depends on the words that make it up and on the syntax that rules it, what is preserved when we exchange them for other words and another syntax? What remains when we replace the sound, structure, cultural bias, linguistic conventions? What do we translate when we speak to one another from tongue to tongue? Neither the endemic sense nor the sound but something else that survives the transformation of both, whatever remains when all is stripped away. I don't know if this essence can be defined but perhaps, as an analogy, we might understand it as the Sirens' song.

Of all its characteristics, the most powerful one is its divinatory nature. All great literature (all literature we call great) survives, more or less painfully, through its reincarnations, its translations, its readings and rereadings, transmitting a sort of knowledge or revelation that in turn expands and illuminates new intuitions and experiences in many of its readers. This creative quality, like the shamanic reading of tortoiseshells or tealeaves, allows us to understand, through the reading of fiction or poetry, something of our own mysterious selves. This procedure entails not just the comprehension of a shared vocabulary but the discernment, in a literary construction, of a newly created meaning. In such cases, it is the reader (not the author) who recomposes and deciphers the text, standing as it were on both sides of the page at once.

In the same section of the *Republic* in which the Sirens appear, Plato imagines that when the great dead heroes of antiquity were told to choose their future reincarnations, the soul of Odysseus, remembering how ambition had made him suffer in his previous life, chose the life of an ordinary citizen, a fate the other souls had disdainfully discarded. In that instant, Odysseus rejects the glory of Troy, the fame of inventor and strategist, the knowledge of the sea, the dialogue with his cherished dead, the love of princesses and witches, the crown of slayer of monsters, the role of honorable avenger, the reputation of faithful husband: all in exchange for a quiet, anonymous life. We may ask if such wisdom, surprising in a man who felt that the adventurous life was his destiny, was not given to him in the moment when, tied to the mast, he heard the Sirens' song.

Tiresias had told him that after the last, mysterious voyage his death would be peaceful, "a gentle, painless death . . . borne down with the years in ripe old age / with all your people there in blessed peace around you." Dante was unable to grant it to him, and neither did the generations of poets who each in his own way translated the Sirens' song. Almost all, from Homer to Joyce and Derek Walcott, demanded that Odysseus/Ulysses be an adventurer. Only a few, Plato among them, intuited that Odysseus alone could change his given destiny after discovering his true self in the song he is made to hear. In the fourth century A.D., the rhetorician Libanius, friend of Julian the Apostate, argued in his *Apology of Socrates* that Homer had written the *Odyssey* in praise of the man who, like Socrates, wished to know himself.

Dante too recognized the necessary ambiguity of the Sirens' song, which allows each listener to hear a different version. In the nineteenth canto of *Purgatorio*, Dante dreams a dream. He sees (in W. S. Merwin's translation),

> a stammering
> woman, cross-eyed, and her feet were crooked,
> her hands mangled, and her color faded.

Dante looks at her, and his gaze renders her beautiful. The woman begins to sing, and her song dazzles the poet.

> "I am," she sang, "I am the sweet siren
> who lures sailors astray out on the sea
> so full of pleasure they are when they hear me.
>
> I turned Ulysses from his wandering course
> with my singing, and he leaves me seldom
> who is at home with me, so wholly do I satisfy him."

Suddenly, "a watchful and holy lady" appears beside them and calls upon Virgil to tell Dante who this apparition really is. Virgil grabs the Siren, tears open her dress, and reveals a pestilential belly whose stench wakes Dante from his dream.

The Siren (as conceived by the poet) is the creation of Dante's erotic desire, a desire that transforms the image he looks on, exaggerating its features until it acquires a haunting but false beauty. The Siren, as Virgil attempts to show his charge, is not a true amorous vision but a reflection of his own perverted longing. The Siren and her song are projections of that which Dante hides from himself, a shadow of his own dark side, unspeakable and hallucinatory, the secret text that Dante's dream conjures up and that his consciousness attempts to decipher. This is a possible interpretation of Dante's Siren. But perhaps more can be read in her changing apparition.

Centuries later, Kafka suggested that, faced with Odysseus's expectations, the Sirens kept still, either because they wished to defeat him with their silence or because they were themselves seduced by the powerful gaze of the hero, and that the clever Ulysses only pretended to hear the magic song which they denied him. In this case, we might add, it was neither the sound nor the words that Ulysses perceived but a sort of blank page, the perfect poem, taught between writing and reading, on the point of being conceived.

Later still, Jorge Luis Borges, attempting to define his *ars poetica,* wrote,

> They say that Ulysses, tired of astonishments
> Wept for love at once again seeing his Ithaca
> Humble and green. Art is like that Ithaca
> Of green eternity, not of mere astonishments.

We too can imagine—why not?—that Ulysses, like Dante in Purgatory, was able to transform, through his amorous desire, the Sirens and their song. We can imagine him, "tired of astonishments," reading the apparition, and its voice or its silence, as something uniquely personal. We can imagine him translating the Sirens' universal language into a singular and intimate tongue in which he then composes an all-encompassing autobiography, past, present and future, a mirrored poem in which Ulysses recognizes, and also discovers, his true self.

Perhaps this is the way in which all literature works.

PART FIVE

The Ideal Reader

At last a bright thought struck her. "Why, it's a Looking-Glass book, of course! And, if I hold it up to a glass, the words will all go the right way again."
Through the Looking-Glass, Chapter I

Notes Towards a Definition
of the Ideal Reader

"Let's hear it," said Humpty Dumpty. "I can explain all the
poems that ever were invented — and a good many that
haven't been invented just yet."
Through the Looking-Glass, Chapter 6

THE IDEAL READER IS THE writer just before the words come together on
the page.

The ideal reader exists in the moment that precedes the moment of creation.

Ideal readers do not reconstruct a story: they re-create it.

Ideal readers do not follow a story: they partake of it.

A famous children's book program on the BBC always started with the
host asking, "Are you sitting comfortably? Then we shall begin." The ideal
reader is also the ideal sitter.

Depictions of Saint Jerome show him poised over his translation of
the Bible, listening to the word of God. The ideal reader must learn how to
listen.

The ideal reader is the translator, able to dissect the text, peel back the
skin, slice down to the marrow, follow each artery and each vein, and then set
on its feet a whole new sentient being. The ideal reader is not a taxidermist.

For the ideal reader all devices are familiar.

For the ideal reader all jokes are new.

"One must be an inventor to read well." Ralph Waldo Emerson.

The ideal reader has an unlimited capacity for oblivion and can dismiss
from memory the knowledge that Dr. Jekyll and Mr. Hyde are one and the

same person, that Julien Sorel will have his head cut off, that the name of the murderer of Roger Ackroyd is So-and-so.

The ideal reader has no interest in the writings of Bret Easton Ellis.

The ideal reader knows what the writer only intuits.

The ideal reader subverts the text. The ideal reader does not take the writer's word for granted.

The ideal reader is a cumulative reader: every reading of a book adds a new layer of memory to the narrative.

Every ideal reader is an associative reader and reads as if all books were the work of one ageless and prolific author.

Ideal readers cannot put their knowledge into words.

Upon closing the book, ideal readers feel that, had they not read it, the world would be poorer.

The ideal reader has a wicked sense of humor.

Ideal readers never count their books.

The ideal reader is both generous and greedy.

The ideal reader reads all literature as if it were anonymous.

The ideal reader enjoys using a dictionary.

The ideal reader judges a book by its cover.

Reading a book from centuries ago, the ideal reader feels immortal.

Paolo and Francesca were not ideal readers since they confess to Dante that after their first kiss they read no more. Ideal readers would have kissed and then read on. One love does not exclude the other.

Ideal readers do not know they are ideal readers until they have reached the end of the book

The ideal reader shares the ethics of Don Quixote, the longing of Madame Bovary, the lust of the Wife of Bath, the adventurous spirit of Ulysses, the mettle of Holden Caulfield, at least for the space of the story.

The ideal reader treads the beaten path. "A good reader, major reader, an active and creative reader is a rereader." Vladimir Nabokov.

The ideal reader is polytheistic.

The ideal reader holds, for a book, the promise of resurrection.

Robinson Crusoe is not an ideal reader. He reads the Bible to find answers. An ideal reader reads to find questions.

Every book, good or bad, has its ideal reader.

For the ideal reader, every book reads, to a certain degree, as an autobiography.

The ideal reader has no precise nationality.

Sometimes a writer must wait several centuries to find the ideal reader. It took Blake 150 years to find Northrop Frye.

Stendhal's ideal reader: "I write for barely a hundred readers, for unhappy, amiable, charming beings, never moral or hypocritical, whom I would like to please; I know barely one or two."

The ideal reader has known unhappiness.

Ideal readers change with age. The fourteen-year-old ideal reader of Pablo Neruda's *Twenty Love Poems* is no longer its ideal reader at thirty. Experience tarnishes certain readings.

Pinochet, who banned *Don Quixote* because he thought it advocated civil disobedience, was that book's ideal reader.

The ideal reader never exhausts the book's geography.

The ideal reader must be willing, not only to suspend disbelief, but to embrace a new faith.

The ideal reader never thinks, "If only . . ."

Writing on the margins is a sign of the ideal reader.

The ideal reader proselytizes.

The ideal reader is guiltlessly whimsical.

The ideal reader is capable of falling in love with one of the book's characters.

The ideal reader is not concerned with anachronism, documentary truth, historical accuracy, topographical exactness. The ideal reader is not an archaeologist.

The ideal reader is a ruthless enforcer of the rules and regulations that each book creates for itself.

"There are three kinds of readers: one, who enjoys without judging; a third, who judges without enjoying; another in the middle, who judges while enjoying and enjoys while judging. The last class truly reproduces a work of art anew; its members are not numerous." Goethe, in a letter to Johann Friedrich Rochlitz.

The readers who committed suicide after reading *Werther* were not ideal but merely sentimental readers.

Ideal readers are seldom sentimental.

The ideal reader wishes both to get to the end of the book and to know that the book will never end.

The ideal reader is never impatient.

The ideal reader is not concerned with genres.

The ideal reader is (or appears to be) more intelligent than the writer; the ideal reader does not hold this against the writer.

There comes a time when every reader considers himself to be the ideal reader.

Good intentions are not enough to produce an ideal reader.

The marquis de Sade: "I only write for those capable of understanding me, and these will read me with no danger."

The marquis de Sade is wrong: the ideal reader is always in danger.

The ideal reader is a novel's main character.

Paul Valéry: "A literary ideal: finally to know not to fill the page with anything except 'the reader.'"

The ideal reader is someone the writer would not mind spending an evening with, over a glass of wine.

An ideal reader should not be confused with a virtual reader.

Writers are never their own ideal reader.

Literature depends, not on ideal readers, but merely on good enough readers.

How Pinocchio Learned to Read

"So do I," the White Queen whispered. And I'll tell you a
secret — I can read words of one letter! Isn't *that* grand?
However, don't be discouraged. You'll come to it in time."
Through the Looking-Glass, Chapter 9

I READ CARLO COLLODI'S *Adventures of Pinocchio* for the first time many
years ago in Buenos Aires, when I was eight or nine, in a vague Spanish translation with Enrico Mazzanti's original black-and-white drawings. I saw the
Disney film some time later and was annoyed to find a multitude of changes:
the asthmatic Shark that swallowed Geppetto had become Monstro the Whale;
the Cricket, instead of disappearing and reappearing, had been given the name
Jiminy and kept pursuing Pinocchio with good advice; grumpy Geppetto had
turned into a nice old man with a goldfish called Cleo and a cat called Figaro.
And many of the most memorable episodes were missing. Nowhere, for instance, did Disney portray Pinocchio (as Collodi did in what was for me the
most nightmarish scene in the book) witnessing his own death when, after
he refuses to take his medicine, four rabbits "as black as ink" come to carry
him off in a small black coffin. In its original version, Pinocchio's passage
from wood to flesh and blood was for me as thrilling a quest as that of Alice
for a way out of Wonderland or of Odysseus for his beloved Ithaca. Except
the ending: when, on the final pages, Pinocchio is rewarded by becoming "a
handsome boy with chestnut brown hair and light blue eyes," I cheered and
yet felt strangely unsatisfied.

I didn't know it then, but I think I loved *The Adventures of Pinocchio*
because they are adventures in learning. The puppet's saga is that of a citizen's education, the ancient paradox of someone who wants to enter common
human society while trying to find out at the same time who he really is, how
he appears not in the eyes of others but in his own. Pinocchio wants to be

155

"a real boy" but not just any boy, not an obedient little version of the ideal citizen. Pinocchio wants to be whoever he really is under the painted wood. Unfortunately (because Collodi stopped Pinocchio's education short of this epiphany), he never quite succeeds. Pinocchio becomes a good little boy who has learned to read, but Pinocchio never becomes a reader.

From the beginning, Collodi sets up a conflict between Pinocchio the Rebel and the society of which he wants to be a part. Even before Pinocchio is carved into a puppet, he proves himself a rebellious piece of wood. He doesn't believe in "being seen and not heard" (the nineteenth-century motto for children) and provokes a quarrel between Geppetto and his neighbor (yet another scene deleted by Disney). He then throws a tantrum when he finds that there is nothing to eat but a few pears, and when he falls asleep by the fire and burns off both his feet, he expects Geppetto (society's representative) to carve him new ones. Hungry and crippled, Pinocchio the Rebel does not resign himself to remaining unfed or handicapped in a society that should provide him with food and health care. But Pinocchio is also aware that his demands from society must be reciprocated. And so, having received food and new feet, he says to Geppetto, "To pay you back for all you've done for me, I'll start school right away."

In Collodi's society, school is the beginning place for proving oneself responsible. School is the training ground for becoming someone able to "pay back" society's concerned care. This is how Pinocchio sums it up: "Today, at school, I'll learn how to read right away, tomorrow I'll learn how to write, and the day after tomorrow I'll learn arithmetic. Then with my skill I'll make lots of money, and with the first money that I get in my pocket I'll buy my father a beautiful woolen jacket. But what am I talking about, wool? I'll get him one all of silver and gold, with diamond buttons. And the poor man really deserves it, because, after all, in order to buy me books and have me educated he's left in short sleeves . . . in the middle of winter!" Because in order to buy a spelling book for Pinocchio (essential for attending school) Geppetto has sold his only jacket. Geppetto is a poor man, but in Collodi's society, education requires sacrifice.

The first step, then, to becoming a citizen is to learn to read. But what does this mean, "to learn to read"? Several things.

• First, the mechanical process of learning the code of the script in which the memory of a society is encoded.

• Second, the learning of the syntax by which such a code is governed.

• Third, the learning of how the inscriptions in such a code can serve to help us know in a deep, imaginative, and practical way ourselves and the world around us.

It is this third learning that is the most difficult, the most dangerous, and the most powerful—and the one Pinocchio will never reach. Pressures of all sorts—the temptations with which society lures him away from himself, the mockery and jealousy of his fellow students, the aloof guidance of his moral preceptors—create for Pinocchio a series of almost insurmountable obstacles to becoming a reader.

Reading is an activity that has always been viewed with qualified enthusiasm by those in government. It is not by chance that in the eighteenth and nineteenth centuries, laws were passed against teaching slaves to read, even the Bible, since (it was correctly argued) whoever could read the Bible could also read an abolitionist tract. The efforts and stratagems devised by slaves to learn to read are proof enough of the relationship between civil freedom and the power of the reader, and of the fear elicited by that freedom and that power in rulers of all kinds.

But in a so-called democratic society, before the possibility of learning to read can be considered, the laws of that society are obliged to satisfy a number of basic needs: food, housing, health care. In a stirring essay on society and learning, Collodi has this to say about the republican efforts to implement a system of obligatory schooling in Italy: "As I see it, until now we have thought more about the heads than the stomachs of the classes that are needy and suffering. Now let us think a little more about the stomachs." Pinocchio, no stranger to hunger, is clearly aware of this primary requirement. Imagining what he might do if he had a hundred thousand coins and were to become a wealthy gentleman, he wishes for himself a beautiful palace with a library "chock-full of candied fruit, pies, panettoni, almond cakes, and rolled wafers filled with whipped cream." Books, as Pinocchio well knows, won't feed a hungry stomach. When Pinocchio's naughty companions hurl their books at him with such bad aim that they fall in the sea, a school of fish hurries to the surface to nibble at the soggy pages, but soon spits them out, thinking, "That's not for us; we're used to feeding on much better fare." In a society in which the citizens' basic needs are not fulfilled, books are poor nourishment; wrongly used, they can be deadly. When one of the boys hurls a thick-bound *Manual of Arithmetic* at Pinocchio, instead of hitting the puppet the book strikes another of the boys on the head, killing him. Unused, unread, the book is a deadly weapon.

Even as it sets up a system to satisfy these basic requirements and establish a compulsory education system, society offers Pinocchio distractions from that system, temptations of entertainment without thought and without effort. First in the shape of the Fox and the Cat, who tell Pinocchio that school has left them blind and lame, then in the creation of Funland, which Pinocchio's friend Lampwick describes in these alluring words: "There are no schools there; there are no teachers there; there are no books there. . . . Now that's the sort of place that appeals to me! That's how all civilized countries should be!" Books, quite rightly, are associated in Lampwick's mind with difficulty, and difficulty (in Pinocchio's world as in our own) has acquired a negative sense which it did not always have. The Latin expression "per ardua ad astra," "through difficulties we reach the stars," is almost incomprehensible for Pinocchio (as for us) since everything is expected to be obtainable with the least possible expenditure.

But society does not encourage this necessary search for difficulty, this increase in experience. Once Pinocchio has suffered his first misadventures and accepted school and become a good student, the other boys begin to attack him for being what we would today call "a nerd" and laugh at him for "paying attention to the teacher." "You talk like a printed book!" they tell him. Language can allow the speaker to remain on the surface of thought, mouthing dogmatic slogans and commonplaces in black and white, transmitting messages rather than meaning, placing the epistemological weight on the listener (as in "you know what I mean?"). Or it can attempt to re-create an experience, give shape to an idea, explore in depth and not only on the surface the intuition of a revelation. For the other boys, this distinction is invisible. For them, the fact that Pinocchio speaks "like a printed book" is enough to label him an outsider, a traitor, a recluse in his ivory tower.

Finally, society places in Pinocchio's way a number of characters who are to serve him as moral guides, as Virgils in his exploration of the infernal circles of this world. The Cricket, whom Pinocchio squashes against the wall in an early chapter but who miraculously survives to assist him much later on in the book; the Blue Fairy who first appears as to Pinocchio as a Little Girl with

Blue Hair in a series of nightmarish encounters; the Tuna, a stoic philosopher who tells Pinocchio, after they have been swallowed by the Shark, to "accept the situation, and wait for the Shark to digest us both." But all these "teachers" abandon Pinocchio to his own suffering, unwilling to keep him company in his moments of darkness and loss. None of them instructs Pinocchio on how to reflect about his own condition, none encourages him to find out what he means by his wish of "becoming a boy." As if reciting from school textbooks without eliciting personal readings, these magisterial figures are merely interested in the academic semblance of instruction in which the attribution of roles—teacher versus student—is meant to suffice for "learning" to take place. As teachers, they are useless, because they believe themselves accountable only to society, not to the student.

In spite of all these constraints—diversion, derision, abandonment— Pinocchio manages to climb the first two steps of society's learning ladder: learning the alphabet and learning to read the surface of a text. There he stops. Books then become neutral places in which to exercise this learned code in order to extract a conventional moral at the end. School has prepared him to read propaganda.

Because Pinocchio has not learned to read in depth, to enter a book and explore it to its sometimes unreachable limits, he will always ignore the fact that his own adventures have deep literary roots. His life (he doesn't know this) is actually a literary life, a composite of ancient stories in which he might one day (when he truly learns to read) recognize his own biography. And this is true for every fully fledged reader. *The Adventures of Pinocchio* echo a multitude of literary voices. It is a book about a father's quest for a son and a son's quest for a father (a subplot of the *Odyssey* that Joyce would later discover); about the search for oneself, as in the physical metamorphosis of Apuleius's hero in *The Golden Ass* and the psychological metamorphosis of Prince Hal in *Henry IV;* about sacrifice and redemption, as taught in the stories about the Virgin Mary and in the sagas of Ariosto; about archetypal rites of passage, as in the fairy tales of Perrault (which Collodi translated) and in the earthy commedia dell'arte; about voyages into the unknown, as in the chronicles of the sixteenth-century explorers and in Dante. Since Pinocchio does not see books as sources of revelation, books do not reflect back to him his own experience. Vladimir Nabokov, teaching his students how to read Kafka, pointed out to them that the insect into which Gregor Samsa is transformed is in fact a winged beetle, an insect that carries wings under its armored back, and that if Gregor had only discovered them, he would have been able to escape. And then Nabokov added, "Many a Dick and a Jane grow up like Gregor, unaware that they too have wings and can fly."

Of this, Pinocchio as well would remain unaware if he happened upon *The Metamorphosis*. All Pinocchio can do, after he learns to read, is parrot the textbook speech. He assimilates the words on the page but does not digest them: the books do not become truly his because he is still, at the end of his adventures, incapable of applying them to his experience of himself and of the world. Learning the alphabet leads him in the final chapter to be born into a human identity and to look upon the puppet he was with amused satisfaction. But in a volume Collodi never wrote, Pinocchio must still confront society with an imaginative language which books could have taught him through memory, association, intuition, imitation. Beyond the last page, Pinocchio is finally ready to learn to read.

Pinocchio's superficial reading experience is exactly the opposite of that of another wandering hero (or heroine). In Alice's world, language is restored to its essential rich ambiguity and any word (according to Humpty Dumpty) can be made to say what its speaker wishes it to say. Though Alice refuses such arbitrary assumptions ("But 'glory' does not mean 'a well-rounded argument,'" she tells him), this free-for-all epistemology is the norm in Alice's world. While in Pinocchio's world the meaning of a printed story is unambiguous, in Alice's world the meaning of "Jabberwocky," for instance, depends on the will of its reader. (It may be useful to recall here that Collodi was writing at a time when the Italian language was being set down officially for the first time, from a choice among numerous dialects, while Lewis Carroll's English had long been "fixed" and could be opened and questioned in relative safety.)

When I speak of "learning to read" (in the fullest sense I mentioned earlier), I mean something that lies between these two styles or philosophies. Pinocchio responds to the strictures of scholasticism, which, up to the sixteenth century, was the official learning method in Europe. In the scholastic classroom, the student was meant to read as tradition dictated, according to fixed commentaries accepted as the authorities. Humpty Dumpty's method is an exaggeration of the humanist interpretations, a revolutionary viewpoint according to which every reader must engage with the text on his or her own terms. Umberto Eco usefully limited this freedom by noting that "the limits of interpretation coincide with the limits of common sense"; to which, of course,

Humpty Dumpty might reply that what is common sense to him may not be common sense to Eco. But for most readers, the notion of "common sense" retains a certain shared clarity that must suffice. "Learning to read" is then to acquire the means to appropriate a text (as Humpty Dumpty does) and also to partake of the appropriations of others (as Pinocchio's teacher might have suggested). In this ambiguous field between possession and recognition, between the identity imposed by others and the identity discovered by oneself, lies, I believe, the act of reading.

A fierce paradox exists at the heart of every school system. A society needs to impart the knowledge of its codes to its citizens so that they can become active in it; but the knowledge of that code, beyond the mere ability of deciphering a political slogan, an advertisement, or a manual of basic instructions, enables those same citizens to question that society, to uncover its evils and attempt a change. In the very system that allows a society to function lies the power to subvert it, for better or for worse. So the teacher, the person appointed by that society to unveil to its new members the secrets of its shared vocabularies, becomes in fact a danger to that same society, a Socrates able to corrupt the youth, someone who must on the one hand rebelliously teach civil disobedience and the art of critical questioning and on the other submit to the laws of the society that has assigned the teacher's position—submit even to the point of self-destruction, as was the case with Socrates. A teacher is forever caught in this double bind: to teach in order to make students think on their own, while teaching according to a social structure that imposes a curb on thinking. School, in Pinocchio's world as in most of ours, is not a training ground for becoming a better, fuller child but an initiation place to the world of grownups, with its conventions, bureaucratic requirements, tacit agreements, and caste system. There is no such thing as a school for anarchists, and yet, in some sense, every teacher must teach anarchism, must teach the students to question rules and regulations, to seek explanations in dogma, to confront impositions without bending to prejudice, to demand authority from those in power, to find a place from which to speak their own ideas, even if this means opposing, and ultimately doing away with, the teacher herself.

In certain societies in which the intellectual act has a prestige of its own, as in many aboriginal societies throughout the world, the teacher (elder, shaman, instructor, keeper of the tribe's memory) has an easier task in fulfilling his or her obligations, since most activities in those societies are subordinate to the act of teaching. But in most societies, the intellectual act has no prestige whatsoever. The budget allotted to education is the first to be cut; most of our leaders are barely literate; our national values are purely economical. Lip service is paid to the concept of literacy and books are officially celebrated, but effectively our schools and universities are becoming mere training grounds for the workforce, instead of places in which curiosity and reflection are fostered. "Think less, work more," was the message delivered on 21 July 2007 by Christine Lagarde, then finance minister of Nicolas Sarkozy. "We have in our libraries enough to talk about for centuries to come," said Madame Lagarde. "This is why I would like to tell you: Enough thinking, already. Roll up your sleeves." In France as elsewhere, our motto, like that of a certain laptop, has become "Faster than thought," a quality Pinocchio's school would no doubt have endorsed. The opposition is valid, since thought requires time and depth, the two essential qualities of the act of reading.

Teaching is a slow, difficult process, two adjectives that have in our time become faults instead of terms of praise. It seems almost impossible to convince most of us today of the merits of slowness and deliberate effort. And yet, Pinocchio will only learn if he is not in a hurry to learn, and will only become a full individual through the effort required to learn slowly. Whether in Collodi's age of parroted school texts or in ours of almost infinite regurgitated facts available at our fingertips, it is relatively easy to be superficially literate, to follow a sitcom, to understand an advertising joke, to read a political slogan, to use a computer. But to go further and deeper, to have the courage to face our fears and doubts and hidden secrets, to question the workings of society in regard to ourselves and to the world, in order to learn to think, we need to learn to read in other ways, differently. Pinocchio may turn into a boy at the conclusion of his adventures, but ultimately he still thinks like a puppet.

Almost everything around us encourages us not to think, to be content with commonplaces, with dogmatic language that divides the world neatly into white and black, good and evil, them and us. This is the language of extremism, sprouting up everywhere these days, reminding us that it has not disappeared. To the difficulties of reflecting on paradoxes and open questions, on contradictions and chaotic order, we respond with the age-old cry of Cato the Censor in the Roman Senate, "Carthago delenda est!" "Carthage must be destroyed!"—the other civilization must not be tolerated, dialogue must be avoided, rule must be imposed by exclusion or annihilation. This is the cry of dozens of contemporary leaders. This is a language that pretends to communicate but, under several guises, simply bullies; it expects no answer except obedient silence. "Be sensible and good," the Blue Fairy tells Pinocchio in the end, "and you'll be happy." Many a political slogan can be reduced to this inane piece of advice.

To step outside that constricted vocabulary of what society considers "sensible and good" into a vaster, richer, and, above all, more ambiguous one is terrifying, because this other realm of words has no boundaries and is equivalent to thought, emotion, intuition. This infinite vocabulary is open to us if we will take the time and make the effort to explore it, and over our many centuries it has wrought words out of experience in order to reflect experience back to us, to allow us to understand the world and ourselves. It is greater and longer lasting than Pinocchio's ideal library of sweetmeats because it includes it, metaphorically, and can lead to it, concretely, by allowing us to imagine ways in which we can change a society in which Pinocchio starves, is beaten and exploited, is refused the state of childhood, is asked to be obedient and to be happy in his obedience. To imagine is to dissolve barriers, to ignore boundaries, to subvert the vision of the world imposed upon us. Though Collodi was unable to grant his puppet this final state of self-discovery, he intuited, I believe, the possibilities of his imaginative powers. And even when asserting the importance of bread over words, he knew well that every crisis of society is ultimately a crisis of the imagination.

Candide in Sanssouci

"I only wanted to see what the garden was like."

Through the Looking-Glass, Chapter 2

OUR FIRST IMPULSE IS TO decipher what we sense around us, as if every-thing in the universe carried meaning. We try to decode not only systems of signs created for that purpose—such as alphabets, hieroglyphs, pictographs, social gestures—but also the objects that surround us, the faces of others and our own reflection, the landscape through which we move, the shapes of clouds and trees, the changes in the weather, the flight of birds, the spoor of insects. Legend has it that cuneiform script, one of the earliest systems of writing we know, was invented by copying the footprints of sparrows in the mud of the Euphrates five thousand years ago, prints which must have seemed to our remote ancestors less casual markings than words in a mysterious and divine language. We lend moods to the seasons, significance to geographic settings, symbolic value to animals. Whether as trackers, poets, or shamans, we have intuited in the unfolding of nature an endless book in which we, like all other things, are written, but which we are also compelled to read.

If nature is a book, it is an infinite book, at least as vast as the universe itself. A garden then, is a scaled-down version of that universe, a comprehen-sible model of that endless text, glossed according to our restricted capabili-ties. According to the Midrash, God put man in the Garden of Eden "to dress it and to keep it," but "that only means he is to study the Torah there and fulfill the commandments of God." Expulsion from the Garden can be understood as a punishment for willfully incorrect reading.

Gardening and reading have a long association. In 1250, the chancellor of the cathedral of Amiens, Richard de Fournival, imagined a book-cataloguing system based on a horticultural model. He compared his library to an orchard wherein his fellow citizens might gather "the fruits of knowledge" and divided it into three flowerbeds corresponding to three major categories: philosophy, the so-called lucrative sciences, and theology. Each bed in turn was divided into a number of smaller plots (*areolæ*) containing a summary of the book's subject matter. Fournival speaks of "cultivating" both his garden and his library.

Not surprisingly, the verb *cultiver* retains in French these two meanings: that of growing a garden and that of becoming learned. The tending of one's garden and the tending of one's books require, in the sense of the word *cultiver*, equal devotion, patience, persistence, and a serviceable sense of order. *Cultiver* is to seek the truth hidden in the apparent chaos of nature or a library, and to render visible its attendant qualities. Furthermore, in both cases, truth is subject to review. Gardener and reader must both be willing to shift purpose according to the exterior or interior weather, to yield to the consequences of new discoveries, to reorganize, redistribute, reconsider, redefine, according not to overwhelming absolutist notions but to individual and quotidian experience.

To a certain extent, the French Revolution is the consequence of a loss of confidence in absolutes. Rather than maintain that universal metaphysical categories rule human lives, or that ideas override experience, or that figures of divine power have the right to rule over individuals, the philosophers of the French Enlightenment preferred to argue what Immanuel Kant was later to call "the categorical imperative": that every human act, at its finest, should in principle become a universal law. A splendid, if impossible, achievement, concerning which a century later Robert Louis Stevenson would note: "Our duty in life is not to succeed, but to continue to fail in the best of spirits."

Voltaire would have agreed. Voltaire, above all the philosophers of the Enlightenment, wished us to act as if we, and not a Divine Commander, were accountable for the consequences of our acts. For him no human action is independent of another. "All events are linked in the best of all possible worlds," the philosopher Pangloss tells Candide at the end of his adventures. "Had you not lost all your sheep in the good land of Eldorado, you would not be here eating pistachios and candied lemons." To which Candide wisely answers, "Well said, but we must tend to our garden."

The garden is then our business, the stage of our essential occupations, nature transformed into the setting in which we are to accomplish our allotted human tasks. The wise Turkish dervish whom Candide consults at the end of his adventures knows or cares nothing of what goes on in the world (for instance, that two viziers and a mufti have been strangled in Constantinople), nor is he concerned with metaphysical questions about the reason for our existence or problems of good and evil. "What then are we to do?" asks Pangloss anxiously. "Shut up," answers the dervish. Shut up and act. "Man is born for action, like fire tends to rise and stones to fall. Not to be occupied and not to exist is all one to man," argues Voltaire against Pascal. And farther on: "Let us be consoled for not knowing the relationship that might exist between a spider and the rings of Saturn, and let us continue to examine that which lies within our reach."

To examine nature, we must therefore render it accessible, lend it a shape and a symmetry that can be grasped by our senses. Faced with the conceptual order of a garden, we can pretend or assume to read it: allot significance to its beds and partitions, garner instruction from its layout, deduce a narrative from its sequence of plantings.

In this sense, every garden is a palimpsest, design over design, season after season. Let us consider, as an example, the garden through which Voltaire wandered during his three years of grace in Prussia: the royal park of Sanssouci. Sanssouci began life in 1715 as a kitchen garden planted on a hill outside Potsdam under the orders of Friedrich Wilhelm I, and it was sarcastically known as the Marlygarten in reference to Louis XIV's costly garden at Marly. In 1744, Friedrich's son Friedrich II added on a vineyard and six parabolic curving terraces for plum and fig trees and vines, each terrace divided by twenty-eight glazed windows and sixteen yew trees trimmed in the shape of pyramids. A year later, the terraces were extended southward by a level space of eight flowerbeds and punctuated by a fountain over which rose a gilded statue of the goddess Thetis and her attendants. Two sphinxes by Franz Georg Ebenhech were added a decade afterwards on the far side of the moat, leading to a plot of agricultural land, and still later a marble parapet topped with a dozen sculptures of children was erected to separate a Dutch garden of terraced beds from a rond-point and its fountain. Beyond this area, the king installed a Neptune Grotto and an Obelisk Portal, each with a small flower parterre, while to the west he erected a Chinese teahouse, a delightful folly designed by Johann Gottfried Büring between 1754 and 1757.

Flowerbeds, allées, parterres, fountains, sculptural groups, hedged paths combine to form a complex landscaped narrative: but in the beginning, the garden of Sanssouci had no other purpose than to express a certain simplicity as a place both pleasing and useful, a garden like the one through which God walked (Genesis tells us) "in the cool of the evening," so peaceful, that it was here where Friedrich II stipulated (in several wills) that he wished to be buried. The model of such a garden is very ancient: in the oldest Mesopotamian texts no distinction is drawn between "orchard" and "garden," since the aesthetic function was not necessarily differentiated from the utilitarian one.

At Sanssouci, however, habitation succeeded cultivation. A year after the establishment of the orchard and because of the beauty of the scenery, the king had a summer palace built on the site to take advantage of the delightful view. What was to have been merely a model of Eden was overwritten with new architectural episodes and their attendant subplots, complicating and multiplying the itineraries and vistas. In the following years, more buildings were added (such as the gardeners' houses and the orangery, later transformed into guest lodgings), and to the north of the Schloss Sanssouci mock ruins were erected following the principle of baroque metaphors in order to hide the water tank that fed the park's fountains. The stone metaphors hid too well their core meaning: only once did the king enjoy the displays of dancing water since the cumbersome mechanics that worked the jets did not become fully operational until the next century, when a steam engine was installed to fuel them. But by then the king was dead and his intricately conceived garden was no longer in fashion. Three kings later, Friedrich Wilhelm IV redesigned Sanssouci in the style of the Italian landscaped park we see today. The older scripts, however, can still be glimpsed beneath the more recent plots, groves, and pathways. As in a palimpsest, the original text never quite disappears.

When Friedrich II installed his orchard in Sanssouci, he was thirty-two years old. Eight summers earlier, as a young man of twenty-four, he had begun a correspondence with Voltaire, asking him to become his guide. "In the entire universe," wrote Friedrich gushingly, "no exception could be made of those of whom you might not be the teacher." Voltaire was almost twenty years the monarch's senior and the most celebrated philosopher in Europe at the time; Friedrich was only the heir apparent to a secondary European monarchy. Friedrich admired Voltaire's ideas, his prose, his poetry, his drama, and above all, the fact that he was French. Years later, in 1880, Friedrich was to publish a pamphlet (in French, like all the thirty-one volumes of his extensive writings) titled *De la littérature allemande, des défaults qu'on peut lui reprocher, quelles en sont les causes, et par quels moyens on peut les corriger* in which he brands his native tongue as "à demi barbare." Kultur was, for Friedrich, unhesitatingly French.

Friedrich's youth had been, to say the least, rebellious. His father had wanted to mold the prince into his own image of a *Soldatenkönig*, a hard-bitten warrior and statesman. When the experiment failed, he tried to force him to resign his rights of succession. Finally, after one humiliation too many, Friedrich attempted to flee to Paris with his friend Lieutenant von Katte. The two young men were caught, Friedrich was locked up in his room, and von Katte was executed under the prince's window. Friedrich then began to see the merits of dissembling. He bought himself some peace by pretending obedience to his father, inspecting the troops and marrying a niece of the Austrian empress Maria Theresa whom he afterwards visited only once every twelve months, on her birthday. For the few years preceding his accession, he lived in the newly rebuilt Palace of Rheinsberg, reading, writing, composing music, playing the flute, and corresponding with Voltaire. If he had modeled his life on a literary figure, it would have been Shakespeare's Prince Hal. Voltaire was his Falstaff, and as Hal with Falstaff, Friedrich parted from his master when he chose to truly assume his role as king. The break between the two men occurred in 1753, three years before the start of the Seven Years' War, which was to grant Friedrich the appellation "Great."

But from 1750 to 1753, Voltaire was Friedrich's guide, while Friedrich lent Voltaire the illusion that the myth of the philosopher-king could indeed become reality. With promises of money and applause, Friedrich lured Voltaire to Sanssouci. Here Voltaire, like his host, led a quiet, regulated, retired life, as if following the midrashic principles of Eden. "What do you do here at Sanssouci?" someone was once asked. "We conjugate the verb 'to be bored,'" was the answer. Voltaire worked at his writing and at pretending to be ill. He was almost sixty years old.

Without truly being conscious of it, Voltaire had granted Friedrich a philosophical justification for being who he was. The small palace of only twelve rooms, with its library, its picture gallery and music room, but above all the gardens, carefully plotted and artfully kept, lent the king the illusion of power over all the forces of nature, allowing him, rather than to explore the vast and secret rules of nature, to render familiar the unfamiliar, that is to say, to translate and simplify, to abridge, explain, and gloss. To ensure an uninterrupted continuity between the palace and the garden, Friedrich had, against the advice of his architect Georg Wenzeslaus von Knobelsdorff, dispensed with a ground story. In this way, the notions of outside and inside broke down and intermingled, the inside becoming part of the wilderness of nature, the outside domesticated by its connection to the interior.

Friedrich had intuited that we render a place artificial merely by being in it. Our presence (as strollers or as residents) humanizes a landscape, and while topiaries and manicured lawns, patterned flowerbeds and staggered terraces frame that which is essentially alien and wild, these artifices simply confirm the original hierarchies of Eden, when Adam was made lord of all flowers and all trees, with one notorious exception. A cultivated place showed the hand of man—so much so that visitors at Sanssouci sometimes complained that they couldn't see the trees for all the gold and marble. Wilderness, instead, is that place, as God says to Job, where the rain falls on the earth "where no man is." It exists by contrast to our presence; it is a closed book whose text does not come into being until it is opened and read.

At about the same time and in other places, gardeners were discovering that same notion. Horace Walpole, writing about the landscape artist William Kent, noted that "he leaped the fence, and saw that all nature was a garden." Kent did what in another context Marcel Duchamp was to do centuries later: he put a frame around the readymades of nature. He called the wilderness a garden simply because he was there to look upon it, and merely redistributed what he found for better effect in a procedure Alexander Pope was to call "landscape painting." A rock was moved, a watercourse diverted, but the general aspect of the garden remained decidedly "wild." Kent's masterstroke took place in 1735, when, under the patronage of Queen Caroline, he planted a dead tree in Richmond Gardens. The gesture was directly equivalent to the use of unattributed quotations in so much eighteenth-century writing, for instance in the work of Laurence Sterne.

In contrast with Kent's "recuperation" of the wilderness in England, Friedrich's Sanssouci was a model of French artifice, a product of human reason. Kent's wilderness was, in some sense, a response to the English Puritans' abhorrence of the geometrical forms in gardens, to the logical constructions that, according to them, prevented the soul from finding its narrow path. Sanssouci, on the other hand, obeyed the baroque impulse born with the Counter-Reformation, the intuition that truth can best be revealed in hiding, in the elaborate volutes and spirals that lend presence to a concept by enclosing it. Looking towards the palace, a visitor would have been able to follow the careful lines of terraced gardens which look, especially in winter when the trellises are visible, like rising rows of bookshelves in a dream library; the viewer would probably reflect for a moment on the circumscribed passages of laid-out parterres, enjoy the convoluted swirls that surrounded the central fountain, remember the stories of the ancient gods illustrated by the sculptures. In his *Essai sur les moeurs,* written at Sanssouci, Voltaire had noted that "it is not in the nature of man to desire that which he does not know" and that therefore he required "not only a prodigious length of time but also felicitous circumstances to rise above his animal state." Sanssouci allowed the visitor to understand how nature could be reasoned, could be read through its unfurled texts revealed in apparently coded flowerbeds and deliberately arranged views, could be reflected in poetical compositions and musical scores, could be understood through baroque emblems and artifices, thereby encouraging an ardent desire for natural knowledge. At least, that was the intention.

But Friedrich became disillusioned with Voltaire's teachings, or with Voltaire the man, or with that part of himself that as a youngster had believed that there was wisdom in art beyond the scope of power and accomplishments in the spirit that no imperial armies could conquer. He had opposed his personal vanity to that of his father, the sophisticated, cultured identity of the heir apparent to the brutish, ambitious identity of Friedrich I. Like Prince Hal, Prince Friedrich suddenly realized that "The tide of blood in me / Hath proudly flow'd in vanity till now: / Now doth it turn and ebb back to the sea, / Where it shall mingle with the state of floods / And flow henceforth in formal majesty." Of such majesty Voltaire wanted no part even though in his *Memoirs* he was to confess: "I could not but be attracted to him, because he was witty, graceful, and also because he was a king, which always proves very seductive, given our human weakness."

According to Novalis, when Adam was sent out of Eden, the shattered remains of Paradise were scattered all over the earth, and that is the reason why Paradise is so difficult to recognize. Novalis hoped that these fragments would somehow be brought together, its skeleton filled out. Perhaps the young Friedrich had entertained the same hope since Voltaire had taught him to believe in the uttermost importance of philosophy and art that sought, in a practical, empirical way, to know the world and the human condition. But the older statesman Friedrich had little faith in such cultured notions. For the student prince, gardens, like books, were ordered fragments of Paradise, reflections of what we know of the world, artificial creations that were nevertheless alive and fruit bearing, ordered spaces for our imagination to roam and for our dreams to take root, the means by which our arts and crafts transcribed the story of creation. If all flesh was as grass, as the Bible told us, then the warning could also be read as an exultation, as the revelation that we too had in us some of the grass's ability to come into being summer after summer, to conquer death by covering the dirt-filled graves, to lead a multitudinous, exuberant, and orderly existence in leaves as numerous as those of the books in the Universal Library. For the middle-aged King Friedrich II, only the political order seemed to matter.

And yet something of Voltaire's teachings must have taken secret root. Four years after the victory of Rossbach that won Friedrich the epithet "Great," the king, aged thirty-nine, reverted to his early literary ambitions and composed a poetic fable which he called "Le Conte du violon" (The Tale of the Fiddle). Jotted down in Breslau, far from the quiet and beauty of Sanssouci, in the last days of 1751, it tells the story of a gifted fiddler who is asked to play on only three strings, then two, then one, and finally on none, with the obvious results. The fable ends like this:

> Through this story, if it please you,
> May you now this wisdom glean:
> That however skilled you may be
> Art falls short without the means.

The Gates of Paradise

"Come, we shall have some fun now!" thought Alice.
Alice's Adventures in Wonderland, Chapter 7

ONE OF THE OLDEST VERSIONS of Beauty and the Beast, told in Latin by
Apuleius sometime in the second century, is the story of a princess ordered
by an oracle to become the wife of a dragon. Fearing for her life, dressed in
mourning, abandoned by her family, she waited at the top of a mountain for
her winged husband. The monster never came. Instead, a breeze lifted her and
bore her down into a peaceful valley, in which stood a house of gold and silver.
Disembodied voices welcomed her, and offered her food and drink, and sang
to her. When night fell, no lights were lit, and in the darkness she felt someone
near her. "I am your lover and your husband," a voice said, and mysteriously
she was no longer afraid. The princess lived with her unseen spouse for many
days.

One evening, the voices told her that her sisters were approaching the
house, searching for her, and she felt a great desire to see them once again and
tell them of the wonderful things that had taken place. The voices warned her
not to go, but her longing was too great. Crying out their names, she hurried
to meet them. At first the sisters seemed overjoyed, but when they heard her
story they cried and called her a fool for allowing herself to be deceived by a
husband who required the cover of darkness. "There must be something monstrous about him, if he will not show himself to you in the light," they said, and
felt pity for her.

That night, steeling herself for a hideous revelation, the princess lit an
oil lamp and crept to where her husband was sleeping. What she saw was not
a dragon, but a young man of extraordinary beauty, breathing softly into the
pillow. Overjoyed, she was about to extinguish the lamp, when a drop of hot
oil fell on the sleeper's left shoulder. He awoke, saw the light, said not a word,
and fled.

Eros vanishes when Psyche tries to perceive him.

As an adolescent, reading about Eros and Psyche one hot afternoon at home in Buenos Aires, I didn't believe in the moral of the story. I was convinced that in my father's almost unused library, where I had found so many secret pleasures, I would find, by magic chance, the startling and unspoken thing that crept into my dreams and was the butt of schoolyard jokes. I wasn't disappointed. I glimpsed Eros through the chiffonnerie of *Forever Amber*, in a tattered translation of *Peyton Place*, in certain poems of Federico García Lorca, in the sleeping-car chapter of Alberto Moravia's *The Conformist*, which I read haltingly at thirteen, in Roger Peyrefitte's *Particular Friendships*.

And Eros didn't vanish.

When a couple of years later I was able to compare my readings to the actual sensation of my hand brushing for the first time over my lover's body, I had to admit that for once, literature had fallen short. And yet the thrill of those forbidden pages remained. The panting adjectives, the brazen verbs were perhaps not useful to describe my own confused emotions, but they conveyed to me, then and there, something brave and astonishing and unique.

This uniqueness, I was to discover, brands all our essential experiences. "We live together, we act on, and react to, one another," wrote Aldous Huxley in *The Doors of Perception*, "but always and in all circumstances we are by ourselves. The martyrs go hand in hand into the arena; they are crucified alone. Embraced, the lovers desperately try to fuse their insulated ecstasies into a single self-transcendence; in vain. By its very nature every embodied spirit is doomed to suffer and enjoy in solitude." Even in the moment of greatest intimacy, the erotic act is a solitary act.

Throughout the ages, writers have attempted to make this solitude a shared one. Through ponderous hierarchies (essays on gender etiquette, texts of medieval love courts), through mechanics (lovemaking manuals, anthropological studies), through examples (fables, novels, poems), every culture has sought to comprehend the erotic experience in the hope that perhaps, if it is faithfully depicted in words, the reader may be able to relive it or even learn it, in the same way that we expect a certain object to preserve a memory or a monument to bring the dead to life.

It is amazing to think how distinguished a universal library of this wishful erotic literature would be. It would include, I imagine, the Platonic dialogues in which Socrates discusses the types and merits of love; Ovid's *Ars amatoria* of imperial Rome, in which Eros is considered a social function, like table manners; the Song of Songs, in which the loves of King Solomon and the black Queen of Sheba become reflections of the world around them; the Hindu Kama Sutra and the Kalyana Malla, in which pleasure is regarded as an element of ethics; the Arcipreste de Hita's *Book of Loving Well* in fourteenth-century Spain, which pretends to draw its wisdom from popular sources; the fifteenth-century *Perfumed Garden* of Sheik al-Nefzawi, which codifies the erotic acts according to Islamic law; the German *Minnereden,* or medieval amatory discourses, in which love, like politics, is given its own rhetoric; and poetic allegories such as the *Roman de la rose* in France and *The Faerie Queene* in Britain, in which the abstract noun *Love* acquires once again, as Eros had, a human or divine face.

There would be other, even stranger works, in this ideal library: the ten-volume novel *Clélie* (1654–60), by Mademoiselle de Scudéry, which includes the *Carte de tendre,* a map charting the erotic course with its rewards and perils; the writings of the marquis de Sade, who, in prolix and tedious catalogues, noted the sexual variations to which a human group can be subjected; the theoretical books of his near-contemporary Charles Fourier, who devised entire utopian societies centered around the sexual activities of its citizens; the intimate journals of Giacomo Casanova, Ihara Saikaku, Benvenuto Cellini, Frank Harris, Anaïs Nin, Henry Miller, and John Rechy, all of whom tried to recapture Eros in autobiographical memoirs.

Curled up in an armchair in my father's library and in other, later armchairs in more houses than I care to remember, I found that Eros kept appearing in all sorts of unexpected places. In spite of the singular nature of the experiences hinted at or described on the private page, these stories touched me, aroused me, whispered secrets to me.

We may not share experiences, but we can share symbols. Transported into another realm, distracted from its subject, erotic writing at times achieves something of that essentially private act, as when the swoons and agonies of erotic desire become a vast metaphorical vocabulary for the mystical encounter. I remember the excitement with which I read, for the first time, the erotic union described by Saint John of the Cross.

This is Roy Campbell's translation:

Oh night that was my guide!
Oh darkness dearer than the morning's pride,

Oh night that joined the lover
To the beloved bride
Transfiguring them each into the other.

Lost to myself I stayed
My face upon my lover having laid
From all endeavour ceasing:
And all my cares releasing
Threw them amongst the lilies there to fade.

And then John Donne, for whom the erotic and mystical act is also an act
of geographical exploration:

License my roving hands and let them go.
Before, behind, between, above, below.
O my America! my new-found-land.

In Shakespeare's time, the erotic borrowing of the geographical vocabulary had become sufficiently common to be parodied. In *The Comedy of Errors*
the slave Dromio of Syracuse describes to his master the dubious charms of
the wench lusting after him — "she is spherical, like a globe; I could find out
countries in her" — and proceeds to discover Ireland in her buttocks, Scotland
in the barren palm of her hand, America upon her nose, "all o'er embellished
with rubies, carbuncles, sapphires, declining their rich aspect to the hot breath
of Spain."

William Cartwright, the nebulous seventeenth-century author of *The
Royal Slave* (a play that once received praise from both Charles I and Ben Jon-
son), deserves to be better remembered for the following lines, which return
spiritual love to its authentic source:

I was that silly thing that once was wrought
To Practise this thin Love;
I climb'd from Sex to Soul, from Soul to Thought;
But thinking there to move,
Headlong I rowl'd from Thought to Soul, and then
From Soul I lighted at the Sex agen.

Occasionally, in my haphazard reading, I found that a single image could render a poem unforgettable. These are lines composed by a Sumerian poet circa 1700 B.C. She writes:

Going to my young husband —
I'll become the apple
clinging to the bough,
surrounding the stem
with my sweet flesh.

In a few cases, all that is required is an absence of description to convey the erotic power of that which has been lost. An anonymous English poet wrote this most famous of quatrains sometime in the late Middle Ages:

Western wind, when will thou blow,
The small rain down can rain?
Christ, that my love were in my arms,
And I in my bed again.

Fiction, however, is another matter.

Of all the erotic literary genres, fiction, I think, has the hardest time of it. To tell an erotic story, a story whose subject is outside words and outside time, seems not only a futile task but an impossible one. It may be argued that any subject, in its sheer complexity or simplicity, makes its own telling impossible, that a chair or a cloud or a childhood memory is just as ineffable, just as indescribable, as lovemaking, as a dream, as music.

Not so.

We have in most languages a varied and rich vocabulary that conveys reasonably well, in the hands of an experienced craftsperson, the actions and the elements with which society is comfortable, the daily bric-a-brac of its political animals. But that which society fears or fails to understand, that which forced me to keep a wary eye on the door of my father's library, that which becomes forbidden, even unmentionable in public is given no proper words with which to approach it. "To write a dream, which shall resemble the real course of a dream, with all its inconsistency, its eccentricities and aimlessness," complained Nathaniel Hawthorne in his *American Notebooks*, "up to this old age of the world, no such thing has ever been written." He could have said the same of the erotic act.

The English language in particular makes things difficult by simply not having an erotic vocabulary. The sexual organs, the sexual acts borrow the words to define them from either the science of biology or the lexicon of vituperation. Clinical or coarse, the words to describe the marvels of physical beauty and the exultation of pleasure condemn, asepticize, or deride that which should be celebrated in wonder. Spanish, German, Italian, and Portuguese suffer from this same weakness. French is, perhaps, a little more fortunate. *Baiser* for copulate, which borrows its semantics from the word "kiss"; *verge* for penis, the same word for "birch," which in its association with trees gives *verger*, "orchard"; *petite mort*, "little death," for the moment of ecstasy after achieving orgasm, in which the diminutive endearment takes the eternity out of dying but retains the sense of blissfully leaving this world have little of the nudge-nudge wink-wink quality of *fuck*, *prick*, and *come*. The vagina (surprise, surprise) receives in French as little respect as it does in English, and *con* is hardly better than *cunt*. To write an erotic story in English, or to translate one into English, requires from the writer new and crafty ways of making use of the medium, so that the reader is led, against the grain of meaning or through an entirely separate imagination of language, into an experience that society has decreed will remain unspoken. "We have placed sex," said the wise Montaigne, "in the precincts of silence."

But why have we decided that Psyche must not look upon Eros?

In the Judeo-Christian world, the banning of Eros finds its canonical voice in Saint Augustine, a voice that echoes through the entire Middle Ages and still rings, distorted, in the censor boardrooms of our day. After a youth of womanizing and carousing (to make use of these fine preacherly words), looking back on his quest for a happy life, Augustine concludes that ultimate happiness, *eudaemonia*, cannot be achieved unless we subordinate the body to the spirit, and the spirit to God. Bodily love, eros, is infamous, and only amor, spiritual love, can lead to the enjoyment of God, to agape, the feast of love itself that transcends both human body and spirit. Two centuries after Augustine, Saint Maximus of Constantinople put it in these words: "Love is that good disposition of the soul in which it prefers nothing that exists to knowledge of God. But no man can come to such a state of love if he be attached to anything earthly. Love," concludes Saint Maximus, "is born from lack of erotic passion." This is a far cry from Plato's contemporaries, who saw Eros as the binding force (in a real, physical sense) that keeps the universe together.

Condemnation of erotic passion, of the flesh itself, allows most patriarchal societies to brand woman as the temptress, as Mother Eve, guilty of Adam's daily fall. Because she is to blame, man has a natural right to rule over her, and any deviance from this law — by woman or by man — is punishable as treacherous and sinful. An entire apparatus of censorship is constructed to protect male-defined heterosexual stereotypes and as a result, misogyny and homophobia are both justified and encouraged, assigning women and homosexuals restricted and depreciated roles. (And children: we excise the sexuality of children from social life, while allowing it to appear in seemingly innocuous guises on the screen and in the fashion pages — as Graham Greene noted when he reviewed the films of Shirley Temple.)

Pornography requires this double standard. In pornography, the erotic must not be an integral part of a world in which both men and women, homosexual and heterosexual, seek a deeper comprehension of themselves and of the other. To be pornographic, the erotic must be amputated from its context and adhere to strict clinical definitions of that which is condemned. Pornography must faithfully embrace official normality in order to contravene it for no other purpose than immediate arousal. Pornography — or "licentiousness," as it used to be called — cannot exist without these official standards. *Licentious*, meaning "sexually immoral," comes from *license*, permission granted (to depart from the rules). That is why our societies allow pornography, which embraces official notions of "normal" or "decent" behavior, to exist in specific contexts but zealously persecute artistic erotic expressions in which the authority of those in power is brought implicitly into question. "Girlie" magazines could be bought in neat brown paper bags while *Ulysses* was being tried on charges of obscenity; hard-core porno films were shown in theaters a few steps away from others at which *The Last Temptation of Christ* or *How to Make Love to a Negro* were being picketed.

Erotic literature is subversive; pornography is not. Pornography, in fact, is reactionary, opposed to change. "In pornographic novels," says Vladimir Nabokov in his post-scriptum to *Lolita*, "action has to be limited to the copulation of clichés. Style, structure, imagery should never distract the reader from his tepid lust." Pornography follows the conventions of all dogmatic literature — religious tracts, political bombast, commercial advertising. Erotic literature, if it is to be successful, must establish new conventions, lend the words of the society that condemns it new meaning, and inform its readers of a knowledge that in its very nature must remain intimate. This exploration of the world from a central and utterly private place gives erotic literature its formidable power.

For the mystic, the whole universe is one erotic object, and the whole body (mind and soul included) the subject of erotic pleasure. The same can be said of every human being who discovers that not only penis and clitoris are places of pleasure but also the hands, the anus, the mouth, the hair, the soles of the feet, every inch of our astounding bodies. That which physically and mentally excites the senses and opens for us what William Blake called "the Gates of Paradise" is always something mysterious, and, as we all eventually find out, its shape is dictated by laws of which we know nothing. We admit to loving a woman, a man, a child. Why not a gazelle, a stone, a shoe, the sky at night?

In D. H. Lawrence's *Women in Love,* Rupert Birkin's object of desire is the vegetation itself: "To lie down and roll in the sticky, cool young hyacinths, to lie on one's belly and cover one's back with handfuls of fine wet grass, soft as a breath, soft and more delicate and more beautiful than the touch of any woman; and then to sting one's thigh against the living dark bristles of the fir-boughs; and then to feel the light whip of the hazel on one's shoulders, sting-ing, and then to clasp the silvery birch-trunk against one's breast, its smooth-ness, its hardness, its vital knots and ridges — this was good, this was all very good, very satisfying."

In John Collier's *His Monkey Wife,* Eros is a chimp called Emily with whom an English schoolmaster, Mr. Fatigay, falls madly in love: "'Emily!' he said. 'My Angel! My Own! My Love!' At this last word, Emily raised her eyes, and extended to him her hand. Under her long and scanty hair he caught glimpses of a plum-blue skin. Into the depths of those all-dark lustrous eyes, his spirit slid with no sound of splash. She uttered a few low words, rapidly, in her native tongue. The candle, guttering beside the bed, was strangled in the grasp of prehensile foot, and the darkness received, like a ripple in velvet, the final happy sigh."

In Cynthia Ozick's "The Pagan Rabbi," Eros is a tree: "I busied my fingers in the interstices of the bark's cuneiform. Then with forehead flat on the tree, I embraced it with both arms to measure it. My hands united on the other side. It was a young narrow weed, I did not know of what family. I reached to the lowest branch and plucked a leaf and made my tongue marvel meditatively along its periphery to assess its shape: oak. The taste was sticky and exaltingly bitter. I then placed one hand (the other I kept around the tree's waist, as it were) in the bifurcation (disgustingly termed crotch) of that lowest limb and the elegant and devoutly firm torso, and caressed that miraculous juncture with a certain languor, which gradually changed to vigor."

This is Marian Engel describing an amorous encounter between a woman and a beast in *Bear:*

> He licked. He probed. She might have been a flea he was searching for. He licked her nipples stiff and scoured her navel. With little nick-erings she moved him south.
>
> She swung her hips and made it easy for him.
>
> "Bear, bear," she whispered, playing with his ears. The tongue that was muscular but also capable of lengthening itself like an eel found all her secret places. And like no human being she had ever known it persevered in her pleasure. When she came, she whimpered, and the bear licked away her tears.

And the English writer J. R. Ackerley describes in these words his love for his dog, Tulip: "I go to bed early to end the dismal day, but she is instantly beside me, sitting upright against my pillow, her back turned, shifting, licking, panting, shifting, peering at my face: pulling at my arm. Sweet creature, what am I doing to you? I stretch out my hand in the gloom and stroke the small nipples. . . . Panting, she slackly sits while my hand caresses her, her ears flattened, her head dropped, gazing with vacant eyes into the night beyond the windows. Gradually, she relaxes, subsides. Gradually, my hand upon her, she sleeps ."

Even the lover's severed head can become an erotic object, as when Stendhal has Mathilde, in *The Red and the Black,* seek out Julien's remains: "He heard Mathilde move hurriedly around the room. She was lighting a number of candles. When Fouqué gathered enough strength to look, he saw that she had placed in front of her, on a little marble table, Julien's head, and was kissing its brow."

Confronted with the task of making art out of a bewildering variety of objects and subjects, acts and variations, feelings and fears; limited by a vo-cabulary specifically designed for other purposes; walking the perilous edge between pornography and sentimentality, biology and purple prose, the coy

and the overexplicit; threatened by societies intent on preserving the aristoc-
racies of established power through the censoring forces of politics, education,
and religion, it is a miracle that erotic literature has not only survived this long
but become braver, brighter, more confident, pursuing a multicolored infinity
of objects of desire.

A postscript: I believe that, like the erotic act, the act of reading should
ultimately be anonymous. We should be able to enter the book or the bed
like Alice entering the Looking-Glass Wood, no longer carrying with us the
prejudices of our past and relinquishing for that instant of intercourse our social trappings. Reading or making love, we should be able to lose ourselves in
the other, into whom — to borrow Saint John's image — we are transformed:
reader into writer into reader, lover into lover into lover. "Jouir de la lecture,"
"to enjoy reading," say the French, for whom reaching orgasm and deriving
pleasure are both expressed in a single common word.

Time and the Doleful Knight

"If you knew Time as well as I do," said the Hatter, "you wouldn't talk about wasting *it*."

Alice's Adventures in Wonderland, Chapter 7

AFTER THE STORY OF DON QUIXOTE has been brought almost to its end, Sansón Carrasco, the pompous intellectual who believes he can cure all this madness, says that he is the Knight of the White Moon and, swearing that his lady is far more beautiful than Dulcinea, forces the old gentleman to challenge him to a duel. Don Quixote charges against his adversary, falls to the ground badly hurt, and, unable to raise himself, hears Carrasco say that he'll admit to Dulcinea's superior charms only if he, Don Quixote, agrees to withdraw to his house for a full year "or until such time by me decided." The defeated Don Quixote gives his consent. A few further events take place on the following pages, further hallucinations and further enchantments, but as a result of the promise Don Quixote returns with Sancho to his village and asks to be taken to his bed, where a week later, having become once again Alonso Quijano (as the distraught author, Cide Hamete Benegeli, tells us), "he gave up his spirit: I mean to say, he died."

The year of abeyance that Sansón Carrasco has Don Quixote promise him is, for our hero, a period of impossible time. To stop being Don Quixote for a year, or even for a moment, is to demand that time come to a halt. Don Quixote cannot simultaneously stop being himself and go on living. Don Quixote is a creation of his own reading, and his world, materially alive in all its brutality and violence, is something that he can only know through his activity as a reader. Nothing exists for Don Quixote that has not previously been read, or rather, nothing exists that does not begin and end in his books. Consequently, Don Quixote cannot refuse himself the acting-out of his reading, to continue the story that his life has become, to behave like a knight in arms, because as soon as Alonso Quijano stops reading his dream book, Don Quixote must die. Don Quixote's time consists of the moments that Alonso Quijano is willing to grant him.

Don Quixote exists (as Alonso Quijano knows) between the covers of Cide Hamete's book: this, for the reader, is the only true story, and there cannot be other concurrent ones. This is why it is not fortuitous that in the last chapters of part 2 the characters discuss the false nature of the sequel to *Don Quixote* published by Avellaneda after the success of Cervantes's first part of the knight's adventures. The maid Altisidora, who pretends to have died because of her unrequited love for the old knight, describes her descent to Hell, saying that there she saw a group of devils playing ball with books, who tore Avellaneda's opus to bits, "a book so bad," says one of the devils, "that if I tried to produce a worse one on purpose, I wouldn't succeed." Neither is it fortuitous that when Alonso Quijano dictates his last will and testament, he instructs his executor to apologize to the apocryphal author for having provided an occasion for writing "such enormous and copious nonsense." Implicit in this apology is that Avellaneda's book was nonsense, not the one the reader now holds in his hands. False fiction (wasted time, untruth, fruitless lies) and true fiction (the chronicle of real time, of things as they essentially are) cannot and must not coexist. And Don Quixote, seemingly a believer in witchcraft and magic, never mistakes reality and untruth. Don Quixote's time is that of the real world, the one we can recognize because we can tell it in a story.

The year of inaction that Sansón Carrasco demands from Don Quixote belongs to false time, to the time of nonexistence. This is the time described by those condemned to real and literary hells, an inhuman time, a species of eternity in which nothing, except pain, has its existence and the sufferer loses everything that allows us to grant ourselves a recognizable identity. It is a time of no mirrors, or of fake mirrors that reflect only emptiness, the time of commercial and political advertising that stultifies and distracts, a time in which the consumer is trained to forget his own self and become another, become someone who identifies his desire with what is merely superficial, useless, sterile. This is the time wished upon us by the wizards of the mercantile world, like the one who, according to Don Quixote, caused his library to vanish (though the library has in fact been walled up by the censorious priest and barber): "Because his arts and his letters have taught him that in time I must come to fight a singular battle with a knight whom he favors, and that I must defeat him."

Against this false time flows the time of Don Quixote, ever-changing in that two-volume space created for us by Cervantes. In this time—true, rich, full of marvels—there is for us, his readers, one moment that, though perhaps no more mysterious than many others, is at least more bewildering and disconcerting. This is the moment in which the reader forgets Miguel de Cervantes, the author, and believes only in the reality of Don Quixote.

Everyone (even those who have not read Cervantes's books) knows Don Quixote. Next to him, Cervantes is almost phantomlike, a very minor character in the novel, an intruder who from time to time emits a comment or an opinion on the events, a leisurely reader who one day found a bundle of papers in a Toledo market and had them translated, thereby allowing us to read the adventures of the memorable knight. Even Cervantes's physical characteristics become in time those of his invention, a usurpation that by the nineteenth century is so firmly established that the illustrators of the novel see both author and fictional hero as identical. The clean-shaven knight of the early engravings vanishes and in his place appears a gentleman with the features of Cervantes: "eagle-faced . . . hawk-nosed . . . silver beard . . . teeth neither tiny nor enormous, because he has only six, and these badly kept and worse disposed . . . the body between two extremes, neither too big nor too small . . . somewhat curved in the shoulders and not very fast on his feet." This is the description that Cervantes makes of himself at the age of sixty-six, as if he had grown into the character of Don Quixote as he described him in the novel: "aged close to fifty . . . dry, nut-colored, moody . . . of tough complexion, wizened, thin faced." The literary creation comes to life in the time of the book, while he author himself fades away in the time of literary history, a ghost in the groves of academe.

Possibly Cervantes guessed that this was to be his fate. When in the sixth chapter of the first part the priest and the barber purge Don Quixote's library before walling it up, and find next to López Maldonado's *Cancionero* the unfinished *Galatea* by Miguel de Cervantes, the first instance of this vertiginous game takes place. Cervantes now exists because Don Quixote has read him and placed his book on the shelf, and *La Galatea* is saved from destruction because the priest says that he is a long-time friend of the author. And so the reader finds himself on the verge of a first abyss: if the pages he is reading are meant to be fiction, then the author of those pages is now part of that fiction, and the witness of the story (the reader who is summoned to take part in the story) no longer belongs to the conventional time of everyday life but to a time of imaginary existences whose flow depends only on an act of faith, faith in the reality of that fiction.

Cervantes (the imaginary figure we call Cervantes) guides and diverts, again and again, this fictitious time. When after barely eight chapters, halfway through an adventure, Cervantes confesses not to know how to continue Don Quixote's story, a miracle occurs. Finding himself one day in Toledo, Cervantes tells us, he finds a folder full of papers written in Arabic characters and since he can't read them, he looks for a *morisco aljaimado* (a Spanish-speaking Arab) to translate them for him. He discovers that the manuscript is by a certain Cide Hamete Benegeli, who has put on paper the entire story of Don Quixote. That is to say: depending on our point of departure, either Cide Hamete Benegeli narrates the story of Don Quixote that a morisco translates for Cervantes — the Cervantes who is a character in the preceding chapters — or the character called Cervantes, author of a book found in Don Quixote's library, has the translator read him the story of what follows the knight's first adventures in the manuscript of an Arabic author who writes in aljaimía, a Romance tongue transcribed in Arabic characters. The book we hold in our hands is such that, at whichever page we open it, conventional time disappears and becomes the time of fiction in order to render it "more real," as Don Quixote himself explains.

So thoroughly does Cervantes's fiction absorb reality to render it "more real" that it ends up devouring its own self. In the second chapter of part 2, Sansón Carrasco lets Sancho know that his adventures are told in a book (which Carrasco has read in Salamanca, a town famous for the seriousness of its academic publications) "under the title *The Ingenious Knight Don Quixote de la Mancha*." Hearing this, Sancho crosses himself in fright; much the same reaction is that of the reader for whom, if the first part of the book he's reading has also been read by the characters of the part he's reading now, then he, a creature of flesh and blood, is also part of that device, that trickery, that imaginary world, a ghost among ghosts, a servant not of his own will but of another man's dreams, a man who is not dust and ashes and who once upon a time was called Miguel de Cervantes.

Cervantes was no doubt aware of the mirror he held up to his readers. Towards the end of part 2, a certain scholarly canon tells Don Quixote that he cannot understand how certain books can delight without teaching unless they are nothing but beautiful. For the canon, "Delight conceived in the soul must be that of loveliness and balance seen or observed in things that sight or imagination bring forward; since anything that carries in itself ugliness or imperfection can produce no contentment whatsoever." The world of which the canon approves is that of perfect sterility, meaningless beauty, vacuous creations, like that of today's fashion models or sitcom characters for whom everything is immaculately aseptic, and time nothing but an interminable state of existence in which there is no responsibility and no distress. To this time without depth and without limits with which society shrouds the real passing of time, Don Quixote opposes a time of ethical action, a time in which every act has its consequences, good or evil, just or unjust. Instead of a vast and anonymous magma in which we exist unconsciously, Don Quixote proposes a time in which we are alive and fertile, in which our consciousness works towards rendering us more fully in our own image, becoming whoever it is the canon's time prevents us from knowing. In this time, in this truly real time, we must live, Don Quixote says, "undoing all manner of wrongs, and placing ourselves in situations and dangers which, once overcome, will grant us eternal renown and fame." This, Cervantes tells us, is the time of the stories we tell in order to be able to affirm that we exist.

Saint Augustine's Computer

"But there's one great advantage in it, that one's memory
works both ways."

Through the Looking-Glass, Chapter 5

IN THE FIRST YEARS OF THE sixteenth century, the elders of the guild of
San Giorgio degli Schiavoni in Venice commissioned the artist Vittore Carpaccio to paint a series of scenes illustrating the life of Saint Jerome, the fourth-
century reader and scholar. The last scene, now set up high on the right as
you enter the small, darkened guildhall, is not a portrait of Saint Jerome but
of Saint Augustine of Hippo, Saint Jerome's contemporary. In a story popular
since the Middle Ages, it was told that Saint Augustine had sat down at his
desk to write to Saint Jerome, asking his opinion on the question of eternal
beatitude, when the room filled with light and Augustine heard a voice telling
him that Jerome's spirit had ascended to the heavens.

The room in which Carpaccio placed Augustine is a contemporary Venetian study, as worthy of the author of the *Confessions* as of the spirit of Jerome,
responsible for the Latin version of the Bible and patron saint of translators:
thin volumes facing forward on a high shelf, delicate bric-a-brac lined beneath
it, a brass-studded leather chair and a small writing desk lifted from the flood-
prone floor, a distant table with a rotating lectern beyond the door at the far
left, and the saint's working space, cluttered with open books and with those
private objects which the years wash onto every writer's desk—a seashell, a
bell, a silver box. Set in the central alcove, a statue of the risen Christ looks
towards a statuette of Venus standing among Augustine's things; both inhabit,
admittedly on different planes, the same human world: the flesh from whose
delights Augustine prayed for release ("but not just now") and the Logos,
God's Word that was in the beginning and whose echo Augustine heard one

afternoon in a garden. At an obedient distance, a small white shaggy dog is expectantly watching.

This place depicts both the past and the present of a reader. Anachronism meant nothing to Carpaccio, since the compunction for historical faithfulness is a modern invention, not later perhaps than the nineteenth century and John Ruskin's Pre-Raphaelite credo of "absolute, uncompromising truth . . . down to the most minute detail." Augustine's study and Augustine's books, whatever these might have been in the fourth century, were, to Carpaccio and his contemporaries, in all essentials much like theirs. Scrolls or codices, bound leaves of parchment, or the exquisite pocket books that Aldus Manutius had printed just a few years before Carpaccio began his work at the guild were variant forms of the book—the book that changed and would continue to change, and yet remained one and the same. In the sense in which Carpaccio saw it, Augustine's study is also like my own, a common reader's realm: the rows of books and memorabilia, the busy desk, the interrupted work, the reader waiting for a voice—his own? the author's? a spirit's?—to answer questions seeded by the open page in front of him.

Since the fellowship of readers is a generous one, or so we are told, allow me to place myself for a moment next to Carpaccio's august reader, he at his desk, I at mine. Has our reading—Augustine's and Carpaccio's and mine—altered in the passing centuries? And if so, how has it altered?

When I read a text on a page or a screen, I read silently. Through an unbelievably complex process or series of processes, clusters of neurons in specific sections of my brain decipher the text my eyes take in and make it comprehensible to me, without the need to mouth the words for the benefit of my ears. This silent reading is not as ancient a craft as we might think.

For Saint Augustine, my silent activity would have been, if not incomprehensible, at the very least surprising. In a famous passage of the *Confessions*, Augustine describes his curious coming upon Saint Ambrose in his cell in Milan, reading silently. "When he read," Augustine recalled, "his eyes scanned the page and his heart explored the meaning, but his voice was silent and his tongue was still." Augustine, in the fourth century, usually read as the ancient Greeks and Romans had read, out loud, to make sense of the attached strings of letters without full stops or capitals. It was possible for an experienced and hurried reader to disentangle a text without speaking the words—Augustine himself was able to do this, as he tells us in his description of the tremendous moment of his conversion, when he picks up a volume of Paul's Epistles and reads "in silence" the oracular line that tells him to "put on Christ like an armor." But reading out loud was not only considered normal, it was also considered necessary for the full comprehension of a text. Augustine believed that reading needed to be made present; that within the confines of a page the *scripta*, the written words, had to become *verba*, spoken words, in order to spring into being. For Augustine, the reader had literally to breathe life into a text, to fill the created space with living language.

By the ninth century, punctuation and the greater diffusion of books had established silent reading as common, and a new element — privacy — had become a feature of the craft. For these new readers, silent reading allowed a sort of amorous intimacy with the text, creating invisible walls around them and the activity of reading. Seven centuries later, Carpaccio would have considered silent reading part and parcel of the scholar's work, and his scholarly Augustine would necessarily be pictured in a private and quiet place.

Almost five centuries later, in our time, since silent reading is no longer surprising and since we are always desperately searching for novelty, we have managed to grant the text on the screen its own disembodied voice. At the reader's request, a computer can now usurp the post-Augustine reader's magical prerogative: it can either be silent as a saint while I scan the scrolling page or lend a text both voice and graphic features, bringing the dead back to life not through a function of memory (as Augustine proposed) but through mechanics, as a ready-made Golem whose appearance will continue to be perfected. The difference is, the computer's reading voice isn't our voice: therefore the tone, modulation, emphasis, and other instruments for making sense of a text have been established outside our understanding. We have not so much given wing to the verba as made the dead scripta walk.

Nor is the computer's memory the same as our own. For Augustine, those readers who read the Scriptures in the right spirit preserved the text in the mind, relaying its immortality from reader to reader, throughout the generations. "They read it without interruption," he wrote in the *Confessions*, "and what they read never passes away." Augustine praises these readers, who "become" the book itself by carrying the text within them, imprinted in the mind as on a wax tablet.

Being able to remember passages from the essential texts for argument and comparison was still important in Carpaccio's time. But after the invention of printing, and with the increasing custom of private libraries, access to books for immediate consultation became much easier, and sixteenth-century readers were able to rely far more on the books' memory than on their own. The multiple pivoting lectern depicted by Carpaccio in Augustine's study extended the reader's mnemonic capacities even further, as did other wonderful contraptions—such as the marvelous "rotary reading desk" invented in 1588 by the Italian engineer Agostino Ramelli, which allowed a reader ready access to ten different books at almost the same time, each one open at the required chapter and verse.

The capacious memory of my computer attempts to provide the same service. In certain ways it is vastly superior to those Renaissance inventions. One example: the ancient texts of the Greeks and Romans, so rare that many of the books we call classics were unknown to Augustine, were lovingly and laboriously collected by Carpaccio's contemporaries. Today all those texts are entirely at my disposal. Two-thirds of all surviving Greek literature up to the time of Alexander, 3.4 million words and twenty-four thousand images, can be found contained in four disks published by Yale University Press (and many of these texts are available in several of the various digital libraries), so that now, with one nibble from my mouse, I can determine, for instance, exactly how many times Aristophanes used the word for "man," and figure out that it was twice as often as he used the word for "woman." To come up with such precise statistics, Augustine would have had to strain very hard his mnemonic capacities, even though the art of memory, arduously developed since the days of Greece and Rome, had by then been perfected to an astonishing degree.

However, what my computerized memory cannot do is select and combine, gloss and associate through a mingling of practice and intuition. It can't, for instance, tell me that in spite of the statistical evidence, it is Aristophanes' female characters—Praxagora in *The Assemblywomen,* the market gossips in *The Poet and the Women,* that old battle-ax Lysistrata—who come to mind when I think of his work, read not online but in the ancient Garnier codices we used at school. The gluttonous memory of my computer is not an active memory, like Augustine's; it is a repository, like Augustine's library, albeit vaster and more readily accessible. Thanks to my computer, I can memorize—but I cannot remember. That is a craft I must learn from Augustine and his ancient codices.

By Augustine's time, the codex, the book of bound sheets, had supplanted the scroll almost completely, since the codex held, over the scroll, obvious advantages. The scroll allowed only certain parts of the text to be shown at a given moment, without permitting the reader to flip through pages or read one chapter while keeping another open with a finger. It therefore laid strictures on the reading sequence. The text was offered to the reader in a predetermined order and only one section at a time. A text such as *Finnegans Wake*, which suggests an endless reading loop, would have been unthinkable in the days of the scroll. Also, the scroll limited the contents of the text far more than the codex would ever do. It is surmised that the division of the *Odyssey* into books corresponds not to the poet's desire but to the necessity of what would fit on one scroll.

Today my electronic screens partake of both book forms: "scrolling" a text and yet, if I wish, capable of flipping simultaneously to another section on a separate window. But in neither case do they have the full characteristics of their elders: they don't tell me, as the scroll did at a glance, the full physical measure of the text's contents. Nor do they allow me, in spite of windows, to skip and choose pages as dexterously as the codex did. On the other hand, my computer is a better retriever: its sniffing-out and fetching functions are infinitely superior to its dog-eared ancestors of parchment and paper.

Augustine knew (and we seldom remember) that every reader creates, when reading, an imaginary space, a space made up of the person reading and the realm of the words read — what Keats called "that purple-lined palace of sweet sin." This reading space exists either in the medium that reveals or contains it (in the book or in the computer) or in its own textual being, incorporeal, as words preserved in the course of time, a place in the reader's mind. Depending on whether the written word lies at the end or the beginning of a given civilization, whether we see it as the result of a creative process (as did the Greeks) or as the source (as did the Hebrews), the written word becomes — or does not become, as the case may be — the driving force of that civilization.

What I mean is this: for the Greeks, who assiduously wrote down their philosophical treatises, plays, poems, letters, speeches, and commercial transactions and yet regarded the written word merely as a mnemonic aid, the book was an adjunct to civilized life, never its core; for this reason, the material representation of Greek civilization was in space, in the stones of Greek cities. For the Hebrews, however, whose daily transactions were oral and whose literature was entrusted largely to memory, the book — the Bible, the revealed word of God — became the core of their civilization, surviving in time, not space, in the migrations of a nomad people. In one of his scriptural commentaries, Augustine, coming directly from the Hebrew tradition, noted that words tend towards the quality of music, which finds its being in time and does not have any particular geographical location.

My computer apparently belongs not to the book-centered Hebrew tradition of Augustine but to the bookless Greek tradition that required monuments in stone. Even though the Web simulates on my screen a borderless space, the words I conjure up owe their existence to the familiar temple of the computer, erected with its portico-like screen above the cobbled esplanade of my keyboard. Like marble for the Greeks, these plastic stones speak (in fact, thanks to its audio functions, they literally speak). And the ritual of access to cyberspace is in certain ways like the rituals of access to a temple or palace, to a symbolic place that requires preparation and learned conventions, decided by invisible and seemingly all-powerful computer buffs.

Augustine's reading rituals, performed around the space of his desk and within the space of his room, were nevertheless dispensable, or at the very least kept changing. He could choose to move about with the text he was reading, or lie in bed with his codex, or leave the room and read in the garden (as he did when he heard the words that led to his conversion) or in the solitary desert. Augustine's book, as a container of the text, was essentially variable. For the humanist reader of Carpaccio's time, this variability was of the essence, leading to Manutius's invention of the companionable pocket book. And throughout the centuries, the book became increasingly portable, multiple, replaceable — able to be read anywhere, in any position, at any time.

My rituals at the computer, though also translatable, depend on a complex technology many times beyond a layperson's knowledge. Even though a laptop or Blackberry can allow me to transport my reading to a cliff in the Grand Canyon (as the ads proclaim), the text still owes its existence to the technology that created and maintains it, and still requires my surrendering to the physical "monument" of the machine itself.

That is why, for Augustine, the words on the page — not the perishable scroll or replaceable codex that held them — had physical solidity, a burning, visible presence. For me, the solidity is in the edifice of the electronic device, not in the fleeting words. When silent, the phantom text, eerily materializing on the screen and vanishing at the drop of a finger, is certainly different from the sturdy, authoritarian black letters meticulously composed on a piece of parchment or stamped on the page. My electronic text is separated from me by a screen, so that I cannot directly kiss the words as Augustine might have done in his devotion, or inhale the perfume of leather and ink as the contemporaries of Carpaccio did in theirs. This accounts for the difference in the vocabulary used by Augustine and myself to describe the act of reading. Augustine spoke of "devouring" or "savoring" a text — a gastronomical imagery derived from a passage in Ezekiel, in which an angel commands the prophet to eat a book, an image repeated later in the Revelation of Saint John. I instead speak of "surfing" the Web, of "scanning" a text. For Augustine, the text had a material quality that required ingestion. For the electronic reader, the text exists only as a surface that is skimmed as he or she "rides the waves" of information from one cyber area to another.

Does all this mean that our reading craft has declined, lost its most precious qualities, become debased or impoverished? Or has it rather improved, progressed, perfected itself since Augustine's hesitant days? Or are these meaningless questions?

For many years now we have been prophesying the end of the book and the victory of the electronic media, as if books and electronic media were two gallants competing for the same beautiful reader on the same intellectual battlefield. First film, then television, later video games and DVDs and virtual libraries have been cast as the book's destroyers, and certain writers — Sven Birkerts, for example, in *The Gutenberg Elegies* — do not hesitate to use apocalyptic language full of calls for salvation and curses against the Antichrist. All readers may be Luddites at heart, but I think this may be pushing our enthusiasms too far. Technology will not retreat, nor, in spite of countless titles predicting the twilight of the printed word, do the numbers of new books printed every year show signs of diminishing.

And yet changes will occur. It is true that before most great turning points in technology, the previous technological form experiences a flourish, a last-minute exuberance. After the invention of the printing press, the number of manuscripts produced in Europe increased dramatically, and canvas painting mushroomed immediately after the invention of photography. It seems more than likely that even though the number of printed books is higher than ever, certain genres now available mainly as codices will give way to other formats, better suited for their purpose. Encyclopedias, for instance, will find more efficient homes in electronic containers, once the technology develops a more intelligent cross-referencing system and not one that simply throws up, with mechanical nonchalance, every example, however irrelevant.

But these are obvious transformations. Essentially, nothing precious need be lost. It may be that the qualities we nostalgically wish to retain in books as they appear now, and as the humanist readers imagined them, will reappear under clever guises in the electronic media. We can already scribble on electronic paper, and there are e-books reduced to fit in the reader's hand. The woman in the subway reading her paperback novel and the man next to her listening to the thud-thud bass of his iPod, the student making notes on the margins of her textbook and the child playing a handheld Nintendo by her side will all combine their instruments (as certain mobile phones do now) in a single portable apparatus that will offer all these textual possibilities: displaying text, reciting, allowing for annotations and proposing playful modes of research on one small portable screen or by some other yet-to-be-invented device—a device that, like Wagner's *Gesamtkunstwerk*, will allow for a sort of mini-opera, in which all the senses must come into play in order to re-create and enhance a text.

So why do we fear the change?

It is unlikely that reading will lose, in the electronic revolution, its aristocratic qualities. In the blurred childhoods of the past, reading appears either as a duty destined to preserve certain notions of authority (as in the scriptoria of Mesopotamia and of the European Middle Ages) or as a leisure-class activity throughout our various histories, accorded to those with means or usurped by those without them. Most of our societies (by no means all) have assembled around a book, and for these the library became an essential symbol of power. Symbolically, the ancient world ends with the destruction of the Library of Alexandria; symbolically, the twentieth century ends with the rebuilding of the library of Sarajevo.

But the notion of true democratic reading is illusory. Andrew Carnegie's nineteenth-century libraries were temples to his class, where the common readers were allowed to enter, mindful of their position, in veneration of established authority. Reading may bring some measure of social change, as Matthew Arnold believed, but it also can become a way of killing time or of slowing down time against the communality of death, arrogantly set against the monotonous cadence of time spent at work, "doing time" as it were in the countless illiterate sweatshops, mines, fields, and factories on which our societies are built.

What will certainly change is the idea of books as property. The notion of the book as an object of "pure value" (the expression belongs to Maurice Blanchot) because of its contents, its history, or its decorations has existed since the days of the scrolls, but it was not until the fourteenth century (in

Europe at least) that the rise of a bourgeois audience, beyond the realms of the nobility and the clergy, created a market in which the possession of books became a mark of social standing and the production of books a profit-making business like any other. A whole modern industry arose to fill this commercial need, causing Doris Lessing to exhort her beleaguered fellow workers: "And it does no harm to repeat, as often as you can, 'Without me the literary industry would not exist: the publishers, the agents, the sub-agents, the sub-sub-agents, the accountants, the libel lawyers, the departments of literature, the professors, the theses, the books of criticism, the reviewers, the book pages — all this vast and proliferating edifice is because of this small, patronized, put-down and underpaid person.'"

But in the days of the new technology, the industry (which will not disappear) will have to work otherwise in order to survive. Essays on the Internet, poems transmitted in blogs, books published electronically have begun to bypass editors and booksellers. Interactive novels question the very notion of authorship. Who will be paid royalties for a text scanned in Salamanca, received on e-mail in Recife, modified in Melbourne, expanded in Ecuador, saved on a key in San Francisco? Who in fact is the author of that multifarious text? Like the many contributors to the construction of a medieval cathedral or to the production of a Hollywood film, the new industry will find, no doubt, ways of securing a profit for someone, Church or multinational. And Doris Lessing's small, underpaid person may have to resign herself to becoming even smaller and more underpaid.

However, in our fear, we forget that as regards a text, *pace* Blanchot, there never was such a thing as "pure value." Every text is, in an essential sense, an interactive text, changing according to a particular reader, at a particular hour, and in a particular place. Every single reading carries the reader into the "spiral of interpretation," as the French historian Jean-Marie Pailler has called it. No reading can avoid it, every reading adds a turn to its vertiginous ascent. There never was "pure writing" or "pure reading": in reading Diderot, the act becomes confused with conversation; in Danielle Steele with titillation; in Defoe with reportage; in others with instruction, with gossip, with lexicography, with cataloguing, with hysterics. There seems to be no platonic archetype of any one reading, as there seems to be no platonic archetype of any one book. The notion of a text being "passive" is only true in the abstract: from the earliest scrolls to the displays of Bauhaus typography, from the cuneiform tablets to the graphic novels of today, every recorded text, every book in whatever shape carries implicitly or explicitly an aesthetic intention. No two manuscripts were ever the same, as the arduous cataloguers of Alexandria remarked, forcing them to choose "definitive" versions of the books they were preserving and establishing in the process the epistemological rule of reading: that every new copy supersedes the previous one, since it must of necessity include it. And while Gutenberg's printing press, re-creating the miracle of the loaves and fishes, multiplied one same text a thousand times, every reader proceeds to individualize his or her copy with scribbles, stains, markings of different sorts, so that no copy, once read, is identical to another. All these myriad variations, all these various runs of thumb-printed copies, have not prevented us, however, from speaking of "my very own copy" of *Hamlet* or *King Lear,* much as we speak of "the one and only" Shakespeare. Electronic texts will find new ways to generalize and define, and new critics will find vocabularies generous enough to accommodate the possibility of change.

The misplaced fear of technology, which once opposed the codex to the scroll, now opposes the scroll to the codex. It opposes the unfurling text on the screen to the multiple pages of the humanist reader's handheld book. But all technology, whether satanic mills or satanic Chernobyls, has a human measure; it is impossible to remove the human strand even from the most inhuman of technological devices. They are our creation, even if we try to deny them (as the Red Queen would say) "with both hands." Recognizing that human measure, like understanding the exact meaning of the colored palm marks on the walls of prehistoric caves, may be beyond our present capabilities. What we require therefore is not a new humanist reader but a more effective one, one who will restore to the text now enmeshed in technological devices the ambiguity that lent it a divinatory capacity. What we need is not to marvel at the effects of virtual reality, but to recognize its very real and useful defects, the necessary cracks through which we can enter a space yet uncreated. We need to be less, not more, assertive. We need to question more. Whether, for the future humanist reader, the book in its present form will remain unchanged is in some ways an idle question. My guess (but it is no more than a guess) is that by and large it will not be transformed drastically because it has adapted so well to our requirements — though these, indeed, may change. . . .

The question I ask myself instead is this: In these new technological spaces, with these artifacts that will certainly coexist with (and in some cases supplant) the book, how will we succeed in still able being to invent, to remember, to learn, to record, to reject, to wonder, to exult, to subvert, to rejoice? By what means will we continue to be creative readers instead of passive viewers?

Years ago, George Steiner suggested that the anti-bookish movement would drive reading back to its birthplace and that there would be reading houses like the old monastic libraries, where those of us quaint enough to wish to peruse an old-fashioned book would go and sit and read in silence. Something of the sort takes place every day in the monastery of the Holy Cross in Chicago's South Side, but not in the way Steiner imagined: here the monks, after morning prayers, switch on their computers and work away in their scriptorium like their ancestors a thousand years ago, copying and glossing and preserving texts for future generations. And even the privacy of devotional reading will not, apparently, retreat into secrecy; it has instead become ecumenical. God Himself can apparently be reached via the Jerusalem "Wailing Wall" site for readers of the Old Testament, or via the Vatican's Pope site for readers of the New.

To these visions of reading, I would like to add three more, imagined not too long ago by Ray Bradbury for our not-so-distant future.

• In one of the stories of *The Martian Chronicles,* "There Will Come Soft Rains," a fully automated house offers as an evening diversion to read a poem to its inhabitants, and when it receives no response it selects and reads a poem on its own, unaware that the entire family has been annihilated in a nuclear war. This is the future of reading without readers.

• Another story, "Usher II," records the saga of a heroic devotee of Poe in an age when fiction is considered not a source of thought but something dangerously real. After Poe's works are outlawed, a passionate reader builds a weird and perilous house as a shrine to his hero, through which he destroys both his enemies and the books he intends to avenge. This is the future of readers without reading.

• The third, the most famous, is in *Fahrenheit 451* and depicts a future in which books are burned and groups of literature lovers have memorized their favorite books, carrying them around in their heads like walking libraries. This is a future in which readers and reading, in order to survive, follow Augustine's precept and become one and the same.

Automated reading that requires no readers; the act of reading left to old-fashioned cranks who believe in books not as monsters but as places for dialogue; books transformed into a memory carried about until the mind caves in and the spirit fails . . . these scenarios suit our new century: the end of books set against the end of time, after the end of the second millennium. At the end of the first, the Adamites burned their libraries before joining their brethren in preparation for the Apocalypse so as not to carry useless wisdom into the promised Kingdom of Heaven.

Our fears are endemic fears, rooted in our time. They do not branch into the unknowable future; they demand a conclusive answer, here and now. "Stupidity," wrote Flaubert, "consists in a desire to conclude." Indeed. As every reader knows, the point, the essential quality of the act of reading, now and always, is that it tends to no foreseeable end, to no conclusion. Every reading prolongs another, begun in some afternoon thousands of years ago and of which we know nothing; every reading projects its shadow onto the following page, lending it content and context. In this way the story grows, layer after layer, like the skin of the society whose history the act preserves. In Carpaccio's painting Augustine sits, as attentive as his dog, pen poised, book shining like a screen, looking straight into the light, listening. The room, the instruments keep changing, the books on the shelf shed their covers, the texts tell stories in voices not yet born.

PART SIX

Books as Business

"I should like to buy an egg, please," she said timidly. "How do you sell them?"

"Fivepence farthing for one — twopence for two," the Sheep replied.

"Then two are cheaper than one?" Alice said in a surprised tone, taking out her purse.

"Only you *must* eat them both, if you buy two," said the Sheep.

Through the Looking-Glass, Chapter 5

Reading White for Black

"Do you know Languages? What's French for fiddle-de-dee?"

"Fiddle-de-dee's not English," Alice replied gravely.

"Who ever said it was?" said the Red Queen.

Through the Looking-Glass, Chapter 9

For Christine Le Boeuf

THROUGHOUT PART OF 1992 AND 1993, I worked on the translation of three short stories by Marguerite Yourcenar. The stories, published in French under the title *Conte bleu*, which I rendered in English as *A Blue Tale*, are early works by the writer who was to become in later life such an accomplished stylist. Understandably, because they were written with the exuberance and know-all of youth, the stories stray from time to time from sober blue to lurid purple. Since translators, unlike writers and God Himself, have the possibility of amending the faults of the past, it seemed to me that to preserve every glitter and volute of Yourcenar's young text would have been nothing but a pedantic undertaking, less intended for lovers of literature than for literary archaeologists. Furthermore, the English language is less patient with ebullience than French. And so it was that a few times—mea culpa, mea maxima culpa—I silently clipped an adjective or pruned a simile.

Vladimir Nabokov, criticized by his friend Edmund Wilson for producing a translation of *Eugene Onegin* "with warts and all," responded that the translator's business was not to improve or comment on the original but to give the reader ignorant of one language a text recomposed in all the equivalent words of another. Nabokov apparently believed (though I find it hard to imagine that the master craftsman meant this) that languages are "equivalent" in both sense and sound, and that what is imagined in one language can be reimagined in another—without an entirely new creation taking place. But the truth is (as every translator finds out at the beginning of the first page) that the phoenix imagined in one language is nothing but a barnyard chicken in another, and to invest that singular fowl with the majesty of the bird born from its own ashes, a different language might require the presence of a different creature, plucked from bestiaries that possess their own notions of strangeness. In English, for instance, the word *phoenix* still has a wild, evocative ring; in Spanish, *ave fénix* is part of the bombastic rhetoric inherited from the seventeenth century.

In the early Middle Ages, translation (from the past participle of the Latin *transferre,* "to transfer") meant conveying the relics of a saint from one place to another. Sometimes these translations were illegal, as when saintly remains were stolen from one town and carried away for the greater glory of another, which is how the body of Saint Mark was transferred from Constantinople to Venice, hidden under a cartful of pork, which the Turkish guards at Constantinople's gates refused to touch. Carrying away something precious and making it one's own by whatever means possible: this definition serves the act of literary translation perhaps better than Nabokov's.

No translation is ever innocent. Every translation implies a reading, a choice both of subject and interpretation, a refusal or suppression of other texts, a redefinition under the terms imposed by the translator, who, for the occasion, usurps the title of author. Since a translation cannot be impartial, any more than a reading can be unbiased, the act of translation carries with it a responsibility that extends far beyond the limits of the translated page, not only from language to language but often within the same language, from genre to genre, or from the shelves of one literature to those of another. In this not all "translations" are acknowledged as such: when Charles and Mary Lamb turned Shakespeare's plays into prose tales for children, or when Virginia Woolf generously herded Constance Garnett's versions of Turgenev "into the fold of English Literature," the displacements of the text into the nursery or into the British Library were not regarded as "translations" in the etymological sense. Lamb or Woolf, every translator disguises the text with another, attractive or detractive meaning.

Were translation a simple act of pure exchange, it would offer no more possibilities for distortion and censorship (or improvement and enlightening) than photocopying or, at most, scriptorium transcription. But that isn't so. If we acknowledge that every translation, simply by transferring the text to another language, space, and time, alters it for better or for worse, then we must also acknowledge that every translation—transliteration, retelling, relabeling — adds to the original text a *prêt-à-porter* reading, an implicit commentary. And that is where the censor comes in.

That a translation may hide, distort, subdue, or even suppress a text is a fact tacitly recognized by the reader who accepts it as a "version" of the original, a process Joachim de Bellay described in 1549, in his *Défense et exemple de la langue française:* "And what shall I say of those more properly called traitors than translators, since they betray those whom they aim to reveal, tarnishing their glory, and seducing ignorant readers by reading white for black?"

In the index to John Boswell's groundbreaking book on homosexuality in the Middle Ages, *Christianity, Social Tolerance and Homosexuality,* the entry for "Translation" reads, "*See* Mistranslation" — or what Boswell calls "the deliberate falsification of historical records." The instances of asepticized translations of Greek and Roman classics are too numerous to mention and range from a change of pronoun which willfully conceals the sexual identity of a character to the suppression of an entire text, such as the *Amores* of the Pseudo-Lucian, which Thomas Francklin in 1781 deleted from his English translation of the author's works because it included an explicit dialogue among a group of men on whether women or boys were erotically more desirable. "But as this is a point which, at least in this nation, has been long determined in favour of the ladies, it stands in need of no further discussion," wrote the censorious Francklin.

"We can only prohibit that which we can name," wrote George Steiner in *After Babel.* Throughout the nineteenth century, the classic Greek and Roman texts were recommended for the moral education of women only when purified in translation. The Reverend J. W. Burgon made this explicit when in 1884, from the pulpit of New College, Oxford, he preached against allowing women into the university, where they would have to study the texts in the original. "If she is to compete successfully with men for 'honours'" (wrote the timorous reverend), "you must needs put the classic writers of antiquity unreservedly into her hands — in other words, must introduce her to the obscenities of Greek and Roman literature. Can you seriously intend it? Is it then a part of your programme to defile that lovely spirit with the filth of old-world civilisation, and to acquaint maidens in their flower with a hundred abominable things which women of any age (and men too, if that were possible) would rather a thousand times be without?"

It is possible to censor not only a word or a line of text through translation but also an entire culture, as has happened time and again throughout the centuries among conquered peoples. Towards the end of the sixteenth century, for instance, the Jesuits were authorized by King Philip II of Spain, champion of the Counter-Reformation, to follow in the steps of the Franciscans and establish themselves in the jungles of what is now Paraguay. From 1609 until their expulsion from the colonies in 1767, the Jesuits created settlements for the native Guaranís, walled communities called *reducciones* because the men, women, and children who inhabited them were "reduced" to the dogmas of Christian civilization. The differences between conquered and conquerors were, however, not easily overcome. "What makes me a pagan in your eyes," said a Guaraní shaman to one of the missionaries, "is what prevents you from being a Christian in mine." The Jesuits understood that effective conversion required reciprocity and that understanding the other was the key that would allow them to keep the pagans in what was called, borrowing from the vocabulary of Christian mystic literature, "concealed captivity." The first step to understanding the other was learning and translating the other's language.

A culture is defined by that which it can name; in order to censor, the invading culture must also possess the vocabulary to name those things belonging to the other. Therefore, translating into the tongue of the conqueror always carries within the act the danger of assimilation or annihilation; translating into the tongue of the conquered, the danger of overpowering or undermining. These inherent conditions of translation extend to all variations of political imbalance. Guaraní (still the language spoken, albeit in a much altered form, by more than a million Paraguayans) had been until the arrival of the Jesuits an oral language. It was then that the Franciscan Fray Luis de Bolaños, whom the natives called "God's wizard" because of his gift for languages, compiled the first Guaraní dictionary. His work was continued and perfected by the Jesuit Antonio Ruiz de Montoya, who after several years' hard labor gave the completed volume the title of *Tesoro de la lengua guaraní* (Thesaurus of the Guaraní Tongue). In a preface to a history of the Jesuit missions in South America, the Paraguayan novelist Augusto Roa Bastos noted that in order for the natives to believe in the faith of Christ, they needed, above all, to be able to suspend or revise their ancestral concepts of life and death. Using the Guaranís' own words, and taking advantage of certain coincidences between the Christian and Guaraní religions, the Jesuits retranslated the Guaraní myths so that they would foretell or announce the truth of Christ. The Last-Last-First-Father, Ñamandú, who created His own body and the attributes of that body from the primordial mists, became the Christian God from the book of Genesis; Tupa, the First Parent, a minor divinity in the Guaraní pantheon, became

Adam, the first man; the crossed sticks, *yvyrá yuasá,* which in the Guaraní cosmology sustain the earthly realm, became the Holy Cross. And conveniently, since Ñamandú's second act was to create the word, the Jesuits were able to infuse the Bible, translated into Guaraní, with the accepted weight of divine authority.

In translating the Guaraní language into Spanish, the Jesuits attributed to certain terms that denoted acceptable and even commendable social behavior among the natives the connotation of that behavior as perceived by the Catholic Church or the Spanish court. Guaraní concepts of private honor, of silent acknowledgment when accepting a gift, of a specific as opposed to a generalized knowledge, and of a social response to the mutations of the seasons and of age, were translated bluntly and conveniently as "Pride," "Ingratitude," "Ignorance," and "Instability." This vocabulary allowed the traveler Martin Dobrizhoffer of Vienna to reflect, sixteen years after the expulsion of the Jesuits in 1783, in his *Geschichte der Abiponer* (History of the Abiponer People), on the corrupt nature of the Guaranís: "Their many virtues, which certainly belong to rational beings, capable of culture and learning, serve as frontispiece to very irregular compositions within the works themselves. They seem like automata in whose making have been joined elements of pride, ingratitude, ignorance, and instability. From these principal sources flow the brooks of sloth, drunkenness, insolence, and distrust, with many other disorders which stultify their moral quality."

In spite of Jesuit claims, the new system of beliefs did not contribute to the happiness of the natives. Writing in 1769, the French explorer Louis Antoine de Bougainville described the Guaraní people in these laconic words: "These Indians are a sad lot. Always trembling under the stick of a pedantic and stern master, they possess no property and are subjected to a laborious life whose monotony is enough to kill a man with boredom. That is why, when they die, they don't feel any regret in leaving this life."

By the time of the expulsion of the Jesuits from Paraguay, the Spanish chronicler Fernández de Oviedo was able to say of those who had "civilized" the Guaraní people what a Briton, Calgacus, is reported to have said after the Roman occupation of Britain: "The men who have perpetuated these acts call these conquered places 'peaceful.' I feel they are more than peaceful — they are destroyed."

Throughout history, censorship in translation has also taken place under more subtle guises, and in our time, in certain countries, translation is one of the means by which "dangerous" authors are submitted to cleansing purges.

(The Brazilian Nélida Piñón in Cuba, the decadent Oscar Wilde in Russia, Native American chroniclers in the United States and Canada, the French enfant terrible Georges Bataille in Franco's Spain have all been published in truncated versions. And in spite of all my good intentions, could not my version of Yourcenar be considered censorious?) Often, authors whose politics might be read uncomfortably are simply not translated and authors with a difficult style are either passed over in favor of others more easily accessible or condemned to weak or clumsy versions of their work.

Not all translation, however, is corruption and deceit. Sometimes cultures can be rescued through translation, and translators become justified in their laborious and menial pursuits. In January 1976, the American lexicographer Robert Laughlin sank to his knees in front of the chief magistrate of the town of Zinacantán in southern Mexico and held up a book that had taken Laughlin fourteen years to compile: the great Tzotzil dictionary that rendered into English the Mayan language of 120,000 natives of Chiapas, known also as the "People of the Bat." Offering the dictionary to the Tzotzil elder, Laughlin said, in the language he had so painstakingly recorded, "If any foreigner comes and says that you are stupid, foolish Indians, please show him this book, show him the 30,000 words of your knowledge, your reasoning."

It should, it must, suffice.

The Secret Sharer

"You might make a joke on *that*," said the little voice close to
her ear: "something about 'you *would* if you could,' you know."

"Don't tease so," said Alice, looking about in vain to see
where the voice came from. "If you're so anxious to have a joke
made, why don't you make one yourself?"
Through the Looking-Glass, Chapter 3

IN 1969, TIMOTHY FINDLEY traveled to New York to work with his American editor on the galleys of his second novel, *The Butterfly Plague*. Canadian
publishers were still not impressed by the efforts of this actor-turned-writer,
but the illustrious American publishing company Viking had expressed interest in this budding author. The editor assigned to Findley's book was Cor-
lies M. Smith, known as "Cork," who was also the editor of the letters of James
Joyce. Smith read *The Butterfly Plague*, the chronicle of a declining Hollywood
family set against the background of Nazi Germany, and although he liked the
book very much, he wasn't satisfied with one aspect of it: he wanted to know
the "meaning" of the butterflies in the story and strongly advised Findley to
make it clear. Findley was young, inexperienced, and afraid to upset the publisher he so much wanted, and bowed to Smith's suggestion. He reworked the
book in order to explain the butterflies, and the novel duly appeared under the
Viking imprint.

The extraordinary point of this anecdote is that most North American
readers would not see it as extraordinary. Even the most inexperienced writers
of fiction know that if they are to be published at all, their manuscripts must
pass through the hands of professionals known as "editors," employed by
publishing companies to read the books under consideration and recommend
changes they think appropriate. (This paragraph you are now reading will not

be the paragraph I originally wrote, since it will have to undergo the inquisition of an editor; in fact, when an earlier version of this essay was published in *Saturday Night* magazine, this sentence was cut out completely.)

Writers, notoriously wary about their craft, are reluctant to speak about this obligatory help except in general terms or off the record. Contemporary literature abounds in examples of both malpractice and redemption, but writers prefer to keep these interventions secret—and rightly so. In the end a work of fiction is the writer's own, and should be seen as such. Writers (and their editors agree) need not make public the seams and patches of their collaboration. Writers want to be sole begetters.

However, underlying this coyness is a paradox. The writer who knows himself to be the single author of a text, wondering a little at its very existence and puzzled more than a little by the mysteries it contains, also knows that before the text is published it will be professionally questioned, and that answers will have to be provided or suggestions accepted; he thereby relinquishes, at least in part, the writer's single-handed authorship. Before going out into the world, every writer of fiction in North America (and most of the British Commonwealth) acquires, as it were, a literary back-seat driver.

Recognition of the profession of editor is not so ancient or widespread as the Anglo-Saxon public might suppose. In the rest of the world it is virtually unknown: even in England it appeared almost two centuries and a half after the introduction of the printing press. *The Oxford English Dictionary* gives 1712 as the earliest date for the mention of *editor* with the meaning "one who prepares the literary work of another," used by Joseph Addison in *The Spectator* to specify someone working on material the author had either finished or left incomplete. Perhaps this was the meaning William Hazlitt, intent on reaffirming the writer's sole responsibility in a text, had in mind when he remarked, "It is utterly impossible to persuade an Editor that he is nobody." The editor, understood as "one who works with the author in the *fashioning* of a work of fiction," didn't come into history until much later, in the first decades of the twentieth century. Before that there were only scattered references to editorial advice: Erasmus giving Thomas More suggestions regarding *Utopia,* Charles Dickens, as the editor of *Household Words,* counseling Wilkie Collins on a plot, etc.

To find a full-fledged editor in the contemporary sense we have to wait until the 1920s, when a now legendary figure appeared in New York: Maxwell

Perkins, editor of F. Scott Fitzgerald, Ernest Hemingway, Erskine Caldwell, and Thomas Wolfe. By all accounts, Perkins was a generous editor, keen to respect what he thought were the author's intentions—though his Samaritan urge has prevented us from knowing what Thomas Wolfe's manuscripts were like before Perkins pared them down to publishable form. With Perkins, editors acquired respectability and a patron saint. (Some might say that the patron saint of editors should be the Greek robber Procrustes, who placed his visitors on an iron bed and stretched them or cut off the overhanging parts until they fitted exactly to his liking.)

To the common reader, the precise task of an editor is something of a mystery. In a small pamphlet signed by several hands, *Author and Editor: A Working Guide* (1983), Rick Archbold, a distinguished Canadian freelance editor, attempted to elucidate: "Editors have several functions," he writes, "which vary in number according to the size and complexity of the publishing house. They may include acquiring rights to publish book projects; selling subsidiary rights; developing plans for promotion and marketing; writing copy for book jackets; . . . overseeing production; and proofreading. And, of course, editing." This is not much help. Leaving aside specialized areas of publishing such as textbooks, magazines, and technical nonfiction, what exactly do editors do when they say that they are "editing"?

At least one part of an editor's job, sometimes performed by a "copy editor," involves simply checking facts, spelling, grammar, compliance with the publishing company's preferred style of punctuation, etc., and asking commonsense questions: Are you aware that your character is fifteen years old on page 21 and eighteen on page 34? Whatever salary an editor receives, it is probably not enough to compensate for all this thankless checking and double-checking.

Still, even this workaday aspect of editing, however necessary it may seem, has a pernicious potential. The writer who knows that his text will be inspected by an editor may see fit to leave the finer tuning unattended, because an editor will in any case try to tune the text to what sounds right to his or her own professional ear. Thomas Wolfe, submitting to Perkins's editing, would simply throw his uncorrected manuscript pages on the floor as he finished them, for the typist to collect and type out and his editor to cut and paste. Gradually the writer runs the danger of seeing himself not so much as carrying his work to where he believes he can go no farther (not finishing but "abandoning" his text, in Valéry's brave phrase) as carrying his text only to the threshold of the classroom where the teacher will check spelling and grammar for him.

Copyediting, then, is an accepted part of the editor's job. But at some point in history, probably even before the days of Maxwell Perkins, the editor bridged the chasm between questioning spelling and questioning sense, and began questioning the meaning of the butterflies. Surreptitiously, the content of fiction became the editor's responsibility.

In *Editors on Editing: An Inside View of What Editors Really Do* (compiled by Gerald Gross), the editor, bookseller, and author William Trag has this to say about what makes an editor an editor: "A working, qualified editor of books must read. He must have read from the earliest days of his childhood. His reading must be unceasing. The lust for printed matter is a biological thing, a visceral and intellectual necessity; the urge must be in the genes." In short, an editor must be a reader.

True enough. Editors must assume this function or not edit at all. But can anyone read beyond his personal inclinations? Because to justify intrusions into an author's virgin text, an editor must surely not be Felix Chuckle who delights in happy endings or Dolores Lachrymose who prefers her endings bitter. The editor must be a sort of platonic idea of a reader; he must embody "readerness"; he must be a Reader with a capital R.

However, can even the ideal Reader help the writer? As every reader knows, literature is an act of shared responsibility. And yet to suppose that this mutual act allows us to know the goal the writer has set herself, a goal that in most cases is not revealed even to the writer, is either simple-minded or fatuously arrogant. To paraphrase another author, a Book is what It is. Whether the writer achieved what she intended, even knew what she intended to achieve, or in fact intended to achieve anything at all except what appears between two covers is a mystery that no one, not even the writer, can answer truthfully. The inappropriateness of the question comes from the richness and ambiguity that are, I believe, the true achievements of literature. "I'm not saying that it isn't in my book," confessed the Italian novelist Cesare Pavese in response to a critic who pointed out a metaphysical theme in his work. "I'm only saying that I didn't put it there."

When editors try to guess an author's "intention" (that rhetorical concept invented by Saint Thomas Aquinas in the thirteenth century), when they question the author about the meaning of certain passages or the reason for certain events, they are assuming that a work of literature can be reduced to a set of rules or explained in a précis. This prodding, this reductive exercise is indeed a threat, because the writer may (as Findley did) pay heed and upset the delicate balance of his creation. Older, more experienced, less afraid to alienate his publishers, Findley finally rebelled. In 1986 he revised *The Butter-fly Plague,* deleting the explanation, and the new version (neither better nor worse, simply the original one) was published by Viking Penguin.

The threat, however, is not universal. Editing understood as "a search for the author's intention" is practiced almost exclusively in the Anglo-Saxon world, and less in the United Kingdom than in North America. In the rest of the world, by and large, editing means only copyediting, a function of publishing, and even this is done with a caution that would send hundreds of editors in Chicago and Toronto in search of more challenging careers. I have worked for publishing companies in Argentina, Spain, France, Italy, and Tahiti, and have visited publishing companies in Brazil, Uruguay, Japan, Germany, and Sweden. Nowhere else is there such a job as intrusive as our North American editors describe, and the literatures of these other countries have, to the best of my knowledge, survived very nicely.

Why is North America the hothouse of editors? I suggest that the answer lies in the mercantile fabric of American society. Because books must be sale-able merchandise, experts must be employed to ensure that the products are profitably commercial. At its worst this unifying task produces mass-market romances; at its best it cuts Thomas Wolfe down to size. In Latin America, where books seldom make money, the writer is left to his own devices and a novel is welcome to stretch to whatever lengths without fear of editorial scissors.

Unfortunately, the American influence has begun to spread. In Germany, Spain, and France, for instance, the *directeur de collection,* who hitherto simply chose the books she wished to publish, now sits with writers and discusses their works in progress. Sometimes the writer digs in his heels and refuses to play along. But few have either the courage or the literary clout of Graham Greene, who, when his American publisher suggested changing the title of his novel *Travels with My Aunt,* replied with an eight-word telegram: "Easier to change publisher than to change title."

In some cases, the writers themselves have sought this kind of professional advice, asking an editor to clarify their own craft. The result is a peculiar collaboration. Commenting on what is perhaps the most famous case of editing in modern poetry, Ezra Pound's reworking of T. S. Eliot's *The Waste Land*, Borges remarked that "both their names should have appeared on the title page. If an author allows someone else to change his text, he is no longer the author—he is one of the authors, and their collaboration should be recognized as such."

Among the many lines crossed out by Pound (deletions which Eliot accepted) are these, now forever absent from the poem:

Something which we know must be dawn—
A different darkness, flowed above the clouds,
And dead ahead we saw, where sky and sea should meet,
A line, a white line, a long white line,
A wall, a barrier, towards which we drove.

The Waste Land, published after Pound's editing, has been called "the greatest poem in the English language," and yet I miss those lines and wonder whether Eliot would not have left them in had it not been for Pound's intervention.

Of course, everywhere in the world, Anglo-Saxon or not, writers show their work before it is published (though Nabokov argued that this was like showing samples of your sputum). A gaggle of unprofessional readers—the author's mother, a neighbor, a friend, a husband or wife—performs the ritual first inspection and offers a handful of doubts or approvals on which the author may choose or not to reflect. This contradictory chorus is not the voice of power and officialdom recommending revision. John Steinbeck would show his wife every new finished chapter on condition that her only comment would be: "This is *wonderful*, dear!"

The professional editor, on the other hand, even the most subtle and understanding (and I have been blessed with a small number of them), tinges her opinion with the color of authority simply because of her position. The difference between a paid editor and someone close to us is the difference between a doctor who proposes a lobotomy and a devoted aunt recommending a strong cup of tea.

The story has often been told of how Coleridge dreamt his "Kubla Khan" in an intoxication of opium, and of how, upon waking, he sat down to write it and was interrupted "by a person on business from Porlock," thereby losing forever the conclusion to that extraordinary poem. Persons from Porlock are professionally employed by the publishing companies of the Anglo-Saxon world. A few are wise and ask questions that speed on the writing; a few distract; a few quibble away at the author's vaporous confidence; a few destroy the work in mid-creation. All interfere, and it is this compulsive tinkering with someone else's text that I question.

Without editors we are likely to have rambling, incoherent, repetitive, even offensive texts, full of characters whose eyes are green one day and black the next (like Madame Bovary); full of historical errors, like stout Cortez discovering the Pacific (as in Keats's sonnet); full of badly strung-together episodes (as in *Don Quixote*); with a badly cobbled-together ending (as in *Hamlet*) or beginning (as in *The Old Curiosity Shop*). But with editors — with the constant and now unavoidable presence of editors without whose *nihil obstat* hardly a book can get published — we may perhaps be missing something fabulously new, something as incandescent as a phoenix and unique, something impossible to describe because it has not yet been born but which, if it were, would admit no secret sharers in its creation.

Honoring Enoch Soames

At last the Dodo said: "*Everybody* has won, and *all* must have prizes."
Alice's Adventures in Wonderland, Chapter 3

ON 3 JUNE 1997, A GROUP OF literary aficionados gathered in the Reading Room of the British Library in London to welcome Enoch Soames, the poet. Perhaps not unexpectedly, he didn't materialize. What prompted the gathering was this: a century earlier, Soames, having sold only three copies of his book of poems, *Fungoids,* had made a pact with the Devil. In exchange for his ambitious soul, he had asked to be allowed to visit the Reading Room a hundred years hence to see how posterity had judged him. Unfortunately for Soames, posterity had not judged him at all; posterity had merely ignored him. There was no record of his work in the library's voluminous catalogue, and in a history of the literature of his period the only mention of his name was in a note that described him as an imaginary character, invented by the English humorist Max Beerbohm. It can only be assumed that for his future readers even his ghost was invisible. So much for the fruits of ambition.

Literary ambition takes on various guises, one of which is the furtive figure dreaded by booksellers and known as the Anxious Author. Cleverly disguised as an ordinary customer, the Anxious Author roams the bookstore in search of his or her own books, berating the salespeople for not having them in stock or rearranging the shelves to give them prominence. Sometimes, the Anxious Author will buy one or two copies, in the endearing belief that where a couple will lead others will follow. Prompted perhaps by such superstitions, in 1999 the Pulitzer Prize–winning reporter David Vise bought not merely a few but nearly twenty thousand copies of his new book *The Bureau and the Mole.* This gesture may be seen as carrying author anxiety too far, but Vise did not buy the volumes for his own enjoyment. Generous to a fault, he decided to share his work with the public at large, offering author-signed copies on his personal Web site. Vise's actions (complicated by a labyrinthine financial strategy that involved bulk discounts and free shipping from Barnes and Noble's online bookstore, calculated massive returns, and the benefit of the bookseller's special prices for new books and fast-selling titles) deserve a moment's consideration.

Though the book had appeared on the *New York Times* best-seller list a few days before Vise's shopping spree, the twenty thousand copies no doubt prompted its appearance on other such lists. When questioned about his actions, Vise declared: "My goal was to increase awareness of *The Bureau and the Mole*."

David Vise is not the first author to invent strategies for getting his book to be read. It seems that the term *best seller* was coined in 1889 in a Kansas City newspaper, but the ideal had certainly taken root in our psyche thousands of years earlier: in the first century, the poet Martial bragged that all Rome was mad about his book, though we don't know what methods he used to get (in his words) "readers to hum the lines and shops to stock it." Closer to our time, Walt Whitman promoted his *Leaves of Grass* with enthusiastic reviews which he wrote himself. Georges Simenon advertised his new detective novels by typing away in the window of a department store. For a tidy sum, Fay Weldon promised to include the trade name Bulgari in her most recent novel. The young Jorge Luis Borges slid copies of one of his first books into the pockets of the journalists' coats hanging in the newspaper's waiting room. In 1913, D. H. Lawrence wrote to Edward Garnett: "If *Hamlet* and *Oedipus* were published now, they wouldn't sell more than 100 copies, unless they were pushed."

And yet, compared to Vise's deployment, those earlier pushy strategies seem like minor skirmishes, less outrageous than amusing and more amusing than effective. At a time when publishers are no longer enthusiasts keen on midwifing books but have become instead accountable managers of companies within companies, forced to compete under the same roof for space and profit; when writers are no longer (with a few Pynchonian exceptions) secluded and private scribblers touched by the muse but rather performing characters who traipse around the country filling space in afternoon chat shows and serving as talking mannequins on shop floor displays; when so many books are not (as Kafka wanted) "the ax for the frozen sea within us" but rather deep-freeze readymades (like *The Bureau and the Mole*) concocted in an agent's office to respond to the current prurience of the public—at such a time, why should a "creative marketing strategy" (as Vise calls it) applied to books surprise us?

In the past, writers sometimes kept a grinning skull on their desk to remind them that the only certain reward for their labors was the grave. In our time, a writer's memento mori is not a skull but a lit-up screen that allows the writers to see, on one of several best-seller lists, that they too share poor Soames's fate, their name assiduously absent from these roll calls of the elect.

There are, however, exceptions to this common fate. In 2000, driven by a sense of charity if not humor, a certain Jeff Bezos, chief executive officer of Amazon.com, Inc., decided to come to the rescue of all those woefully neglected writers. Thanks to a gesture that can only be described as truly democratic, Amazon.com's best-seller lists were now no longer limited to a puny top twenty names but enshrined instead three million titles in order of bestsellerdom—a modest figure dictated only by the number of titles held in the generous memory of Amazon.com, Inc.

Thanks to the new technology, the writer's memento mori has become a vanity chest. You have published a book, you reasonably suppose it is among the three million offered by Amazon.com, you type out its title, and, presto! You are given the exact ranking of your book among its peers. Think of the satisfied sneer (like that of the last passenger to make it into the last *Titanic* lifeboat) with which best-selling author number 3,000,000 can now look down on Soames's anonymous fellow sufferer, lost in the unlisted 3,000,001st place.

Laws stranger than those of chance determine which authors are in and which are out, and, ever since 1895, when the first best-seller list appeared in the pages of *The Bookman*, books make the grade for reasons that apparently not even the Devil himself can fathom. Of course, if your name in lights is all you want, there are methods to procure you this modest satisfaction. For example, ask each of your friends to buy, on the same afternoon, a copy of your book, and you are likely to shimmer, for one exquisite hour, on the Amazon. com ranking. But for those unwilling to take such steps, it may be salutary to skim through the names enshrined in the best-seller lists of just a couple of years ago. With few exceptions, who are these people? Who are these Ozymandiases whose now utterly forgotten books presumably sold in the hundreds of thousands, were counted among the blessed by the compilers of bestseller lists, and then vanished without a trace?

But it is we, the readers, and not casual performers such as Vise and Bezos, who are the paradox. When Sam Goldwyn was negotiating with George Bernard Shaw the sale of the rights to one of celebrated author's plays, the mogul expressed surprise at the fee demanded. Shaw answered, "The problem, Mr. Goldwyn, is that you are interested in the art, while I am interested in the money." Like Goldwyn, we demand that everything we do yield a financial profit, and yet we like to think that intellectual activities should be free from such material concerns; we have agreed that books should be bought and sold and taxed just like any other industrial product, and yet we feel offended when our obscene commercial tactics are applied to prose and poetry; we are keen to admire the latest best sellers and speak of "the shelf life of a book," but we are disappointed to find that most books are no more immortal than an egg. In spite of Bezos's efforts, the saga of Vise is a cautionary tale whose moral was enshrined many years ago by the writer Hilaire Belloc: "When I am dead, I hope it may be said: / 'His sins were scarlet, but his books were read.'"

It is perhaps unfair to ask what all this counting means. Lists are delightful things in themselves, the very essence of poetry (as W. H. Auden once remarked), and it would be mean-spirited to deny the author of *Fungoids* the pleasure of introducing himself at a dinner party with "Hello, I'm best-selling author number 2,999,999. My book sold seven copies!"

But it may be that a little vanity is a requisite quality in literary endeavors. "Seven copies," reflects the protagonist of Thomas Love Peacock's early-nineteenth-century novel *Nightmare Abbey,* "have been sold. Seven is a mystical number, and the omen is good. Let me find the seven purchasers of my seven copies, and they shall be the seven golden candlesticks with which I will illuminate the world." In these days, when greed is considered a virtue, who would dare quarrel with such modest ambition?

Jonah and the Whale

"You don't know how to manage Looking-Glass cakes," the Unicorn remarked. "Hand it round first, and cut it afterwards."
Through the Looking-Glass, Chapter 7

OF ALL THE SNARLING OR moaning prophets who haunt the pages of the Old Testament, I believe that none is so curious as the prophet known as Jonah. I like Jonah. I have a fondness for Jonah, in spite of his posthumous reputation as a purveyor of bad luck. I think I've discovered what it was about Jonah that made people nervous in his presence. I think Jonah had what in the nineteenth century was called an artistic temperament. I think Jonah was an artist.

The first time I heard the story of Jonah, it was from a great-uncle of mine, who had the disagreeable habit of spitting into his handkerchief when he talked. He had a small claim to Jewish scholarship, which we believed did not go far beyond the few verses he taught us to memorize for our bar mitzvah. But sometimes he could tell a good story, and if you didn't look too closely at the spittle forming at the corners of his mouth, the experience could be quite entertaining. The story of Jonah came about one day when I was being especially pigheaded, refusing to do something or other I had been asked to do for the one hundredth time. "Just like Jonah," said my great-uncle, holding his handkerchief to his mouth, spitting heartily, and tucking the handkerchief deep into his pocket. "Always no, no, no. What will you grow up to be? An anarchist?" For my great-uncle, who in spite of the pogroms had always felt a curious admiration for the tsar, there was nothing worse than an anarchist, except perhaps a journalist. He said that journalists were all Peeping Toms and Nosy Parkers, and that if you wanted to find out what was going on in the world you could do so from your friends in the café. Which he did, day in, day out, except, of course, on Shabbat.

The story of Jonah was probably written sometime in the fourth or fifth century B.C. The book of Jonah is one of the shortest in the Bible—and one of the strangest. It tells how the prophet Jonah was summoned by God to go and cry against the city of Nineveh, whose wickedness had reached the ears of Heaven. But Jonah refused because he knew that through his word the Ninevites would repent and God would forgive them, and thus escape the punishment he thought they deserved. To escape the divine order, Jonah jumped on a ship sailing for Tarshish. A furious storm arose, the sailors moaned in despair, and Jonah, somehow understanding that he was the cause of this meteorological turmoil, asked to be thrown into the sea to calm the waves. The sailors obliged, the storm died down, and Jonah was swallowed by a great fish, appointed for this purpose by God Himself. There in the bowels of the fish Jonah remained for three long days and three long nights. On the fourth day, the Lord caused the great fish to vomit the prophet out onto dry land and, once again, the Lord ordered Jonah to go to Nineveh and speak to the people. Resigned to God's will, this time Jonah obeyed. The king of Nineveh heard the warning, immediately repented, and the city of Nineveh was saved. But Jonah was furious with the Lord and stormed out into the desert to the east of the city, where he set up a sort of booth and sat and waited to see what would become of the repentant Nineveh. The Lord then caused a plant to sprout up and protect Jonah from the sun. Jonah expressed his gratitude for the divine gift but, next morning, the Lord caused the plant to wither. The sun and the wind beat hard on Jonah, and faint with heat he told the Lord that it was better for him to die. Then the Lord spoke to Jonah and said: "You are upset because I killed a simple plant and yet you wished me to destroy all the people of Nineveh. Should I have spared a plant but not spared these people 'who do not know their right hand from their left,' and also much cattle?" With this unanswered question, the book of Jonah ends.

I am fascinated by the reason for Jonah's refusal to prophesy in Nineveh. The idea that Jonah would keep away from performing his divinely inspired piece because he knew his audience would repent and be therefore forgiven must seem incomprehensible to anyone except an artist. Jonah knew that Ninevite society dealt in one of two ways with its artists: either it saw the accusation in an artist's work and blamed the artist for the evils of which the society stood accused or it assimilated the artist's work because, valued in dinars and nicely framed, the art could serve as a pleasant decoration. In such circumstances, Jonah knew, no artist can win.

Given the choice between creating an accusation or a decoration, Jonah would have probably preferred the accusation. Like most artists, what Jonah really wanted was to stir the languid hearts of his listeners, to touch them, to awaken in them something vaguely known and yet utterly mysterious, to trouble their dreams and to haunt their waking hours. What he certainly did not want, under any circumstances, was their repentance. Having the listeners simply say to themselves, "All's forgiven and forgotten, let's bury the past, let's not talk about injustice and the need for retribution, our cuts in education and health programs, our unequal taxation and unemployment, our financial schemes that ruin millions; let exploiters shake hands with exploited, and on to our next glorious money-making hour"—no, that was something Jonah certainly did not want. Nadine Gordimer, of whom Jonah had never heard, said that there could be no worse fate for a writer than *not* being execrated in a corrupt society. Jonah did not wish to suffer that annihilating fate.

Above all, Jonah was aware of Nineveh's ongoing war between the politicians and the artists, a war in which Jonah felt that all the artists' efforts (beyond the efforts demanded by their craft) were ultimately futile because they took place in the political arena. It was a well-known fact that Ninevite artists (who had never tired in the pursuit of their own art) grew quickly weary of the struggle with bureaucrats and banks, and the few heroes who had continued the fight against the corrupt secretaries of state and royal lackeys and investment bankers had done so many times at the expense of both their art and their sanity. It was very difficult to go to your studio or to your clay tablets after a day of committee meetings and official hearings. The bureaucrats of Nineveh counted on this, of course, and one of their most effective tactics was delay: delaying agreements, delaying the attribution of funds, delaying contracts, delaying appointments, delaying outright answers. If you waited long enough, they said, the rage of the artist would fade, or rather mysteriously turn into creative energy: the artist would go away and write a poem or do an installation or dream up a dance. And these things represented little danger to banks and private corporations. In fact, as businesspeople well knew, many times this artistic rage became marketable merchandise. "Think," the Ninevites often said, "how much you'd pay today for the work of painters who in their time hardly had enough money to buy paint, let alone food. Think of the protest songs by musicians who died in the poorhouse, sung today at national festivities. For an artist," they added knowingly, "posthumous fame is its own reward."

But the great triumph of Ninevite politicians was their success in getting the artists to work against themselves. So imbued was Nineveh with the idea that wealth was the city's goal and that art, since it was not an immediate producer of wealth, was an undeserving pursuit, that the artists themselves came to believe that they should pay their own way in the world, producing cost-efficient art, frowning on failure and lack of recognition, and above all, trying to gratify those who, being wealthy, were also in positions of power. So visual artists were asked to make their work more pleasing, composers to write music with a hummable tune, writers to imagine not-so-depressing scenarios.

In times long gone by, in short periods during which the bureaucrats slumbered, certain funds had been granted to artistic causes by soft-hearted or soft-headed Ninevite kings. Since those times, more conscientious officials had been redressing this financial oversight and vigorously pruning down the allotted sums. No official would, of course, recognize any such change in the government's support of the arts, and yet the Ninevite secretary of finance was able to cut the actual funds allotted to the arts down to almost nothing, while at the same time advertising a committed increase of those same funds in the official records. This was done by the use of certain devices borrowed from the Ninevite poets (whose tools the politicians happily pilfered, while despising the poets who invented them). Metonymy, for instance, the device by which a poet uses a part or an attribute of something to stand in its place (*crown* for *king,* for example), allowed the secretary of provisions to cut down on the funds spent on subsidizing artists' work materials. All any artist now received from the city, whatever his needs, was a number 4 rat-hair paintbrush, since in the secretary's official vocabulary *brush* was made to stand for "the ensemble of an artist's equipment." Metaphors, the most common of poetic tools, were employed to great effect by these financial wizards. In one celebrated case, a sum of ten thousand gold dinars had been set aside long ago for the lodging of senior artists. By simply redefining camels, used in public transport, as "temporary lodgings," the secretary of finance was able to count the cost of the camels' upkeep (for which the city of Nineveh was responsible) as part of the sum allotted to artists' lodgings, since the senior artists did indeed use subsidized public camels to get from place to place.

"The real artists," said the Ninevites, "have no cause to complain. If they are really good at what they do, they will make a buck no matter what the social conditions. It's the others, the so-called experimenters, the self-indulgers, the prophets, who don't make a cent and whine about their condition. A banker who doesn't know how to turn a profit would be equally lost. A bureaucrat who didn't recognize the need to clog things down would be out of a job. This is the law of survival. Nineveh is a society that looks to the future."

True: in Nineveh, a handful of artists (and many con artists) made a good living. Ninevite society liked to reward a few of the makers of the products it consumed. What it would not recognize, of course, was the vast majority of the artists whose attempts and glitterings and failures allowed the successes of others to be born. Ninevite society didn't have to support anything it didn't instantly like or understand. The truth was that this vast majority of artists would carry on, of course, no matter what, simply because they couldn't help it, the Lord or the Holy Spirit urging them on night after night. They carried on writing and painting and composing and dancing by whatever means they could find. "Like every other worker in society," the Ninevites said.

It is told that the first time Jonah heard this particular point of Ninevite wisdom, he drummed up his prophetic courage and stood in the public square of Nineveh to address the crowds. "The artist," Jonah attempted to explain, "is not like every other worker in society. The artist deals with reality: inner and outer reality transformed into meaningful symbols. Those who deal in money deal in symbols behind which stands nothing. It is wonderful to think of the thousands and thousands of Ninevite stockbrokers for whom reality, the real world, is the arbitrary rising and falling of figures transformed in their imagination into wealth—a wealth that exists only in their imagination. No fantasy writer, no virtual-reality artist could ever aspire to create in an audience such an all-pervading trust in fiction as that which takes place in an assembly of stockbrokers. Grownup men and women who will not for a minute consider the reality of the unicorn, even as a symbol, will accept as rock-hard fact that they possess a share in the nation's camel bellies, and in that belief they consider themselves happy and secure." By the time Jonah had reached the end of this paragraph, the public square of Nineveh was deserted.

For all these reasons, Jonah decided to escape both Nineveh and the Lord, and jumped on a ship headed for Tarshish. Now, the sailors in the ship that carried Jonah were all men from Joppa, a port not far from Nineveh, an outpost of the Ninevite empire. Nineveh was, as you have no doubt surmised, a society besotted by greed. Not ambition, which is a creative impulse, something all artists possess, but the sterile impulse to accumulate for the sake of accumulation. Joppa, however, had for many decades been a place where prophets had been allowed a tolerable amount of freedom. The people of Joppa accepted the yearly influx of bearded, ragged men and disheveled, wild-eyed women with a certain degree of sympathy, since their presence procured Joppa free publicity when the prophets traveled abroad to other cities, where they often mentioned the name of Joppa in not unkind terms. Also, the recurrent prophesying season brought curious and illustrious visitors to Joppa, and neither the innkeepers nor the owners of the caravanserais complained of the demands made on their bed and board.

But when times were hard in Nineveh and the economic hardships of the city rippled out all the way to the little town of Joppa, when business profits were down and the wealthy Joppites were constrained to sell one of their orna-mented six-horse chariots or close down a couple of their upland sweatshops, then the presence in Joppa of the prophesying artists was openly frowned upon. The tolerance and whimsical generosity of wealthier days seemed now sinfully wasteful to the citizens of Joppa, and many of them felt that the art-ists who came to their quaint little haven should make no demands at all and feel grateful for whatever they got: grateful when they were lodged in the frumpiest buildings of Joppa, grateful when they were denied appropriate working tools, grateful when they were allowed to finance themselves their new projects. When they were forced to move out of their rooms to accom-modate paying guests from Babylon, the artists were told to remember that they, as artists, should know that it was an honorable thing to lie under the stars wrapped in smelly goat hides just like the illustrious prophets and poets of the days before the Flood.

And yet even during those difficult times, most Joppites retained for the prophets a certain sincere fondness, somewhat akin to the affection we feel for old pets who have been around since our childhood, and they tried in several ways to accommodate them even when the going was not good, and attempted not to hurt their artistic sensibilities by being too blunt in their dealings. Thus it was that when the storm rose and the ship from Joppa was tossed by furious waves, the Joppite sailors felt uneasy, and hesitated before blaming Jonah, their artistic guest. Unwilling to take any drastic measures, they tried praying to their own gods, who they knew commanded the heavens and the seas — but with no visible results. In fact, the storm only got worse, as if the Joppite gods had other things to think about and were annoyed by the sailors' whiny re-quests. Then the sailors appealed to Jonah (who was in the hold, sleeping out the storm, as artists sometimes do) and woke him and asked him for advice. Even when Jonah told them, with a touch of artistic pride, that the storm was all his fault, the sailors felt reluctant to toss him overboard. How much of a gale could one scraggy artist raise? How angry could one miserable prophet make the deep, wine-dark sea? But the storm grew worse, the wind howled through the riggings, the planks groaned and cried out when the waves hit them, and in the end, one by one, the sailors remembered the old Ninevite truisms, learned in Joppa at their grandmother's knee: that all artists were, by and large, freeloaders, and that all Jonah and his ilk did all day was compose poems in which they kvetched about this and moaned about that, and said threatening things about the most innocent vices. And why should a society in which greed is the driving force support someone who does not contribute to the immediate accumulation of wealth? Therefore, as one of the sailors explained to his mates, don't blame yourselves for bad seamanship, simply accept Jonah's mea culpa and throw the bastard into the water. He won't resist. In fact, he just about asked for it.

Now, even if Jonah had had second thoughts, and had argued that perhaps a ship, or a ship of state, could in fact do with a few wise prophecies to serve as ballast and keep it steady, the sailors had learned from long familiarity with Ninevite politicians the craft of turning a deaf ear to artistic warnings. Zigzagging their way across the oceans of the world in search of new lands on which to conduct free and profitable trade, the sailors assumed that whatever an artist might say or do, the weight of money would always provide a steadier ballast than any artistic argument.

When they threw Jonah overboard and the sea became calm again, the sailors fell on their knees and thanked the Lord, the God of Jonah. No one enjoys being tossed about in a rocking boat, and since the rocking had stopped as soon as Jonah hit the water, the sailors immediately concluded that he was indeed to blame and that their action had been fully justified. These sailors had obviously not had the benefit of a classical education or the gift of foresight or they would have known that the argument for the elimination of the artist had once enjoyed and was again to acquire in the centuries to come a venerable reputation. They would have known that there is an ancient impulse, running through the very foundations of every human society, to shun that uncomfortable creature who keeps attempting to shift the tenets of our certitudes, the rock on which we like to believe we stand. For Plato, to begin with, the real artist is the statesman, the person who shapes the state according to a divine model of Justice and Beauty. The ordinary artist, on the other hand, the writer or the painter, does not reflect this worthy reality but produces instead mere fantasies, which are unfit for the education of the young. This notion,

that art is only useful if it serves the state, was heartily embraced by succes-
sions of diverse governments: Emperor Augustus banished the poet Ovid because of something the poet had written which Augustus felt was secretly
threatening. The Church condemned artists who distracted the faithful from
the sacred dogma. In the Renaissance, artists were bought and sold like cour-
tesans, and in the eighteenth century they were reduced (at least in the public
imagination) to garret-living creatures dying of melancholy and consumption.
Flaubert penned the nineteenth-century bourgeois view of the artist in his
Dictionary of Clichés: "Artists: All clowns. Praise their selflessness. Be astonished at the fact they dress like everyone else. They earn fabulous sums but
they squander every last cent. Often invited to dinner at the best houses. All
female artists are sluts." In our time, the descendants of the Joppite sailors
have issued a fatwa against Salman Rushdie and hanged Ken Saro-Wiwa in
Nigeria. Their motto regarding artists is the one coined by the Canadian immigration officer in charge of receiving Jewish refugees during World War II:
"None is too many."

So Jonah was thrown into the water and was swallowed by a big fish. Life
in the dark soft belly of the fish was actually not that bad. During those three
days and three nights, lulled by the rumblings of ill-digested plankton and
shrimp, Jonah had time to reflect. This was a luxury artists seldom have. In the
belly of the fish there were no deadlines, no grocer's bills to pay, no diapers
to wash, no dinners to cook, no family conflicts to be dragged into just as the
right note comes to complete the sonata, no bank managers to plead with, no
critics to gnash teeth over. So during those three days and three nights Jonah
thought and prayed and slept and dreamed. And when he woke up, he found
himself vomited onto dry land and the nagging Voice of the Lord was at him
again: "Go on, go seek out Nineveh and do your bit. It doesn't matter how
they react. Every artist needs an audience. You owe it to your work."

This time Jonah did as the Lord told him. Some degree of confidence in
the importance of his craft had come to him in the fish's dark belly, and he felt
moved to put his art on display in Nineveh. But barely had he begun his performance piece, barely had he said five words of his prophetic text, when the
king of Nineveh fell on his knees and repented, the people of Nineveh ripped
open their designer shirts and repented, and even the cattle of Nineveh bel-
lowed out in unison to show that they too, repented. And the king, the people,
and the cattle of Nineveh all dressed in sackcloth and ashes, and assured one
another that bygones were bygones, and sang Ninevite versions of "Auld Lang

Syne" together, and wailed their repentance to the Lord above. And seeing this orgiastic display of repentance, the Lord withdrew His threat over the people and cattle of Nineveh. And Jonah, of course, was furious. What my great-uncle would have called the "anarchic" spirit rebelled inside Jonah, and he went off to sulk in the desert at some distance from the forgiven city.

You will remember that God had caused a plant to grow from the bare soil to shade Jonah from the heat, and that this charitable gesture of God's made Jonah once again thankful, after which God withered the plant back into the dust and Jonah found himself roasting in the sun for a second time. We don't know whether God's trick with the plant—first placing it there to shade Jonah from the sun, and then killing it off—was a lesson meant to convince Jonah of God's good intentions. Perhaps Jonah saw in the gesture an allegory of the funds first given to him and then withdrawn after the cuts by the Nineveh Arts Council—a gesture that left him to fry unprotected in the midday sun. I suppose he understood that in times of difficulty—in times when the poor are poorer and the rich can barely keep in the million-dollar tax bracket—God wasn't going to concern Himself with questions of artistic merit. Being an Author Himself, God had no doubt some sympathy with Jonah's predicament: wanting time to work on his thoughts without having to think about his bread and butter; wanting his prophecies to appear on the *Nineveh Times* best-seller list and yet not wanting to be confused with the authors of potboilers and tearjerkers; wanting to stir the crowds with his searing words, but to stir them into revolt, not submission; wanting Nineveh to look deep into its soul and recognize that its strength, its wisdom, its very life lay not in the piles of coins growing daily like funeral pyramids on the financiers' desks but in the work of its artists and the words of its poets, and in the visionary rage of its prophets, whose job it was to keep the boat rocking in order to keep the citizens awake. All this the Lord understood, as He understood Jonah's anger, because it isn't impossible to imagine that God Himself sometimes learns something from His artists.

However, though God could draw water from a stone and cause the people of Nineveh to repent, He still could not make them think. The cattle, incapable of thought, He could pity. But speaking to Jonah as Creator to creator, as Artist to artist, what was God to do with a people who, as He said with such divine irony, "don't know their right hand from their left"?

At this, I imagine, Jonah nodded and was silent.

The Legend of the Dodos

"Why," said the Dodo, "the best way to explain it is to do it."

Alice's Adventures in Wonderland, Chapter 3

IN *LE MONDE* OF 23 MARCH 2007, I read that Francis Esmenard, president of the commercial publisher Albin Michel, declared, at the Salon du Livre of Paris, that "there are too many small publishers" and that they "clutter the shelves of our bookstores." To which Antoine Gallimard, president of the venerable publishing company that bears his name, added that small publishers "are responsible for the surplus production of books." These interesting comments reminded me of an old Mauritanian legend:

A long time ago, the dodos, flightless birds with enormous appetites, discovered that on a certain island, which was the nesting ground of the local tits, pumpkins grew to a colossal size. Delighted with the prospect of a gargantuan meal, the dodos built a small raft and crossed the narrow strait that separated them from the island. There they feasted for days on the pumpkins (which were indeed huge, and very stodgy and sweet), trampling carelessly on the small berries and grains, too delicate for their large beaks, which they left to the tits, who, with patience and care, planted some in the ground and carried others off to their nests to feed their young. After only a few weeks, there were no more pumpkins left, and the dodos decided to return home. Barely able to walk after all they had eaten, they dragged their fat bellies onto the raft and pushed off to sea. A few moments later, quantities of water began to wash over the deck. "I think we've eaten too many pumpkins," said one of the younger dodos in a quaking voice. "I'm afraid we're sinking." The eldest dodo pointed an angry feather at the top of the mast where a tiny tit had settled with a red berry in its beak. "That's the culprit," shouted the dodo. "He's much too heavy for the raft. There's not enough room for all of us. Get rid of him at once!"

And they all started jumping up and down to frighten it away. Hearing all the noise, the tit flew off towards the land, and the raft sank in the shark-infested waters.

And that is how the dodos became extinct.

PART SEVEN

Crime and Punishment

"There's the King's Messenger. He's in prison now,
being punished: and the trial doesn't even begin till next
Wednesday: and of course the crime comes last of all."

"Suppose he never commits the crime?" said Alice.

"That would be all the better, wouldn't it?" the Queen
said.

Through the Looking-Glass, Chapter 5

In Memoriam

"I went to the Classical master, though. He was an
old crab, he was."

"I never went to him," the Mock Turtle said with a
sigh. "He taught Laughing and Grief, they used to say."

"So he did, so he did," said the Gryphon, sighing in his
turn; and both creatures hid their faces in their paws.
Alice's Adventures in Wonderland, Chapter 9

WHERE TO BEGIN? Almost every Sunday, from 1963 to 1967, I had lunch not at my parents'
home but in the house of the novelist Marta Lynch. She was the mother of one
of my schoolmates, Enrique, and she lived in a residential suburb of Buenos
Aires, in a big villa with a red-tiled roof and a flower garden. Enrique had discovered that I wanted to be a writer, and he offered to show his mother some
of my stories. I agreed. A week later Enrique handed me a letter. I remember
the blue paper, the wobbly typing, the big, ungainly signature, but most of all I
remember the overwhelming generosity of those few pages and the warning at
the end: "My son," she wrote, "congratulations. And I pity you more than you
can know." Only one other person, a Spanish teacher at school, had told me
that literature could be so important. Together with the letter was an invitation
to lunch on the following Sunday. I was fifteen.

I hadn't read Marta's first novel, a semi-autobiographical account of her
political and amorous involvement with one of the few civilian presidents who
came to power after Perón's ousting. It had won an important literary prize
and procured for her the kind of fame that made journalists ring her up for
opinions on the Vietnam War and the length of summer skirts, and her large,

sensuous face, made dreamy by big eyes that seemed always half closed, appeared every other day in a magazine or a newspaper.

So every Sunday, before lunch, Marta and I sat on a large flowered couch and, in an asthmatic voice that I thought breathless with excitement, she talked about books. After lunch, Enrique, I, and a few others — Ricky, Estela, Tulio — would sit around a table in the attic and discuss politics, the Rolling Stones complaining in the background. Ricky was my best friend, but Enrique was the one we envied because he had a steady girlfriend, Estela, who was then twelve or thirteen, and whom he eventually married.

To us, in our adolescence, politics were part of everyday life. In 1955 my father had been arrested by the military government that had overthrown Perón, and as coup followed government coup we grew accustomed to the sight of tanks rolling down the street as we walked to school. Presidents came and went, school principals would be replaced according to party interests, and by the time we reached high school the vagaries of politics had taught us that the subject called "Civic Education" — an obligatory course taught in school on the democratic system — was an amusing fiction.

The high school Enrique and I attended was the Colegio Nacional de Buenos Aires. The year we entered, 1961, a genius in the Ministry of Education had decided that a pilot scheme would be tested here. The courses, instead of being taught by ordinary high school teachers, would be in the hands of university professors, many of whom were writers, scientists, and poets as well as critics and historians. These teachers had the right (were in fact encouraged) to teach us very specialized aspects of their subject. This meant that besides acquiring an overview of, say, Spanish literature, we would spend a whole year studying in great detail a single book. We were extremely lucky: we were given essential information, and we were taught how to think about particulars, a method we could later apply to the world at large and to our own agonizing country in particular. Discussing politics was unavoidable. None of us thought that our studies stopped at the end of a textbook.

I've mentioned that prior to Marta Lynch's encouragement, one other person had told me that literature was a serious activity. Our parents had explained to us that artistic endeavors were not truly valid occupations. Sports were good for the body, and a little reading, like Brasso, gave one a nice shine, but the real subjects were mathematics, physics, chemistry, and at a pinch history and geography. Spanish was lumped together with music and the visual arts. Because I loved books (which I collected with miserly passion) I felt the

guilty shame of someone in love with a freak. Ricky, who accepted my quirk
with the magnanimity of a true friend, always gave me books for my birthday.
Then one year, on the first day of class, a new teacher walked into the room.

I will call him Rivadavia. He was nothing like some of the other professors
of my high school years, such as the Spanish Renaissance specialist who introduced me to *Don Quixote*. Rivadavia walked in, barely said good afternoon,
didn't tell us what the course would be or what his expectations were, and
opening a book, began to read something which began like this: "Before the
door stands a doorkeeper on guard. To this doorkeeper there comes a man from
the country who begs admittance to the Law. But the doorkeeper says that he
cannot admit the man at that moment . . ." We had never heard of Kafka, we
knew nothing of parables, but that afternoon the floodgates of literature were
opened for us. This was nothing like the dreary bits of classics we had had to
study in our grade five and six readers; this was mysterious and rich, and it
touched on things so personal that we would never have acknowledged they
concerned us. Rivadavia read us Kafka, Cortázar, Rimbaud, Quevedo, Akuta-
gawa; mentioned what the new critics were reviewing and quoted from Walter
Benjamin and Maurice Merleau-Ponty and Maurice Blanchot; encouraged us to
see *Tom Jones* even though it was rated R; told us about having heard Lorca recite his own poems one day in Buenos Aires "in a voice full of pomegranates."
But above all, he taught us how to read. I don't know whether all of us learned,
probably not, but listening to Rivadavia guide us through a text, through the
relationships between words and memories, ideas and experiences, encouraged
me towards a lifetime of addiction to the printed page from which I have never
managed to wean myself. The way I thought, the way I felt, the person I was in
the world, and that other, darker person I was all alone by myself were for the
most part born on that first afternoon in which Rivadavia read to my class.

Then, on 28 June 1966, an army coup led by General Juan Carlos Onganía
overturned the civil government. Troops and tanks surrounded the government palace, only a few blocks from our school, and President Arturo Illia,
old and frail (cartoonists portrayed him as a tortoise), was kicked out into the
streets. Enrique insisted that we organize a protest. Dozens of us stood on
the steps of the school chanting slogans, refusing to go to class. A few of the
teachers joined the strike. There were scuffles. One of our friends got his nose
broken in a fight with a pro-military group.

In the meantime, the meetings at Enrique's house continued. Sometimes
we were joined by Estela's younger brother, sometimes only Enrique and

Ricky attended. I became less interested. On a few Sundays I left after lunch with some uneasy excuse. Marta Lynch published several more novels. She was now one of the best-selling authors in Argentina, but she longed for some success abroad, in the United States, in France. It never happened.

After graduation, I spent a few months at the University of Buenos Aires studying literature, but the plodding pace and the unimaginative lectures made me sick with boredom. I suspect that Rivadavia and the critics he had introduced us to had spoilt my enjoyment of a straightforward course: after being told, in Rivadavia's thundering voice, of Ulysses' adventures through a Borges story, "The Immortal," in which the narrator is Homer, alive throughout the ages, it was difficult to listen for hours to someone drone on about the textual problems in early transcriptions of the *Odyssey*. I left for Europe on an Italian ship in the early months of 1969.

For the next fourteen years Argentina was flayed alive. Anyone living in Argentina during those years had two choices: either to fight against the military dictatorship or allow it to flourish. My choice was that of a coward: I decided not to return. My excuse (there are no excuses) is that I would not have been good with a gun. During my European peregrinations I kept hearing, of course, about the friends I'd left behind.

My school had always been known for its political activities, and throughout history many notable Argentinean politicians had come from the same classrooms in which I had sat. Now it seemed as if the government had specifically targeted not only the school but my schoolmates. News about them began to trickle out, month after month. Two friends (one had taught himself to play the oboe and gave impromptu performances in his room; the other had observed that those performances were "more boring than dancing with your own sister") were shot dead at a petrol station just outside Buenos Aires. Another friend, whose name now seems to have vanished with her, so small she seemed to be about twelve when I last saw her, aged sixteen, was gunned down in a military prison. Estela's brother, barely fifteen, disappeared one afternoon on his way to the movies. His corpse was delivered, inside a mailbag, to his parents' doorstep, so badly mangled it was hardly recognizable. Enrique left for Spain. Ricky escaped to Brazil. Marta Lynch committed suicide. She shot herself in the kitchen while outside a taxi was waiting to take her to an interview at a radio station. The note she left read simply, "I can bear all this no longer."

A few years ago I found myself in Brazil on a stopover. Back in Buenos

Aires, one of my brothers had run into Ricky's mother, and she had given him Ricky's address in Rio, which my brother then forwarded to me. I called him. He was now married, with kids, teaching economics at the university. I kept trying to understand what had changed in him because he didn't look older, merely different. I realized that everything he did now seemed slowed down — his speech, his gestures, the way he moved. A certain flabbiness had overtaken him; little seemed to excite him.

He had made a home in Brazil now — his wife, his children were Brazilian — but it was still a foreign country. He told me that in exile, as he called it, a number of refugees had set up "memory groups." Memory groups, he explained, were in charge of recording political crimes so that nothing might be forgotten. They had lists of names of torturers, spies, informants. The Commission on the *Desaparecidos* in Argentina, set up by President Alfonsín in 1983 to investigate the fate of the thousands who disappeared during the military dictatorship, later recorded the testimony of the surviving victims. The memory groups kept records of the victimizers, in the hope that one day they would be brought to justice. I suspect that some of Ricky's despondency came from the fact that he foresaw the outcome of the trials Alfonsín had promised: a few sentences, a few reprimands, and then the general amnesty proclaimed in 1991 by the new president, Carlos Menem.

I mentioned how extraordinary it seemed that our friends, our school, had been a target of the government. Ricky said that the military had depended on informants. That inside the school there were those who provided the torturers with details about our activities, with names, addresses, character descriptions. I agreed that there were those who had always publicly supported the military, but that there was a fair distance between waving a pro-military banner and actually collaborating with torturers.

Ricky laughed and said that I obviously had no idea of how those things worked. The military hadn't depended on a group of reactionary kids chanting things like "Homeland, Family, Church." They needed intelligent, resourceful people. Such as Rivadavia. Ricky said his group had solid proof that for several years Professor Rivadavia had passed on to the military government detailed information about us — his students. Not simply the names, but careful notes on our likes and dislikes, on our family backgrounds and school activities. He knew us all so well.

Ricky told me this a few years ago, and I have never stopped thinking about it. I know Ricky wasn't mistaken. In my mind, I have three options:

• I can decide that the person who was of the uttermost importance in my life, who in a way allowed me to be who I am now, who was the very essence of the illuminating and inspiring teacher, was in fact a monster and that everything he taught me, everything he had encouraged me to love, was corrupt.

• I can try to justify his unjustifiable actions and ignore the fact that they led to the torture and death of my friends.

• I can accept that Rivadavia was both the good teacher and the collaborator of torturers, and allow that description to stand, like water and fire.

I don't know which of these readings is the right one.

Before saying good-bye, I asked Ricky if he knew what had become of Rivadavia. Ricky nodded and said that Rivadavia had left the school and entered a small publishing company in Buenos Aires, and that he wrote book reviews for one of the major Argentinean newspapers.

As far as I know, he's still there.

God's Spies

"They're putting down their names," the Gryphon whispered
in reply, "for fear they should forget them before the end of
the trial."

Alice's Adventures in Wonderland, Chapter 11

AS OUR READING TEACHES US, our history is the story of a long night
of injustice: Hitler's Germany, Stalin's Russia, the South Africa of apartheid,
Ceauşescu's Romania, the China of Tiananmen Square, Senator McCarthy's
America, Castro's Cuba, Pinochet's Chile, Stroessner's Paraguay, endless
others form the map of our time. We seem to live either within or just on this
side of despotic societies. We are never secure, even in our small democracies.
When we think of how little it took for upright French citizens to jeer at con-
voys of Jewish children being herded into trucks, or for educated Canadians
to throw stones at women and old men in the reservation of Oka when the
natives protested the building of a golf course, then we have no right to feel
safe.

The trappings with which we rig our society so that it will remain a society must be solid, but they must also be flexible. That which we exclude and
outlaw or condemn must also remain visible, must always be in front of our
eyes so that we can live by making the daily choice of not breaking these social bonds. The horrors of dictatorship are not inhuman horrors: they are profoundly human — and therein lies their power. "There is a remedy in human
nature against tyranny," wrote optimistically Samuel Johnson, "that will keep
us safe under every form of government." And yet any system of government
based on arbitrary laws, extortion, torture, slavery lies at a mere hand's grasp
from every so-called democratic system.

Chile has a curious motto, "By Reason or by Force." It can be read in
at least two ways: as a bully's threat, with an accent on the second part of

the equation, or as an honest recognition of the precariousness of any social system, adrift (as the Mexican poet Amado Nervo said) "between the clashing seas of force and reason." We, in most Western societies, believe we have chosen reason over force, and for the time being we can depend on that conviction. But we are never entirely free from the temptation of power. At best, our society will survive by upholding a few common notions of humanity and justice, dangerously sailing, as our Canadian motto has it, "A mari usque ad mare," between those two symbolic seas.

Auden declared that "Poetry makes nothing happen." I don't believe that to be true (nor, probably, did he). Not every book is an epiphany, but many times we have sailed guided by a luminous page or a beacon of verse. What role poets and storytellers have on our precarious journeys may not be immediately clear, but perhaps some form of an answer emerged in the aftermath of one particular dictatorship, one that I followed closely over the bloody decade of its rule.

I can't remember her name (so unfaithful are the promises of memory), but she was one grade below mine at the Colegio Nacional de Buenos Aires. I met her in my second year of high school, on one of the excursions our zealous monitors liked to organize for us during which we discovered the art of rigging up tents, a taste for reading around the campfire, and the mystery of politics. What exactly these politics were we never quite found out, except that at the time they echoed, somewhat bombastically, our vague notions of freedom and equality. In time, we read (or tried to read) arid books on economy and sociology and history, but for most of us *politics* remained a serviceable word that named our need for comradeship and our contempt for authority. The latter included the school's conservative headmaster; the remote landowners of vast areas of Patagonia (where, at the foot of the Andes, we went camping and where, as I've mentioned, we saw peasant families living out their distant and for us inconceivable lives); and the military, whose tanks, on 28 June 1966, we saw lumber through the streets of Buenos Aires, one of many such processions towards the presidential palace on Plaza de Mayo. She was sixteen that year; in 1969 I left Buenos Aires and never saw her again. She was small, I remember, with black and curly hair which she had cut very short. Her voice was unemphatic, soft and clear, and I could always recognize her on the phone after just one syllable. She painted, but without much conviction. She was good at math. In 1982, shortly before the Malvinas War and towards the end of the military dictatorship, I returned to Buenos Aires for a brief visit. Asking for news of

old friends, so many dead and disappeared in those terrible years, I was told
that she was among the missing. She had been kidnapped leaving the university where she had sat on the student council. Officially, there was no record
of her detention, but someone had apparently seen her at El Campito, one of
the military concentration camps, in a brief moment when her hood had been
removed for a medical inspection. The military usually kept their prisoners
hooded so that later on they would not be able to recognize their torturers.

On 24 April 1995, Victor Armando Ibáñez, an Argentinean sergeant who
had served as a guard at El Campito, gave an interview to the Buenos Aires
newspaper *La Prensa*. According to Ibáñez, between 2,000 and 2,300 of those
imprisoned there, men and women, old people and adolescents, were "executed" by the army at El Campito during the two years of his service, from
1976 to 1978. When the prisoners' time came, Ibáñez told the newspaper, "they
were injected with a strong drug called pananoval, which made a real mess of
them in a few seconds. It produced something like a heart attack. [The injec-
tions would leave the prisoners alive but unconscious.] Then they were thrown
into the sea. We flew at a very low altitude. They were phantom flights, without registration. Sometimes I could see very large fish, like sharks, following
the plane. The pilots said that they were fattened by human flesh. I leave the
rest to your imagination," Ibáñez said. "Imagine the worst."

Ibáñez's was the second "official" confession. A month earlier, a retired
navy lieutenant commander, Adolfo Francisco Scilingo, had confessed (also in
La Prensa) to the same method of "disposing of the prisoners." In response to
his confession, Argentinean president Carlos Menem called Scilingo a "criminal," reminded the press that the commander had been involved in a shady
automobile deal, and asked how the word of a thief could be counted as true.
He also ordered the navy to strip Scilingo of his rank.

Since his election in 1989, Menem had been trying to shelve the whole
question of military culpability during the so-called "dirty war" that ravaged
Argentina from 1973 to 1982, and during which more than thirty thousand
people were killed. Not content with the deadline for filing charges against the
military (which his predecessor, Raul Alfonsín had set as 22 February 1988),
on 6 October 1989 Menem had offered most of the military involved in human
rights abuses a general pardon. A year later, three days after Christmas, Menem
issued a general amnesty to all involved in the events that had bled the country
for nine long years. Accordingly, he released from prison Lieutenant General
Jorge Videla (who was later re-arrested) and General Roberto Viola, both of

whom had been appointed to the presidency by the military junta, from 1976 to 1981 and for ten months in 1981, respectively. In legal terms, a pardon implies not an exoneration or acquittal but only a relief from punishment. An amnesty, on the other hand (such as the military had granted itself in extremis in 1982, and which was repealed by Alfonsín), is, in effect and intention, a recognition of innocence that wipes away any imputation of crime. After the declarations of Scilingo and Ibáñez, President Menem briefly threatened the military with a retraction of the 1990 amnesty.

Until the confessions of 1995, the Argentinean military authorities had recognized no wrongdoing in their so-called anti-terrorist activities. The extraordinary nature of guerrilla war demanded, the authorities said, extraordinary measures. In this declaration they were well advised. In 1977, following a joint report from Amnesty International and the U.S. State Department's Human Rights Bureau accusing the Argentinean security forces of being responsible for hundreds of disappearances, the military hired an American public relations company, Burson-Marsteller, to plan its response. The thirty-five-page memorandum presented by Burson-Marsteller recommended that the military "use the best professional communications skills to transmit those aspects of Argentine events showing that the terrorist problem is being handled in a firm and just manner, with equal justice for all." A tall order, but not impossible in the Age of Advertising. As if moved by the hackneyed motto "The pen is mightier than the sword," Burson-Marsteller suggested that the military appeal for "the generation of positive editorial comment" from writers "of conservative or moderate persuasions." As a result of their campaign, Ronald Reagan declared in the *Miami News* of 20 October 1978 that the State Department's human rights office was "making a mess of our relations with the planet's seventh largest country, Argentina, a nation with which we should be close friends."

Over the years, others answered the advertisers' appeal. In 1995, shortly after Ibáñez's and Scilingo's confessions, an article appeared in the Spanish newspaper *El Pais*, signed by Mario Vargas Llosa. Under the title "Playing with Fire," Vargas Llosa argued that, horrible though the revelations might be, they were not news to anyone, merely confirmations of a truth "atrocious and nauseating for any half-moral conscience." "It would certainly be wonderful," he wrote, "if all those responsible for these unbelievable cruelties were taken to court and punished. This, however, is impossible, because the responsibility far exceeds the military sphere and implicates a vast spectrum of Argentinean society, including a fair number of those who today cry out, condemning retrospectively the violence to which they too, in one way or another, contributed."

"It would certainly be wonderful": this is the rhetorical topos of false regret, denoting a change from shared indignation at the "atrocious and nauseating" facts, to the more sober realization of what they "really" mean—the impossibility of attaining the "wonderful" goal of impartial justice. Vargas Llosa's is an ancient argument, harking back to notions of original sin: no one soul can truly be held responsible because every soul is responsible "in one way or another" for the crimes of a nation, whether committed by the people themselves or by their leaders. More than a hundred years ago, Nikolai Gogol expressed the same absurdity in more elegant terms: "Seek out the judge, seek out the criminal, and then condemn both."

Using the case of his own country as a history lesson, Vargas Llosa concluded his *cri de coeur:* "The example of what has happened in Peru, with a democracy which the Peruvian people have distorted—because of the violence of extremist groups and also because of the blindness and demagogy of certain political forces—and which they let fall like a ripe fruit in the arms of military and personal power, should open the eyes of those imprudent justice-seekers who, in Argentina, take advantage of a debate on the repression in the seventies to seek revenge, to avenge old grievances or continue by other means the insane war they started and then lost."

Burson-Marsteller could not have come up with a more efficient publicist for its cause. What would a common reader, confident in Vargas Llosa's intellectual authority, make of this impassioned conclusion? After hesitating, perhaps, at the comparison between Argentina and Peru (where the novelist-turned-politician thunderingly lost the presidential election), which seems to protest too much, too obviously, the reader is led into a far subtler argument: these "justice-seekers," the seekers of that justice which, according to Vargas Llosa, is desirable but utopian—are they not in fact hypocrites who not only must share the guilt for the atrocities but are also to blame for starting a war which they then lost? Suddenly the scales of responsibility are tipped ominously to the victims' side. Not a need for justice, not an urge to acknowledge wrongs officially, but an itch for revenge or, even worse, sheer spite apparently drives these so-called justice-seekers. The thirty thousand disappeared are not to be lamented; they were troublemakers who started it all. And those who survived—the Mothers of Plaza de Mayo, the thousands forced into exile, the hundreds of tortured men and women who crowd the pages of the 1984 *Report on the Disappeared* by the National Commission on Disappeared People, with their sober accounts of utterly indescribable sufferings—should not seek redress lest they themselves be called to judgment. And furthermore, the seventies are now so long ago . . . Would it not be better to forget?

Fortunately, there were readers who were not so confident. Mario Vargas Llosa's article was reprinted in *Le Monde* on 18 May 1995. A week later (25 May), the Argentinean writer Juan José Saer published an answer in the same newspaper. After correcting a number of important factual errors in Vargas Llosa's piece—calling Isabel Perón's presidency a "democratic government," ignoring the fact that between 1955 and 1983 Argentina enjoyed barely six years of freely elected leaders—Saer notes that Vargas Llosa's arguments coincide, point by point, with those of the military leaders themselves, who argued that the official tactics of murder and torture had not been their choice but the choice of those who provoked them and forced them to make use of "extreme measures." Saer also points out that Vargas Llosa's notion of "collective responsibility" might place Vargas Llosa himself in a delicate position since, at a time when Argentinean intellectuals were being tortured or forced into exile, the Peruvian novelist continued to publish willingly in Argentina's official press.

Saer responded to Vargas Llosa's role, accusing him of being a spokesman for the military: he dismissed or ignored his arguments, which are based on a number of false assumptions. And yet, since these arguments must stand, thanks to Vargas Llosa's craft, as the most eloquent of those penned by the defenders of a military amnesty, they deserve, perhaps, a closer examination.

> • The notion of guilt shared between the military government, which came to power by force and used torture and murder to fight its opposers, and the victims, including guerrilla fighters, political objectors, and ordinary civilians with no political associations, is fallacious. While it could be argued that in a sense the army of insurrectionists and the official Argentinean army were equal forces (though, even here, the numbers appear to be on the order of 1 to 1,000), no argument can find a balance of power between the organized military forces and the intellectuals, artists, union leaders, students, and members of the clergy who expressed disagreement with them. The civilian who voices an objection to the actions of the government is not guilty of any crime; on the contrary, vigilance is

an essential civic duty in any democratic society, and every citizen must become, as it were, God's spy. "And take upon's the mystery of things," says King Lear, "As if we were God's spies; and we'll wear out / In a walled prison, packs and sects of great ones / That ebb and flow by th' moon."

But the repression overflowed even the realm of civilian opposition. The National Commission on Disappeared People, led by the novelist Ernesto Sabato, concluded its report in September 1984: "We can state categorically—contrary to what the executors of this sinister plan maintain—that they did not pursue only the members of political organizations who carried out acts of terrorism. Among the victims are thousands who never had any links with such activity but were nevertheless subjected to horrific torture because they opposed the military dictatorship, took part in union or student activities, were well-known intellectuals who questioned state terrorism, or simply because they were relatives, friends, or names included in the address book of someone considered subversive."

• Any government that uses torture and murder to enforce the law invalidates both its right to govern and the law it enforces, since one of the few basic tenets of any society in which citizens are granted equal rights is the sacredness of human life. "Clearly," wrote G. K. Chesterton, "there could be no safety for a society in which the remark by the Chief Justice that murder was wrong was regarded as an original and dazzling epigram." Any government that does not recognize this truth, and does not hold accountable those who torture and murder, can make no claims for its own justice. No government can rightly mirror the methods of its criminals, responding in kind to what it might deem an act against the nation's laws. It cannot be guided by an individual sense of justice, or revenge, or greed, or even morality. It must encompass them all, these individual deeds of its citizens, within the parameters established by the country's constitution. It must enforce the law with the law, and within the letter of the law. Beyond the law, a government is no longer a government but a usurped power, and as such it must be judged.

• Trust in the ultimate power of the law sustained many of the military dictatorship's victims during those terrible years. In spite of the pain and the bewilderment caused by the officialized abuses, the belief remained that in a not-too-distant future these acts would be brought to light and judged according to the law. The wish to torture the torturer and to kill the murderer must have been overwhelming, but even stronger was the sense that such acts of revenge would become indistinguishable from the acts that caused them and would be transformed, in some abominable way, into a victory for the abusers. Instead, the victims and their families continued to believe in some form of ultimate earthly judgment, in which the society that had been wronged would bring the guilty ones to trial according to the laws of that society. Only on the basis of such justice being done did they believe that their country might have another chance. Menem's amnesty denied them that long-awaited possibility.

• This "absence of justice" was reflected with ghoulish symmetry in the "disappearing" tactics employed by the military, by which their victims — kidnapped, tortured, thrown from airplanes, dropped into unmarked graves — became not officially dead but merely "absent," leaving the anguished families with no bodies to mourn. Julio Cortázar, speaking in 1981, described in these words the dictatorship's method: "On the one hand, a virtual or real antagonist is suppressed; on the other, conditions are created so that the family and friends of the victims are often forced to remain silent as the only possibility of preserving the life of those whom their hearts won't allow them to presume dead." And he added, "If every human death entails an irrevocable absence, what can we say of this other absence that continues as a sort of abstract presence, like the obstinate denial of the absence we know to be final?" In that sense, Menem's amnesty didn't heal the sickness of the past — it merely prolonged that sickness into the present.

• Menem's revisionist attempt is not original. One of the earliest instances of perfecting the present by erasing the tensions of the past took place in the year 213 B.C., when the Chinese emperor Shi Huangdi ordered that every book in his realm be thrown into the fire so as to destroy all traces (as one legend has it) of his mother's adultery. But no deed, however monstrous or trivial, can ever be abolished once committed — not even by a Chinese emperor, even less by an Argentinean president. This is the adamantine law of our life. The immutability of the past does not depend on the volubilities of government, nor on cravings for revenge or for diplomacy. No deed can be undone. It can be pardoned, but the pardon must come from the offended person and from no one else if it is to have any emotional validity. Nothing changes in the deed itself after a pardon: not the circumstances, not the gravity, not the guilt, not the wound. Nothing except the relationship between the torturer and the victims, when the victims reaffirm their sovereignty, "not weighing our merits," as the Book of Common Prayer has it, "but by pardoning our offences." Pardon is the victim's prerogative, not the torturer's right — and this Menem's government and his supporters, such as Vargas Llosa, have apparently forgotten.

• The pardon granted by a victim — the dripping quality of mercy — has no bearing on the mechanics of justice. Pardon does not change or even qualify the act, which will cast its shadow forward, throughout eternity, into every new present. Pardon does not grant oblivion. But a trial, according to the laws of society, can at least lend the criminal act a context; the law can contain it, so to speak, in the past so that it no longer contaminates the future, standing at a distance as a reminder and a warning. In a mysterious way, the application of a society's laws is akin to a literary act: it fixes the criminal deed on a page, defines it in words, gives it a context which is not that of the sheer horror of the moment but of its recollection. The power of memory is no longer in the hands of the criminal; now it is society itself that holds that power, writing the chronicle of its own wicked past, able at last to rebuild itself not over the emptiness of oblivion but over the solid, recorded facts of the atrocities committed. This is a long, dreary, fearful, agonizing process, and the only possible one. This sort of healing always leaves scars.

• Menem's amnesty, bowing to the demands of acknowledged murderers and torturers, has postponed the healing for what appears to be a very long time. As it stands today, since all the torturers and murders in the military regime have not been brought to justice, Argentina is a country bereft of rights: its right to social justice ignored, its right to moral education invalidated, its right to moral authority forfeit. The need to "carry on," the need to "reconcile differences," the need to "allow the economy to flourish once again" have all been invoked by Menem and his successors as good reasons for forgiving and forgetting. Supported by literate voices such as that of Vargas Llosa, Menem apparently believed that history could be paid off; that the memory of thousands of individuals like my friend from school could be left to yellow on forgotten shelves in dim bureaucratic offices; that the past could be recovered without expenditure of effort, without making official amends, without redemption.

While waiting for the act of justice now denied, the victims of Argentina's military dictatorship can still hope for another, older form of justice — less evident, but in the end longer-lasting. The maze of a politician's mind has seldom held the promise of redemption, but that of a gifted writer is almost exclusively built on such a promise, and in spite of Auden's dictum, it allows no forgetting.

Thanks to certain books (a catalogue too long and personal to be of use here), both the torturers and their victims may know that they were not alone, unseen, unassailable. Justice, beyond the requirements of literary conventions that demand a happy ending is in some essential way our common human bond, something against which we can all measure ourselves. As the old English law has it, justice must not only be done but be seen to be done.

Auden's lack of confidence in the writer's ability to change the world is apparently a modern perception. Robert Graves noted that the Irish and Welsh distinguished carefully between poets and satirists: the poet's task was creative or curative, that of the satirist was destructive or noxious, and both changed the course of worldly events. Even nature was supposed to bow to Orpheus's words, and Shakespeare recalled the power of the Irish bards, "rhyming rats to death"; in the seventh century, the great Senchán Torpéist, having discovered that rats had eaten his dinner, slaughtered ten on the spot by uttering a verse that began:

Rats have sharp snouts
Yet are poor fighters.

Whether against rats or dictators, writers can bring about a wild form of justice in their role as God's spies. "Many brave men lived before Agamemnon's time," wrote Horace in the first century B.C., "but they are all, unmourned and unknown, covered by the long night, because they lacked a poet." As Horace implied, we are luckier. Poems and stories that will redeem us (or in which we will find redemption of a kind) are being written, or will be written, or have been written and are awaiting their readers and, throughout time, again and again, assume this: that the human mind is always wiser than its most atrocious deeds, since it can give them a name; that in the very description of our most loathsome acts something in good writing shows them as loathsome and therefore not unconquerable; that in spite of the feebleness and randomness of language, an inspired writer can tell the unspeakable and lend a shape to the unthinkable, so that evil loses some of its numinous quality and stands reduced to a few memorable words.

Once Again, Troy

Tweedledum looked round him with a satisfied smile. "I don't
suppose," he said, "there'll be a tree left standing, for ever
so far round, by the time we've finished!"
Through the Looking-Glass, Chapter 4

MY GEOGRAPHY IS MAPPED by my readings. Experience, memory, desire
color and shape it, but my books define it. My Oregon belongs to Ursula K.
Le Guin, my Prague to Gustav Meyrink, my Venice to Henry James, my Alge-
ria to Rachid Boudjedra. But when I think of Beirut, three images come to
mind. The first is the one my mother described to me after visiting the city in
the early fifties. She had been to Paris, to Rome, to Venice: she thought there
was no city as lovely as Beirut, as elegant, as welcoming. Whenever things
would go wrong in Buenos Aires (and they would go wrong often) she would
complain and shake her head and, instead of repeating "Moscow, Moscow!"
like one of Chekhov's three sisters, she would sigh, "Beirut, Beirut!" as if her
life in that paradise would have been different had she stayed. Perhaps it would
have, because Beirut was for her an impossibility. Impossible things tend to
be perfect.

The second is the city I visited in 2004. The friendship of the people, their
extraordinary courtesy, the constant shift in tone bred from the variety of cultural backgrounds, the pride and relief in seeing their city built up again after
the war, the lack of shame with which they showed the scars, their ingrained
and shared belief in the vital importance of poetry, music, good food, intelligent conversation left me, as I returned home, with a sudden nostalgia for
what I had experienced as civilization.

The third is the bombed city shown on the evening news in 2008. Like any
ravaged city, it is both a place of incommunicable daily personal suffering and
also the image of every city in no matter what war: a place in which walls that

took so long to build lie crumbled in the streets and someone stares at a fallen roof underneath which lies a brother, a sister, a friend, a parent, a child, and soldiers race past.

But there is a fourth Beirut, I think. It is made less of stones rebuilt and stones demolished than of the perseverance of memory. One of the most moving aspects of the *Iliad* for someone reading it today is the sudden realization that, though the teller's voice is Greek, the tragedy is shared. That is to say: the excuse for the conflict is a kidnapping (of Helen by Paris), and the allied forces, under the insistence of the most powerful of the warlords (Agamemnon), agree to continue the siege and the fighting until their property is restored, but, as the poem makes it very clear, the awful consequences of the war are felt on either side, and both Patroclus the Greek and Hector the Trojan are victims of its savagery. The author (or authors) of the *Iliad* has felt that his allegiance lies with both.

The Greeks exalted war as a heroic activity, relished by the gods who sit watching the show (book 7 tells us explicitly, in Robert Fagles's translation) "for all the world like carrion birds, like vultures." But the fact that it was (or could be) heroic did not blind them to the horror or the suffering. And against the bloodthirsty whims of the gods, the Greeks never failed to recall that human beings are (or can be) compassionate. In Sophocles' play *Ajax*, after Athena gleefully tells Odysseus, her protégé, that his foe is cursed with endless misfortune, Odysseus speaks a few heartbreaking words which suddenly render the Greek hero far nobler than the wise and gory goddess: "The unfortunate man might well be my enemy," he says, "yet I pity him when I see him weighed down with misfortune. Indeed, it is towards myself more than towards him that I direct my thoughts, since I see clearly that we are, all of us who live upon this earth, nothing but ghosts or weightless shadows." Memory of who he is dignifies both Ajax's destiny and Odysseus's own.

Memory lends context to what we are and what we see. In one of the last books of the *Iliad*, the murderous Achilles runs after Hector, the murderer of Achilles' friend Patroclus. Both are soldiers, both have blood on their hands, both have loved ones who have been killed, both believe that their cause is just. One is Greek, the other Trojan, but at this point their allegiances hardly matter. They are two men intent on killing each other. They run past the city walls, past the double springs of the river Scamander. And at this point, Homer (that ancient presence we call Homer) breaks off his description of the fighting and pauses to remind us:

    And here, close to the springs, lie washing-pools
    scooped out in the hollow rocks and broad and smooth
    where the wives of Troy and their lovely daughters
    would wash their glistening robes in the old days,
    the days of peace before the sons of Achaea came

    .   .   .   .

    Past these they raced. [trans. Robert Fagles]

Past these they race still.

Art and Blasphemy

"I shall do nothing of the sort," said the Mouse, getting up
and walking away. "You insult me by talking such nonsense!"

"I didn't mean it!" pleaded poor Alice. "But you're so easily
offended, you know!"

Alice's Adventures in Wonderland, Chapter 3

READING IMAGES CAN BE A perilous enterprise. No one ignores that in
2005 the publication of several caricatures of Muhammad in a number of periodicals around the world (first in Denmark, as a joke, then in other countries,
as an act of defiance) ignited the furious protest of various Islamic groups.
History repeats itself: faith, which is supposed to be the unmovable pillar of a
true believer, seems to shiver and shake when confronted with a mere artistic
creation, with a brushstroke or a few scribbled words, while, in the name of
the Supreme Being, His followers announce the imminence of a fit of divine
temper.

That a cruel or violent act might infuriate the Creator of the Universe (or
His Prophet) is understandable, since no author (with or without a capital A)
enjoys seeing his work mangled or destroyed. To kill, to torture, to humiliate,
to abuse a fellow creature is no doubt a crime in the eyes of God, and I suppose
that believers have every right to see in the fact that a new Universal Deluge
does not take place every month proof of the inexhaustible divine patience.
That creatures such as Augusto Pinochet, George W. Bush, and Osama bin
Laden are allowed to lead a comfortable existence shows that God certainly
possesses a most inhuman patience.

But to declare, at the same time, that a cartoon, a joke, a play on words
might offend Him for whom eternity is like a day, or His blessed elect among
all men, seems to me the greatest of blasphemies. We, feeble human beings,
may feel bothered by someone making fun of us; but surely that can't be the

reaction of a being we imagine supreme, incorruptible, omniscient. Borges suggested that of God's literary tastes we know nothing; it is difficult to imagine that Someone who knows everything and whose generous aesthetic sense led Him both to the creation of the poetic antelope and the tasteless joke of the hippopotamus, would ban from His night table the works of Denis Diderot, of Mark Twain, of Salman Rushdie. Muhammad was all for laughter: "Keep your heart light at every moment, because when the heart is downcast the soul becomes blind."

The great religious figures of the past, because they were also intelligent human beings, did not lack a sense of humor. Christ (in Jerome's Latin version) made fun of Peter with a silly pun. "Your name is Peter (*Petrus*) and upon this rock (*petram*) I'll build my church." When Buddha was about to cross a desert, the gods, with the intention of protecting Him from the sun, threw down parasols from their various heavens. So as not to offend any of them, the Buddha politely multiplied Himself and each of the gods saw a Buddha carrying the parasol he had sent Him. According to the Midrash, Moses was asked why God (who knows everything) had asked, "Adam, where are you?" when He sought him out in the Garden after the episode with the apple. Moses answered: "Thereby did God attempt to teach us good manners, since it is not polite to enter someone else's house without announcing yourself first." In the first volume of the *Al-Mustatraf* it is told that a poor man came to see Muhammad and asked him to grant him a camel to ride. "I'll grant you the young of a camel," said Muhammad. "But the young of a camel will not stand my weight!" the man complained. "You asked for a camel," Muhammad answered. "Don't you know that every camel is by force the young of another camel?"

The word *blasphemy* comes from the Greek and means "to offend someone." In Greek mythology, blasphemy depends on the sensitivity of the blasphemed god. Athena punishes the young Arachne by turning her into a spider because she had boasted of being a better weaver than the goddess. For the Catholic Church of the Middle Ages, the notion of blasphemy becomes confused with that of heresy, except that, thanks to a bureaucratic nicety, Muslims and Jews could not be accused of heresy because they had never confessed to being believers. They could, however, be accused of insulting God and His saints, and not only through words and actions (by saying, for instance, that fortune, not God, rules our lives) but also through thought, what was known as "blaspheming with the heart." An edict of 538, signed by the emperor Justinian, declared that the punishment for blasphemy was death, but the sentence was rarely carried out. In the Judeo-Christian world, the notion of blasphemy is today still legally valid: in the United States, for instance, various religious groups have succeeded in having withdrawn from school libraries books that in their opinion insult their God. This is how writers as diverse as Roald Dahl, J. D. Salinger, and J. K. Rowling have seen themselves included among such banished classics as Jonathan Swift and William Faulkner.

The famous tenth surah of the Qur'an (10:100) reads, "No soul may believe except by the will of God." In the beginning of the eighth century, the illustrious theologian Hasan Al-Basri understood this to mean that "we cannot desire good without God desiring it for us." Believers must therefore be content with the conviction that they have been chosen by divine grace and not demand from those whom God has not seen fit to be elected an equal devotion. Let the others mock: that too (if we continue the argument) is due to God's will (whose reasons are inscrutable). The faithful say that their God demands from them sacrifice and resilience. No doubt, proof of this is that He has decreed the existence of a few court jesters, heirs to Voltaire, to Erasmus, to Rabelais, who, following the advice of Horace (another of God's creations) advocate teaching through laughter.

At the Mad Hatter's Table

"In *that* direction," the Cat said, waving its right paw
round, "lives a Hatter; and in *that* direction," waving the other
paw, "lives a March Hare. Visit either you like: they're both mad."

"But I don't want to go among mad people," Alice remarked.

"Oh, you can't help that," said the Cat: "we're all mad here."
Alice's Adventures in Wonderland, Chapter 6

AS MOST PERCEPTIVE READERS will agree, the distinctive characteristic of the human world is its insanity. Ants scuttle in ordered lines, back and forth, with impeccable propriety. Seeds grow into trees that shed their leaves and bud again with conventional circularity. Birds migrate, lions kill, turtles mate, viruses mutate, rocks crumble into dust, clouds shape and reshape mercifully unconscious of what they build and destroy. We alone live consciously knowing that we live and, by means of a half-shared code of words, are able to reflect on our actions, however contradictory or inexplicable. We heal and help, we sacrifice ourselves and show concern and compassion, we create wonderful artifices and miraculous devices to better understand the world and ourselves. And at the same time, we build our lives on superstitions, hoard for no purpose except greed, cause deliberate pain to other creatures, poison the water and the air we need to live, and finally bring our planet to the verge of destruction. We do all this with full awareness of our actions, as if walking through a dream in which we do what we know we should not be doing and refrain from doing what we know we should do. "May we not then sometimes define insanity as an inability to distinguish which is the waking and which the sleeping life?" wrote Lewis Carroll in his diary on 9 February 1856.

In the seventh chapter of her travels through the insane world of Wonderland, Alice comes upon a table placed under a tree and laid out with many settings. Though the table is a large one, the March Hare, the Mad Hatter, and the Dormouse are crowded together at one corner, having tea, the sleeping Dormouse serving as a cushion for the comfort of the others. "No room! No room!" they cry out when they see Alice coming. "There's *plenty* of room!" Alice says indignantly and sits down in a large armchair at one end.

The table manners of Alice's reluctant hosts are obviously mad. First she is offered wine by the March Hare. But "I don't see any wine," she remarks, looking around. "There isn't any," the March Hare says, and offers her more tea. "I've had nothing yet," Alice replies in an offended tone, "so I can't take more." "You mean you can't take *less*," intervenes the Hatter, "it's very easy to take *more* than nothing." Then the seating arrangements are constantly shifted to suit the Mad Hatter's whimsy. Whenever he wants a clean cup, everyone must move one place along to one with a soiled setting; obviously, the only one to get any advantage out of the changes is the Hatter himself. Alice, for instance, is "a good deal worse off than before," as the March Hare has upset the milk jug into his plate.

As in the real world, everything in Wonderland, however mad, has a logical underpinning, a system of rules that are often themselves absurd. The conventions of Alice's society have led her to believe that the behavior of her elders and betters, wherever she might find herself, is rational. Therefore, attempting to understand the logic of her strange dreamworld, Alice expects rational behavior from the creatures she meets, but, again and again, she is merely confronted by their "logical" madness. "Throughout my life," said Bertrand Russell on his ninetieth birthday, "I have been told that man is a rational animal. In all these many years, I have not once found proof that this is so." Alice's world mirrors Russell's assertion.

An amateur anthropologist, Alice assumes that an understanding of the social conventions of Wonderland will allow her to understand the logic of the inhabitants' behavior, and therefore attempts to follow the proceedings at the table with some measure of reason and good manners. To the absurdities presented, she counters with rational questions; to the questions asked, however absurd, she tries to find rational answers. But to no avail. "Really, now you ask me," she says, "I don't think—" "Then you shouldn't talk," snaps back the Hatter.

As in our world, the manners of the inhabitants of Wonderland carry implicit notions of responsibility and value. The Hatter, emblematic of the perfect egotist, opposes free speech (except his own) and disposes of property to which he has no claim (the table belongs, after all, to the March Hare). Nothing matters to him except his own comfort and profit, and he therefore shows himself unwilling to admit even to his own possessions for fear of being held accountable. (During the trial at the end of the book, he refuses to take off his hat because, he says, it isn't his: "I keep them to sell," he explains, "I've none of my own. I'm a hatter.") By valuing what he has only for what he can sell it for, the Hatter need not care about the consequences of his actions, whether they concern a trail of dirty dishes or the established conventions of a court of law.

The Hatter appears only once in the second Alice book, *Through the Looking-Glass* (jailed for a crime he may or may not one day commit), but his philosophy has spread far and wide across Alice's dreamworlds. Halfway through chapter 3, when Alice suddenly finds herself inside a railway carriage confronting an angry Guard who demands to see her ticket, the Hatter's notion of value is echoed by a mysterious chorus of invisible evaluators.

"Now then! Show your ticket, child!" The Guard went on, looking angrily at Alice. And a great many voices all said together ("like the chorus of a song," thought Alice) "Don't keep him waiting, child! Why, his time is worth a thousand pounds a minute!"

"I'm afraid I haven't got one," Alice said in a frightened tone: "there wasn't a ticket-office where I came from." And again the chorus of voices went on. "There wasn't room for one where she came from. The land there is worth a thousand pounds an inch!"

"Don't make excuses," said the Guard: "you should have bought one from the engine-driver." And once more the chorus of voices went on with "The man that drives the engine. Why, the smoke alone is worth a thousand pounds a puff!"

Alice thought to herself, "Then there's no use speaking." The voices didn't join in, *this* time, as she hadn't spoken, but, to her great surprise, they all *thought* in chorus (I hope you understand what *thinking in chorus* means—for I must confess that *I* don't), "Better say nothing at all. Language is worth a thousand pounds a word!"

"I shall dream about a thousand pounds tonight, I know I shall!" thought Alice.

Whether the vastness of time or the immensity of space, whether a mere puff of smoke or the words we speak, everything has, according to the invisible multitude that echoes the Hatter's code, a monetary value — in this case, of a thousand pounds. For these financially minded Furies, everything can be bought and sold, everything (like the Hatter's hat) can be turned into a negotiable commodity.

There is a scene in our own history that could have found its place in Alice's books. Exhausted from the continuing battles, convinced that further struggle was now useless, having decided to attempt capitulation rather than lose not only his freedom but his life, in the summer of 1520 the Aztec king Montezuma, prisoner of the Spaniards, agreed to hand over to Hernán Cortés the vast treasure that his father, Axayactl, had laboriously assembled, and to swear allegiance to the king of Spain, that distant and invisible monarch whose power Cortés represented. Commenting on the ceremony, the Spanish chronicler Fernández de Oviedo reported that Montezuma was in tears throughout the procedure, and, pointing out the difference between a bond willingly accepted by a free agent and one performed in sorrow by someone in chains, Oviedo quoted the Roman poet Marcus Varro: "What is given by force is not service but larceny."

The royal Aztec treasure was, by all accounts, magnificent, and when it was assembled in front of the Spaniards, it towered in three golden heaps made up, for the most part, of exquisite utensils whose secret purpose suggested sophisticated social ceremonies; intricate collars, bracelets, wands, and fans decorated with many-colored feathers, precious stones, and pearls; and carefully wrought birds, insects, and flowers, which, according to Cortés himself, "were, beyond their value, so marvelous, that their very novelty and strangeness rendered them priceless, nor could it be believed that any of the known Princes of this World might possess things like these, and of such quality."

Montezuma had intended the treasure to be a tribute from his court to the Spanish king. Cortés's soldiers, however, demanded that the treasure be treated as booty and that they each receive a fair part of the gold. A fifth of the treasure belonged by rights to the king of Spain, and an equal portion to Cortés himself. A large sum was destined to indemnify the governor of Cuba for the cost of the expedition. The garrison at Veracruz and the leading caballeros were expecting their part, as well as the cavalry, the harquebusiers, and the crossbow men, who were entitled to double pay. This left the common soldiers with about one hundred gold pesos each, a sum so insignificant, compared to their expectations, that many eventually refused to accept it.

Bending to his men's wishes, Cortés sent for the famed goldsmiths of Azcapozalco to turn Montezuma's precious objects into ingots, which were then stamped with the royal arms. The task took the goldsmiths three full days of work. Today, engraved in stone over the door of the Museum of Gold in Santafé de Bogotá, the visitor can read the following verse, addressed by an Aztec poet to the Spanish conquerors: "I am amazed by your blindness and folly, that you undo such beautifully wrought jewels to make bricks out of them."

The question of value is an ancient one. For Cortés, the value of a work of art whose "very novelty and strangeness" rendered it "priceless," was superseded by the value of the raw material from which the work was made and which had been granted a (however fluctuating and symbolic) market price. Since gold itself was the measure of the value of his social transactions, he deemed himself justified in turning the Aztec artworks into ingots. (In our time, the businessman who bought van Gogh's *Sunflowers* and locked up the painting in a safe proceeded under exactly the same conviction.)

Of course, other values exist. The German language, for instance, employs several words to denote value and its different meanings, such as *Gewalt* (the quality of power), *Wert* (the agreed-upon importance of something), *Geltung* (the current validity), *Gültigkeit* (the official worth or usefulness) in the fields of morality, aesthetics, scholarship, and epistemology. But for Cortés, the monetary value superseded them all. Such an overriding notion allowed the baron de Montesquieu, two centuries later, to suggest mockingly that if buying and selling have become our evaluating scales, "a man is worth the price he would be sold for in Algiers."

By assuming, like Cortés, the precedence of economic values, we change our relationship to all creative activities. If financial profit is the final goal, then perfection of a kind is what we are after: the production of artifacts that are easily converted into money. That is to say, in a world in which monetary value is the measure of all things, works of art that do not carry in themselves immediate financial gratification, that require mostly long and laborious procedures, that cannot be defined by tags or sound bytes, and that may or may not result in commercial benefits through convoluted aesthetic, ethical, or philosophical byways must be discarded or, at least, given very little consideration. Failure, the acceptance of which is inherent in any creative activity, is regarded in such a light as anathema, as are the poetic creations Shelley called "nurslings of immortality," since economic law demands that whatever is created carry within itself its own mortality, its "sell by" date, which will enable the chain of production to continue to sell its products. The artistic qualities of a work must be subjected to the taste of the majority or, in certain cases, to a supposed "elitist" taste which the majority are told they might, for a price, attain. Under the common evaluation of economic worth, all other values blur or dissolve.

This need to consume is created, not through the opening of new fields of intellectual and emotional exploration by the work of art itself, but by planned campaigns that, inspired by census taking and market research, effectively invent a prehistory of longing for something that will be later deliberately produced to satisfy it. Readers don't know that they "need" the *Alice* books until they have discovered and read Carroll's work and see how his writing lends words to their own unuttered experience. However, it is possible to produce books to appease a spiritual "need" after advertising prefabricated pseudo-mysticisms available to all, filling bookstores with apocalyptic warnings and conspiracy theories based, of course, on real collective anguish and fear. But while Carroll, even when portraying our most nightmarish experiences, does not provide consolatory solutions, only rich questions in the style of the ancient oracles, the ersatz *Alice*-texts shower us with tidy answers, clipped and rounded and superficially satisfying, catechisms that lend their readers the illusion of having solved immemorial riddles which, because of their very nature, must remain unresolved.

In our time, in order to create and maintain the huge and efficient machinery of financial profit, we have collectively chosen speed over deliberate slowness, intuitive responses over detailed critical reflection, the satisfaction of reaching snap conclusions rather than the pleasure of concentrating on the tension between various possibilities without demanding a conclusive end. If profit is the goal, creativity must suffer. Discussing the lack of support for scientific research outside the private industries, I once heard a scientist comment, "Electricity was not invented by attempting to produce better lamps."

Notoriously, every age develops its own artistic genre for its own brand of fools. In the Middle Ages, the charlatan's sermons and fortune-teller's prophecies were two of the most popular; in Carroll's day, it was the three-volume "silly" novel and the moral tales. In ours, the fool's art par excellence is the art of advertising—commercial, political, or religious—the ability to create desire for the preys of moth and rust. Advertising begins with a lie, with the assertion that Brand X is more important, or more necessary, or merely better than other brands, and that its possession, like that of the magic objects in fairy tales, will make the owner wiser, more beautiful, more powerful, than his or her neighbor. The willing suspension of disbelief that Coleridge demanded from the reader is tempered in advertising by an induced and simultaneous suspension of belief: the goods or services advertised require not so much belief or disbelief as a kind of bland faith in the imaginary thing created, in which colorful, innocuous images, conventional but voided symbols, simple reassurances or commands lull the viewer into a state of vacuous longing. These images surround us now at all times and everywhere. When we speak of a modern "culture of images," we forget that such a culture was present since the days of our prehistoric ancestors, only the images on caves, in medieval churches, or on Aztec temple walls carried profound and complex meanings, while ours are deliberately banal and shallow. It is not fortuitous that advertising companies control the contemporary art market in which that same deliberate banality and shallowness have been transformed into qualities that justify the monetary value of a work.

Both qualities, however, respond to a view of the world. The world, as we recognize from the moment we are born, is a library of signs, an archive of mysterious texts, a gallery of compelling images, some arbitrary or haphazard, some deliberately created, which we feel we are meant to decipher and read. A natural inclination, what Professor Giovanna Franci calls "the anxiety to interpret," leads us to believe that everything is language, pictures of a vocabulary whose key may be lost, or never existed, or must be wrought again to unlock the pages of the universal book. Plants, animals, clouds, the faces and gestures of others, landscapes and sea currents, constellations and forest tracks have their equivalent in pictographs and ideograms, in letters and coded signals with which we attempt to mirror our experience of the world. The Aztecs called their colored manuscripts *maps*, a better word to make explicit this relationship than our neutral *text*.

But there is also such a thing as a false map that leads nowhere except back to itself. The Hatter has been father to a huge mass of such cartography produced in the past twenty or thirty years by philosophers, sociologists, and economists, who, couching their arguments in elegant language and protected by some version of freedom of speech, defend the virtues of greed and self-enrichment and lend intellectual weight to those who use their power to achieve them. Holding on to what he has and yet always grasping for something else, the Hatter offers others nothing and, pointing to his laid-out table, tells the others to take more, and to believe that "it's very easy to take *more* than nothing . . ." It is not very easy to take more than nothing, as millions on our planet know. But the rules of the mad tea party are those of the world we have constructed so that we can keep for ourselves vast spaces meant for many, so that we can offer wine that is not there and "more" tea to someone who has had none, so that we can appropriate fresh territory after we have spoiled the one we have been occupying. To amass more than we can possibly need or enjoy, to propose to others participation in a common culture that is being eroded daily and gradually replaced with "nothing," to suggest to the poor and needy that they help themselves to "more" of the common wealth when they had none in the first place, to clear-cut, mine out, or fish dry vast areas of our planet and then move on to others, leaving behind our spillage and waste, are the methods of our global madness, regardless of whether we are dealing with fellow human beings, forests, seas, the earth we inhabit, or the air we breathe. They are methods by which we appear to share fortunes and misfortunes with others when in reality we share nothing, we hand over nothing, we hide our wine and hold on to our tea and feel comforted by what we believe we see.

"When we look into a mirror," wrote Harold Pinter in his Nobel Prize lecture, "we think the image that confronts us is accurate. But move a millimetre and the image changes. We are actually looking at a never-ending range of reflections. But sometimes a writer has to smash the mirror—for it is on the other side of that mirror that the truth stares at us. I believe that despite the enormous odds which exist, unflinching, unswerving, fierce intellectual determination, as citizens, to define the *real* truth of our lives and our societies is a crucial obligation which devolves upon us all. It is in fact mandatory. If such a determination is not embodied in our political vision we have no hope of restoring what is so nearly lost to us—the dignity of man."

At the Mad Hatter's table sit today not the imaginary creatures met by Alice but painfully real beings: the inheritors of Cortés, reducing all creation to sticks and stones; the merchants for whom the only measure of value is that of financial profit and who believe that the surest way to bigger earnings is the lowering of the public's intellectual level; the catechists, for whom art is not a dialogue and an exchange of questions but a series of simpleminded and stifling answers; the rag-and-bone vendors who can turn anything into a salable commodity; the philosophers who, in the name of personal considerations or abstract notions of justice, lend arguments to those in power, and false justification; the egotists who, under the protection of civic freedom, believe that tolerance is a virtue that allows for the distinction between "those above" and "those below"; the advertisers of trite virtues and creators of false needs; the religious leaders who believe that the deity has granted their church, and no other, grace, illumination, and a privileged position above that of all other creeds; the revolutionaries for whom there can be no purification without destruction; the political leaders for whom wealth and power are proof of righteousness and moral authority. In a word, the enemies of "the dignity of man."

Alice and her Wonderland shadows play out for us the parts we enact in the real world. Their folly is tragic or amusing, they are themselves exemplary fools or they are eloquent witnesses to the folly of their shadowy brethren, they tell us stories of absurd or mad behavior which mirrors our own so that we may better see and understand it. The difference is that their folly, unlike ours, is framed by the margins of the page, contained by the however-uncertain imagination of their author. Crimes and evil deeds in the real world have sources so deep and consequences so distant that we can never hold them entirely in our understanding, we can merely clip them in a moment, box them in a judicial file, or observe them under the lens of psychoanalysis. Our deeds, unlike those of the great mad creatures of literature, seep far and wide into the world, infecting everything and every place beyond all help and purpose.

The folly of the world is unintelligible. We can (and do, of course) experience it, suffer it in the flesh and in the mind, fall under its merciless weight and be crushed by its implacable movement towards the precipice. We can even, in certain enlightened moments, rise through it to acts of extraordinary humanity, irrationally wise and insanely daring. For such acts, no words suffice. And yet, through language at its best, our folly can be trapped in its own doings, made to repeat itself, made to enact its cruelties and catastrophes (and even its glorious deeds) but this time under lucid observation and with protected emotion, beneath the aseptic covering of words, lit by the reading lamp set over the open book.

The flesh-and-blood beings at the Mad Hatter's table—the military leaders, the torturers, the international bankers, the terrorists, the exploiters—cannot be forced to tell their story, to confess, to beg forgiveness, to admit that they are rational beings guilty of willful cruelty and destructive acts. But tales can be told and books can be written about them that might allow for a certain understanding of what they have done and for a judicious empathy. Their deeds bear no rational explanation, follow absurd logical rules, but their madness and their terror can be trapped for us, in all their consuming and illuminating fire, inside stories or "maps" where they can mysteriously lend our folly a kind of enlightened rationality, transparent enough to clarify our behavior and ambiguous enough to help us accept the indefinable.

PART EIGHT

The Numinous Library

"Now I declare that's too bad!" Humpty Dumpty cried, breaking into a sudden passion. "You've been listening at doors — and behind trees — and down chimneys — or you couldn't have known it!"

"I haven't indeed!" Alice said very gently. "It's in a book."

Through the Looking-Glass, Chapter 6

Notes Towards a Definition
of the Ideal Library

And noticed that they were filled with cupboards and bookshelves.

Alice's Adventures in Wonderland, Chapter 1

THE IDEAL LIBRARY IS MEANT for one particular reader. Every reader must feel that he or she is the chosen one.

Above the door of the ideal library is written a variation of Rabelais's motto: "LYS CE QUE VOUDRA," "Read what you will."

The ideal library is both virtual and material. It allows for every technology, every container, every manifestation of the text.

The ideal library is of easy access. No high stairs, no slippery esplanades, no confusing multiplicity of doors, no intimidating guards must stand between the reader and the books.

The ideal library has comfortable but supportive seats with armrests and a curved back, like those of the lamented Salle Labrouste at the Bibliothèque nationale de France. The ideal library has ample desks, preferably with smooth leather tops, sockets for electronic equipment (on condition that they perform in utter silence), and soft individual lights that remind you of the green-glass reading lamps at the Colegio Nacional de Buenos Aires.

In 1250, Richard de Fournival compared the ideal library to a *hortus conclusus*, a walled garden.

The ideal library has warm walls of brick or wood, and also cool glass windows that open onto peaceful vistas. The ideal library is never a hortus entirely conclusus.

The ideal library holds mainly, but not only, books. It also collects maps, pictures, objects, music, voices, films, and photographs. The ideal library is a reading place in the broadest meaning of the term.

The ideal library allows every reader access to the stacks. A reader must be granted the freedom of chance encounters.

No shelf in the ideal library is higher or lower than the reach of the reader's arm. The ideal library does not require acrobatics.

In the ideal library it is never too warm or too cold.

The ideal library organizes without labeling.

No section in the ideal library is conclusive.

The map of the ideal library is its catalogue.

The ideal library has easy and plentiful access to food, drink, and photo-copying machines.

The ideal library is both secluded and public, intimate and open to social intercourse, meant for meditation and for dialogue, parsimonious and gener-ous, erudite and questioning, full of the despair of plenty and the hope of what has not yet been read.

The ideal library holds the promise of every possible book.

Every book in the ideal library has its echo in another.

The ideal library is an everlasting, ever-renewed anthology.

The ideal library has no closing hours.

The ideal library allows scribbling in its books.

The ideal library is both popular and secret. It holds all the acknowledged classics and all the classics known to only a few readers. In the ideal library Dante's *Commedia* sits next to Phil Cousineau's *Deadlines,* Montaigne's *Essays* next to Eduardo Lourenço's *Montaigne,* Flaubert's *Madame Bovary* next to Edgardo Cozarinsky's *The Bride of Odessa,* Dostoyevsky's *The Brothers Kara-mazov* next to Lázló Flöldényi's *Dostoyevsky Reads Hegel in Siberia and Bursts into Tears.*

In the ideal library, the reader's task is to subvert the established order.

The number of books in the ideal library varies. The Library of Alexandria is said to have held seven hundred thousand scrolls; Jorge Luis Borges's book-shelves contained barely five hundred volumes; the Birkenau concentration camp for children had a clandestine library of eight precious books that had to be hidden away in a different place every night.

Even when built out of walls and shelves and books, the ideal library is in the mind. The ideal library is the remembered library.

The ideal library suggests one continuous text with no discernable begin-ning and no foreseeable end.

In the ideal library there are no forbidden books and no recommended books.

The ideal library is familiar both to Saint Jerome and to Noam Chomsky.

In the ideal library no reader ever feels unwanted.

Every page in the ideal library is the first. None is the last.

Like Paul Valéry's boxes in the brain, the ideal library has sections inscribed thus: *To study on a more favorable occasion. Never to be thought about. Useless to go into further. Contents unexamined. Pointless business. Known treasure that can only be examined in a second life. Urgent. Dangerous. Delicate. Impossible. Abandoned. Reserved. Let others deal with this! My strong point. Difficult. Etc.*

The ideal library disarms the curse of Babel.

The ideal library symbolizes everything a society stands for. A society depends on its libraries to know who it is because libraries are society's memory.

The ideal library can grow endlessly without demanding more physical space, and can offer knowledge of everything without demanding more physical time. As a beautiful impossibility, the ideal library exists outside time and outside space.

Ancient ossuaries bore the inscription "What you are, we once were; what we are, you shall be." Much the same can be said of the ideal library's books and of their readers.

The ideal library is not an ossuary.

Some of the earliest libraries were kept by Egyptian priests, who furnished the departed souls with books to guide them through the kingdom of the dead. The ideal library maintains this soul-guiding function.

The ideal library both renews and preserves its collection. The ideal library is fluid.

There are certain books that, in themselves, are an ideal library. Examples: Melville's *Moby-Dick*, Dante's *Commedia*, Chateaubriand's *Mémoires d'outre-tombe*.

No compass is necessary in the ideal library. Its physical appearance is also its intellectual structure.

The architect of the ideal library is, first and foremost, an ideal reader.

The impossible task of every tyrant is to destroy the ideal library.

The impossible task of every reader is to rebuild the ideal library.

The ideal library (like every library) holds at least one line that has been written exclusively for you.

The Library of the
Wandering Jew

"A slow sort of country!" said the Queen. "Now, *here*, you see,
it takes all the running *you* can do, to keep in the same place.
If you want to get somewhere else, you must run at least twice
as fast as that."
Through the Looking-Glass, Chapter 2

WHEN I WAS FIVE YEARS OLD, my family spent a summer in Garmisch-
Partenkirchen, a postcard Alpine village with geranium-filled balconies, heart-
shaped openings in the shutters, and orange cows that waddled through the
little streets at dusk, sounding their copper bells. In those days, I had no sense
of my social or cultural identity: I didn't know that my family was Jewish, and
therefore I had no notion of how strange it was for a Jewish family to choose,
as a holiday destination less than a decade after the war, a village that had
been one of Hitler's favorite haunts. Deep-blue woods rose on the surrounding
slopes, and often we trekked up the shaded paths to one of the hilltops for a
picnic. One of these paths was a via Crucis, each station sculpted in wood and
set high up on a pole: fourteen little scenes that led, as through a comic strip,
from Christ's trial and sentencing to the laying out of his body in the tomb.
My nurse (a Czech Jew who had escaped the Nazis, and who possessed little
imagination and less humor) knew the story of the Passion only vaguely, and
her explanation of the various images never quite satisfied me. One scene,
however, that of Christ's third fall, she seemed to know well. Christ, having
stumbled twice under the weight of the Cross, stumbles once more, this time
by the door of a Jewish cobbler called Ahasuerus. The cobbler pitilessly pushes
Christ away, telling him to move on. "I will move on," Christ answers, "but
you will tarry till I come!" From that day onwards, Ahasuerus is condemned to

wander the earth and is only allowed to stop here and there for short respites. His shoes and his clothes never wear out completely, and every hundred years he is miraculously rejuvenated. His beard hangs down to his feet, he carries five coins in his pocket that match the five wounds of the man he offended, and he is able to speak every language in the world. Since he is a little over two thousand years old, he has witnessed countless events of historical importance and knows every story there is to tell.

Though the Eternal Wanderer, condemned because of a sin committed or a promise not kept, has a few precursors in Jewish, Islamic, and early Christian and even Buddhist literature, the story as we know it first makes its appearance some time in the thirteenth century. The earliest datable telling is Italian, tucked away in a Bolognese chronicle spanning the years 781 to 1228. In 1223, according to the chronicle, a group of pilgrims arrived at the abbey of Ferrara and informed the abbot that when traveling in Armenia, they had met a certain Jew who had revealed to them that he had been present at the Passion and had driven Christ from his door, and was thus cursed till the Second Coming. "This Jew," the chronicle explains, "is said, every hundred years, to be made young to the age of thirty, and he cannot die until the Lord returns."

Five years after the Italian chronicle, Roger of Wendover, an Englishman staying at the monastery of Saint Albans, northwest of London, described a similar encounter in his *Flores historiarum*. Obviously based on the Bolognese account, Wendover's story, told in much greater detail, was considered for centuries to be the authentic one, though the name of the man and the circumstances of his curse differ from the version we know today. According to Wendover, in 1228 an Armenian bishop visiting Saint Albans told his hosts that back in Armenia, a very pious man named Joseph (nothing is said of his being Jewish) had often eaten at the bishop's table. This Joseph had been present at the trial of Christ, and when, after Pilate's judgment, Christ was dragged away to be crucified, one of Pilate's porters, a certain Cartaphilus, struck him on the back with his hand and said mockingly: "Go quicker, Jesus, go quicker; why do you loiter?" And Jesus, looking on him with severity, replied, "I'm going, and you will wait till I return." After Christ's death, Cartaphilus was baptized by Ananias (who also baptized the apostle Paul) and was called Joseph. He lives mainly in Armenia, preaches the word of the Lord, and places his hope of salvation on the fact that he sinned through ignorance.

Roger of Wendover's chronicle gave rise to a number of variant versions. In the Mediterranean countries, Cartaphilus became Buttadeus (He Who Beats

or Pushes God); in French, Boutedieu; in Italian, Botadeo, which in turn became Votadeo (Devoted to God), translated into Spanish as Juan Espera en
Dios, into Portuguese as João Espera em Dios, and again into Italian, this time
as Giovanni Servo di Dio. Under these various names, the Wandering Jew appears in the work of many major Western writers, from Chaucer to Cervantes,
from Francisco Rodrigues Lobo to Mark Twain, from Eugène Sue to Fruttero
& Lucentini.

The most influential of all the early versions of the legend, in that it lent
the Wandering Jew a tangible contemporary presence, was a small German
pamphlet published in 1602 under the title *Kurtze Beschreibung und Erzehlung
/sic/ von einem Juden mit Namen Ahasuerus* (Short Description and Narrative
of a Jew Called Ahasuerus). It tells how the bishop of Schleswig, in his youth,
had visited Hamburg in the year 1542 and there had seen in church one Sunday "a man who was a very tall person, with long hair reaching down over his
shoulders, standing barefoot by the chancel." The soles of his feet were hard as
horn, and so thick that one could measure them with two fingers held across.
The stranger turned out to be Ahasuerus, the Jew who drove Christ away
from his door. He told the bishop that at the time of Christ's Passion he was a
shoemaker, and after he was cursed he had wandered without respite through
the world. To the bishop's astonishment, Ahasuerus was able to describe in
detail "the lives, sufferings, and deaths of the holy apostles." Years later, in
1575, the Schleswig ambassadors to Spain reported back to the bishop that they
had seen a stranger with similar traits in Madrid, and he spoke good Spanish.
(Later versions lend him the power to speak all the languages that sprang up
in Babel.) "What are we to think of this man?" concludes the pamphlet. "One
may be free in his judgment. The works of God are wonderful and inscrutable,
and as time goes on they will be more so, and more things hitherto hidden will
be revealed, particularly . . . on the approaching Day of Judgment and end of
the world."

The story of the tireless wanderer haunted my dreams. I did not feel his
fate as a curse; I thought how wonderful it would be to travel alone and endlessly, to visit every country in the world and to meet all sorts of extraordinary
people; above all, to be able to read any book that fell into my hands. Until the
age of eight, my only languages were English and German. I had enviously
scrutinized the Hebrew letters in my father's coffee-table Haggadah, and the
Arabic inscriptions on the boxes of Egyptian dates that my mother ordered
from Cairo, and the Spanish words in the storybooks sent to me from Buenos

Aires by an enterprising aunt who hoped they would encourage me to learn my native language. All these scripts were as tantalizing and mysterious as the secret codes that appeared in the Sherlock Holmes stories. I envied the Wandering Jew's ability to read in the universal library.

Because behind every idea of universality lies that of the knowledge of that universality. Behind every overwhelming nightmare of an almost infinite universe lies the mad dream of Babel, to reach its unattainable limit, and the mad dream of Alexandria, to hold under one roof all that can be known of its mysterious nature. A blend of Babel and Alexandria, every library, however small, is a universal library in potentia, since every book declares its lineage of all other books, and every shelf must admit its helplessness to contain them. The essence of a library is that it humbly and magnificently proclaims at the same time its ambitions and its shortcomings. Every time a reader opens a book on the first page, he is opening the countless series of books that line our shelves from the morning on which writing was invented to the last afternoon of the future. It is all there, every story, every experience, every terrible and glorious secret: we lack only the perspicacity, the patience, the strength, the space, the time. All of us, except the Wandering Jew.

To see the Wandering Jew's fate not as a curse but as a blessing may be less odd than we might think. Two conflicting impulses rule our short time on earth: one draws us forward, towards the distant horizon, curious to find out what awaits beyond; the other roots us to one place and weds us to one sky. Both impulses are ours, define us as human beings as much as self-consciousness and its corollary, language. The impulse to move on and the impulse to stand still shape our sense of place; the urge to know who we are and the urge to question that knowledge define our sense of time.

Stateless wanderers and city dwellers, cattle herders and crop farmers, explorers and householders (or, in literary terms, Enkidu and Gilgamesh, Cain and Abel, Odysseus and Penelope) have, throughout time, embodied these two longings, one for what lies outside, the other for what lies within. And two moments in Christ's Passion, two stations in his via Crucis, symbolize, I think, these opposing forces. The moving and the questioning are acted out in the ninth station, when the meeting with Ahasuerus takes place; the standing still and the mirroring of self occur in the sixth station, when Veronica places a cloth on Christ's agonized face and finds his traits miraculously embedded in the fabric.

These vital forces compete with and complement each other. To move away from the place we call ours allows us a better sense of our true identity but at the same time distracts us from self-reflection; to sit at a steadfast point helps us unveil that identity in communion with the numinous but also renders the task impossible by blinding us to what defines us in the surrounding, tangible world. We must move to meet those others who provide the shifting mirrors by means of which we piece together our self-portrait. And yet there must be a steadfast place in which we can stand and, by seeing what Yeats called "the face I had before the world was made," pronounce the word *I*.

As a child, I made no clear distinction between my own identity and that which books created for me. What I mean is that I didn't consciously differentiate between the roles books invented for me (Sinbad or Crusoe) and those which became mine through family circumstances and genetic makeup. I was that first-person singular whom I read and dreamt about, and the world overflowed from the page into conventional reality and back again. Space was that which Sinbad's magic carpet forded, and time the long years Crusoe spent waiting to be rescued. Later, when the differences between everyday life and nighttime stories crept up on me, I realized that in a certain measure I had been given, thanks to my books, the words that helped make the one meaningful and the other intelligible, and offered a degree of consolation for both.

It may be that, of all the instruments we have invented to help us along the path of self-discovery, books are the most useful, the most practical, the most concrete. By lending words to our bewildering experience, books become compasses that embody the four cardinal points: mobility and stability, self-reflection and the gift of looking outward. The old metaphor that sees the world as a book we read and in which we too are read merely recognizes this guiding, all-encompassing quality. In a book, no one point is exclusively the north, since whichever is chosen, the other three remain actively present. Even after Ulysses has returned home to sit by his quiet hearth, Ithaca remains a port of call on the shores of the beckoning sea, one among the countless volumes of the universal library; Dante, reaching the supreme vision of love holding bound "into one volume all the leaves whose flight / Is scattered through the universe around" (legato con amore in un volume, / ciò che per l'universo si squaderna), feels his will and his desire turned by that love "that moves the sun and the other stars" (ma già volgeva il mio disio e l'*velle*, / sì come rota ch'igualmente è mossa, / l'amor che move il sole e l'altre stelle). Likewise the reader who in the end finds the page written for him, a part of the vast, monstrous volume made up by all the libraries and lending sense to the universe.

And yet, almost all the depictions of the Wandering Jew show him bookless, keen on finding salvation in the world of flesh and stone, not that of words. This feels wrong. In the most popular of the fictionalized versions, Eugène Sue's nineteenth-century *roman-feuilleton, Le Juif errant,* the underlying theme is the wicked Jesuit plot to govern the world; the intellectual undertakings of the timeless Wanderer himself are not explored. On Ahasuerus's ongoing journey (according to Sue) libraries are merely gathering rooms in aristocratic houses, and books either pious tracts or evil catalogues of sin under the guise of Jesuitical confession manuals.

But it is hard to believe that a merciful God would condemn anyone to a worldwide waiting room without reading material. Instead, I imagine Ahasuerus granted two thousand years of itinerant reading; I imagine him visiting the world's great libraries and bookstores, exhausting and replenishing his book bag with whatever new titles appear during his travels, from Marco Polo's *Il milione* to Cervantes's *Don Quixote,* from Xueqin Cao's *Dream of Red Mansions* to Virginia Woolf's *Orlando,* in which (like all readers) he will find traces of his own curious destiny. Closer to our time, so as not be overladen, the Wanderer travels perhaps with an e-book, which he periodically recharges at an Internet café. And in his reader's mind, the pages, printed and virtual, overlay and blend and create new stories from a colossal mass of remembered and half-remembered readings, multiplying his books by a thousand, again and again.

And yet, even in the Universal Library, the Wandering Jew, like the Ideal Reader, can never be satisfied, can never be limited by the circumference of one Ithaca, of one quest, of one book. For him the horizon of every page must always—thankfully, we say—exceed his wit and his grasp, so that every last page becomes the first. Because, as we have said, every book once ended leads to another lying patiently in wait, and every rereading grants the book a Protean new life. Ahasuerus's library (which, like all the best readers, he carries mainly in his head) echoes through mirrored galleries that gloss and comment on every text. Every library is a library of memory: first, because it holds the experience of the past, and second, because it lives on in the mind of each of its readers.

The Jews know this practice well. Long after the destruction of the Temple of Jerusalem, Jews in scattered lands continued to carry out the appointed rituals, moving about in a space that no longer existed in stone and mortar, but only in the words set down for their guidance. That is the nature of all exile: it affirms the perseverance of memory. Expelled from their native al-Andalus, the Arabs of Córdoba, Toledo, and Granada continued to recite the verses that their Spanish landscape had inspired; as refugees in South America and Canada, the Armenians who survived the Turkish massacre rewrote the libraries destroyed in their Anatolian homeland; the survivors of the military dictatorships in Chile and Argentina created publishing companies in their new countries for the literature that continued to be written in spite of the blood-imposed silence; in Paris, the Cubans who fled Castro's regime borrowed the French language and tailored it to suit the retelling of their stories; in London, Mahmoud Darwich blended the Palestinian cadence of his verses with his readings of Borges, Paul Eluard, and Emily Dickinson; Vladimir Nabokov carried with him into his American exile the Russian dictionary which held, he said, the building blocks of all his childhood reading. The examples are, unfortunately, countless. The condemned crowds outside the city walls, Ahasuerus's traveling companions in the detention camps of Calais, Lampedusa, Málaga, and scores of other places carrying with them the tattered libraries of their past, are so vast and varied that our protected inner citadels seem desolate and despoiled by comparison. In our anxiety to punish our enemies and protect ourselves, we have forgotten what it is that we are meant to be securing. In our exacerbated fear, we have allowed our own rights and freedoms to be distorted or curtailed. Instead of locking the other out we have locked ourselves in. We have forgotten that our libraries should open onto the world, not pretend to isolate us from it. We have become our own prisoners.

That is the deeper meaning of the Wandering Jew's punishment, and its inevitable consequence, because no curse is ever one-sided. The legend of the man condemned to wander because of an uncharitable act became an uncharitable act in which many men were condemned to wander. Pogroms, expulsions, ethnic cleansings, genocides regardless of nationality or creed are the abominable extensions of this reading of the legend. But I suggest there might be others, like the one I intuited as a child when I first heard the story.

Eternal wandering as a punishment or as an enlightening exploration of the world; a fine and private place as a reward or as the dreaded and silent grave; the "other" as an anonymous enemy or as a reflection of ourselves; ourselves as single, solitary creatures or as part of a multitudinous, timeless, world-conscious being. Perhaps Christ's words to the Jewish cobbler were meant not to punish but to teach that charity is of the essence, because, as we are told by Saint Paul, charity "rejoiceth in truth." Perhaps what Christ meant was that in order to learn why the underdog must not be mocked and why the needy must not be pushed away from our door we must go out into the world and live among our neighbors and be the underdog, the needy, and understand that, whoever and wherever we are, we always wander outside a city wall.

I said that libraries carry in their essence the ambition of Babel to conquer space and of Alexandria to outlive time. I said that they are our collective memory, divided into the myriad memories of generations and generations of individual readers. I want to add that, as if the knowledge were embedded in their genes, libraries understand that the walls that surround them are mere scaffolding and that their place is the wide, open world of those readers who, in desert plains, first recorded their experience and imagination on hand-held clay tablets. Because of the power that reading grants us, to see with the eyes of others and speak with the tongues of the dead, because of the possibilities of enlightenment and of witnessing and of wisdom that libraries hold, our fears invented for us, as readers, the image of the ivory tower, of the Sleeping Beauty castle that keeps us bound by pretty words, far away from the world of reality. The contrary, of course, is true. Don Quixote's reading may make him see windmills as giants and sheep as enemy soldiers, but these, as he himself secretly guesses, are only imaginary constructs, metaphors to better recognize the true suffering of flesh and blood, and the imperative to be just in an unjust world. Madame Bovary finds in books the ideal romances that she will never find in life, but that lying perfection lends her the strength to refuse unhappiness and subservience as her lifelong lot. Children know that Little Red Riding Hood isn't real and that wolves don't habitually haunt the woods, but the frightening story confirms an ineffable knowledge that childhood is a dangerous place where dark things roam and nothing is as it seems. Books force us to look upon the world.

But whether we wander to lose or to find ourselves, in libraries and on roads, depends on our own will, not on the hostile or welcoming cities that lie behind and before us. We can allow ourselves to be anchored in a shallow page, never moving forward or, like the Wandering Jew, steer forward with the flow, on and on, towards the enlarging horizon. "For my part," wrote Robert Louis Stevenson, one of the most charitable of men, "I travel not to go anywhere, but to go. I travel for travel's sake. The great affair is to move."

The Library as Home

She contented herself with turning round, looking at the shelves
as she came to them . . . but the oddest part of it all was that,
whenever she looked hard at any shelf, to make out exactly what
it had on it, that particular shelf was always quite empty, though
the others round it were crowded as full as they could hold.
Through the Looking-Glass, Chapter 5

FOR THE PAST SEVEN YEARS, I have lived in an old stone presbytery in
France, south of the Loire Valley, in a village of fewer than ten houses. I chose
the place because next to the house itself was a barn, partly torn down centuries ago, large enough to accommodate my library of some thirty thousand
books, assembled over six itinerant decades. I knew that once the books found
their place, I would find mine.

My library is not a single beast but a composite of many others, a fantastic
animal made up of the several libraries built and then abandoned, over and
over again, throughout my life. I can't remember a time in which I did not
have a library of some sort. The present library is a sort of multilayered autobiography, each book holding the moment in which I read it for the first time.
The scribbles on the margins, the occasional date on the flyleaf, the faded bus
ticket marking a page for a reason today mysterious all try to remind me of
who I was then. For the most part, they fail. My memory is less interested in
me than in my books, and I find it easier to remember the story read once than
the young man who then read it.

One of my earliest memories (I must have been two or three at the time)
is of a shelfful of books on the wall above my cot from which my nurse would
choose a bedtime story. This was my first library; when I learned to read by
myself a year or so later, the shelf, transferred now to safe ground level, be-

came my private domain. I remember arranging and rearranging my books according to secret rules that I invented for myself: all the Golden Books series had to be grouped together, the fat collections of fairy tales were not allowed to touch the minuscule Beatrix Potters, stuffed animals were not permitted to sit on the same shelf as the books. I told myself that if these rules were upset, terrible things would happen. Superstition and the art of libraries are tightly entwined.

My first library stood in a house in Tel Aviv, where my father was the Argentinean ambassador; my next library grew in Buenos Aires during my adolescence. Before returning to Argentina, my father had asked his secretary to buy enough books to fill the shelves of his library in our new house; obligingly, she ordered cartloads of volumes from a secondhand dealer but found, when trying to place them on the shelves, that many of them wouldn't fit. Undaunted, she had them trimmed down to size and then bound in deep-green leather, a color which, combined with the dark oak, lent the place the atmosphere of a soft forest. I pilfered books from that library to stock my own, which covered three of the walls in my bedroom. Reading these circumcised books required the extra effort of supplanting the missing bit of every page, an exercise that no doubt trained me to read later the "cut-up" novels of William Burroughs.

The library of my adolescence contained almost every book that still matters to me today; few essential books have been added. Generous teachers, passionate booksellers, friends for whom giving a book was a supreme act of intimacy and trust helped me build it. Their ghosts kindly haunt my shelves, and the books they gave still carry their voices, so that now, when I open Isak Dinesen's *Gothic Tales* or Blas de Otero's early poems, I have the impression not of reading the book myself but of being read to out loud. This is one of the reasons I never feel alone in my library.

I left my books behind when I set off for Europe in 1969, some time before the military dictatorship. I suppose that had I stayed, like so many of my friends, I would have had to destroy my library for fear of the police, since in those terrible days one could be accused of subversion merely for being seen with a book that looked suspicious (someone I knew was arrested as a Communist for carrying with him *The Red and the Black*). Argentinean plumbers found that there was an unprecedented call for their services, since many readers tried to burn their books in their toilet bowls, causing the porcelain to crack.

In every place I settled, a library began to grow almost on its own. In Paris and in London, in the humid heat of Tahiti, where I worked as a publisher for five long years (my Melville still shows traces of Polynesian mold), in Toronto and in Calgary, I collected books and then, when the time came to leave, packed them up in boxes to wait patiently inside tomblike storage spaces in the uncertain hope of resurrection. Every time I would ask myself how it had happened, this exuberant accumulation of paper and ink that once again would cover my walls like ivy.

The library as it now stands, between long walls whose stones carry in some places the signature of their fifteenth-century masons, houses under a ceiling of weathered beams the remnants of all those previous libraries, including, from my earliest one, Grimm's *Fairy Tales* in two volumes, printed in somber Gothic script, and a scribbled copy of *The Tailor of Gloucester*. There are only a few books that a serious bibliophile would find worthy: an illuminated Bible from a thirteenth-century German scriptorium (a gift from the novelist Yehuda Elberg), half a dozen contemporary artists' books, a few first editions and signed copies. But I have neither the funds nor the knowledge to become a professional collector, and in my library shiny young Penguins sit happily side by side with severe-looking leather-bound patriarchs.

Because unlike a public library mine requires no common codes that other readers must understand and share, I have organized it simply according to my own requirements and prejudices. A certain zany logic governs its geography. Its major divisions are determined by the language in which the books are written: that is to say, without distinction of genre, all books written originally in Spanish or French, English or Arabic come together on the same shelves. I allow myself, however, many exceptions. Certain subjects—books on the history of the book, biblical studies, versions of the legend of Faust, Renaissance literature and philosophy, gay studies, medieval bestiaries—all have their separate sections. Certain authors are privileged: I have thousands of detective novels but very few spy stories, more Plato than Aristotle, all Zola and hardly any Maupassant, almost all of John Hawkes and Cynthia Ozick but hardly any of the authors on the *New York Times* best-seller list. I have dozens of very bad books which I don't throw away in case I ever need an example of a book I think is bad. The only book I ever banished from my library was Bret Easton Ellis's *American Psycho*, which I felt infected the shelves with its prurient descriptions of deliberately inflicted pain. I put it in the garbage; I didn't give it to anyone because I wouldn't give away a book I wasn't fond of. Nor do I lend books. If I want someone to read a book, I'll buy a copy and offer it as a gift. I believe that to lend a book is an incitement to theft.

Like every library, mine will eventually exceed the space allotted to it. Barely seven years after it was set up, it has already spread into the main body of house, which I had hoped to keep free of bookshelves. Travelogues, books on music and film, anthologies of various kinds cover now the walls of several rooms. My detective novels fill one of the guest bedrooms, known now familiarly as the Murder Room. There is a story by Julio Cortázar, "House Taken Over," in which a brother and sister are forced to move from room to room as something unnamed occupies inch by inch their entire house, eventually forcing them out into the street. I foresee a day in which my books, like that anonymous invader, will complete their gradual conquest. I will then be banished to the garden, but, knowing the way of books, I fear that even that seemingly safe place may not be entirely beyond my library's hungry ambition.

The End of Reading

"There's no use trying," she said: "one can't believe
impossible things."

"I daresay you haven't had much practice," said the
Queen. "When I was your age, I always did it for half-an-hour
a day. Why, sometimes I've believed as many as six impossible
things before breakfast."

Through the Looking-Glass, Chapter 5

"WHY SHOULD WE HAVE LIBRARIES filled with books?" asked a smiling
young futurologist at a recent library convention. (Futurology, for those who
don't read science-fiction, is a branch of electronics that forecasts future technologies and their prospective uses.) "Why waste valuable space to store endless masses of printed text that can be easily enclosed in a minuscule and re-
silient chip? Why force readers to travel all the way to a library, wait to find
out if the book they want is there, and, if it is, lug it back to keep for a limited
time only? Why deny readers access to thousands of titles that their nearest
library doesn't hold? Why yield to the threats of acid corrosion, brittle bind-
ings, fading ink, moths, mice, and worms, theft, fire, and water when all of
Alexandria can be had at your fingertips from the comfort of any place you
choose? The truth is that reading as we knew it is no longer a universal necessity, and libraries should relinquish those noble but antiquated receptacles of
text we call books and adopt once and for all the electronic text, as they once
relinquished clay tablets and parchment scrolls in favor of the codex. Accept
the inevitable: the age of Gutenberg has come to an end."

Unfortunately, or fortunately, the speech I have paraphrased is based on
a misconception. The notion of a scattered library reborn in all its richness
wherever a reader might find himself has a certain Pentecostal loveliness, each

reader receiving, like the fire that rained on the apostles from Heaven, the gift of numberless tongues. But just as a certain text is never expressed identically in different tongues, books and electronic memories, like electronic memories and the memories we hold in our mind, are different creatures and possess different natures, even when the text they carry is the same. As I argued in "Saint Augustine's Computer," they are instruments of particular kinds, and their qualities serve diverse purposes in our attempt to know the world. Therefore any opposition that forces us to eliminate one of them is worse than false: it is useless. To be able to find, in seconds, a half-remembered quotation from Statius or to be able to read at a moment's notice a recondite letter from Plato is something almost anyone can do today, without the erudition of Saint Jerome, thanks to the electronic technology. But to be able to retire with a dog-eared book, revisiting familiar haunts and scribbling on the margins over previous annotations, comforted by paper and ink, is something almost anyone should still be able to do, thanks to the persistence of the codex. Each technology has its own merits, and therefore it may be more useful to leave aside this crusading view of the electronic word vanquishing the printed one and explore instead each technology according to its particular merits.

Perhaps it is in the nature of traditional libraries that, unlike the human brain, the container is less ambitious than the contents. We are told that the cerebral neurons are capable of much more knowledge than however much information we store in them, and that, in the maze of our lobes, many of the immeasurable shelves running along our secret corridors remain empty for the whole of our lives—causing librarians to lose their proverbial composure and seethe with righteous envy. From birth to death we accumulate words and images, emotions and sensations, intuitions and ideas, compiling our memory of the world, and however much we believe that we cram our minds with experience, there will always be space for more, as in one of those ancient parchments known as palimpsests, on which new texts were written over the old ones, again and again. "What is the human brain," asked Charles Baudelaire in 1869, "but an immense and natural palimpsest?" Like Baudelaire's almost infinite palimpsest, the library of the mind has no discernable limits. In the libraries of stone and glass, however, in those storerooms of the memory of society, space is always lacking, and in spite of bureaucratic restraint, reasoned selection, lack of funds, and willful or accidental destruction, there is never enough room for the books we wish to keep. To remedy this constraint, thanks to our technical skills, we have set up virtual libraries for which space approaches infinity. But even these electronic arks cannot rescue for posterity more than certain forms of the text itself. In those ghostly libraries, the concrete incarnation of the text is left behind, and the flesh of the word has no existence.

Virtual libraries have their advantages, but that does not mean that solid libraries are no longer needed, however hard the electronic industry may try to convince us of the contrary, however hard Google and its brethren may present themselves as philanthropical entities and not as exploiters of our intellectual patrimony. The World Digital Library, an international library supported both by UNESCO and by the U.S. Library of Congress, the Bibliothèque nationale de France, and other national libraries, is a colossal and important undertaking, and even though part of the funding comes from Google, it is (for the time being) free from commercial concerns. However, even when such remarkable virtual libraries are being built, traditional libraries are still of the essence. An electronic text is one thing, the identical text in a printed book is another, and they are not interchangeable, any more than a recorded line can replace a line embedded in an individual memory. Context, material support, the physical history and experience of a text are part of the text, as much as its vocabulary and its music. In the most literal sense, matter is not immaterial.

And the problems of traditional libraries—biased selection and subjective labeling, hierarchical cataloguing and its implied censorship, archival and circulating duties—continue to be, in any society that deems itself literate, essential problems. The library of the mind is haunted by the knowledge of all the books we'll never read and will therefore never rightfully call ours; the collective memorial libraries are haunted by all the books that never made it into the circle of the librarians' elect: books rejected, abandoned, restricted, despised, forbidden, unloved, ignored.

Following this pendular motion that rules our intellectual life, one question seems to tick away repeatedly, addressed both to the reader who despairs at the lack of time and to the society of readers who despair at the lack of space: to what purpose do we read? What is the reason for wanting to know more, for reaching towards the ever-retreating horizon of our intellectual exploring? Why collect the booty of such adventures in the vaults of our stone libraries and in our electronic memories? Why do it at all? The question asked by the keen futurologist can be deepened, and rather than wonder, Why is reading coming to an end? (a self-fulfilling assumption), we might ask instead, What is the end of reading?

Perhaps a personal example may help us examine the question.

Two weeks before Christmas 2008, I was told that I needed an urgent operation, so urgent in fact that I had no time to pack. I found myself lying in a pristine emergency room, uncomfortable and anxious, with no books except the one I had been reading that morning, Cees Nooteboom's delightful *In the Dutch Mountains,* which I finished in the next few hours. To spend the following fourteen days convalescing in a hospital without any reading material seemed to me a torture too great to bear, so when my partner suggested getting from my library a few books, I seized the opportunity gratefully. But which books did I want?

The author of Ecclesiastes and Pete Seeger have taught us that for everything there is a season; likewise, I might add, for every season there is a book. But readers have learned that not just any book is suited to any occasion. Pity the soul who finds itself with the wrong book in the wrong place, like poor Roald Amundsen, discoverer of the South Pole, whose book bag sank under the ice, so that he was constrained to read, night after freezing night, the only surviving volume: Dr. John Gauden's indigestible *Portraiture of His Sacred Majesty in His Solitudes and Sufferings.* Readers know that there are books for reading after lovemaking and books for waiting in the airport lounge, books for the breakfast table and books for the bathroom, books for sleepless nights at home and books for sleepless days in the hospital. No one, not even the best of readers, can fully explain why certain books are right for certain occasions and why others are not. In some ineffable way, like human beings, occasions and books mysteriously agree or clash with one another.

Why, at certain moments in our life, do we choose the companionship of one book over another? The list of titles Oscar Wilde requested in Reading Gaol included Stevenson's *Treasure Island* and a French-Italian conversation primer. Alexander the Great went on his campaigns with a copy of Homer's *Iliad.* John Lennon's murderer thought it fit to carry J. D. Salinger's *The Catcher in the Rye* when planning to commit his crime. Do astronauts take Ray Bradbury's *Martian Chronicles* on their journeys or, on the contrary, do they prefer André Gide's *Les Nourritures terrestres?* During Mr. Bernard Madoff's prison sentence, will he demand Dickens's *Little Dorrit* to read about how the embezzler Mr. Merdle, unable to bear the shame of being found out, cut his throat with a borrowed razor? Pope Benedict XIII, will he retire to his *studiolo* in the Castello Sant'Angelo with a copy of *Bubu de Montparnasse,* by Charles-Louis Philippe, to study how the lack of condoms provoked a syphilis epidemic in nineteenth-century Paris? The practical G. K. Chesterton imagined that if stranded on a desert island he would want to have with him a simple shipbuilding manual; under the same circumstances, the less practical Jules Renard preferred Voltaire's *Candide* and Schiller's *Die Räuber*.

And I, what books would I choose best to keep me company in my hospital cell?

Though I believe in the obvious usefulness of a virtual library, I'm not a user of e-books, those modern incarnations of the Assyrian tablets, nor of the Lilliputian iPods, nor the nostalgic Game Boys. I believe, as Ray Bradbury put it, that "the Internet is a big distraction." I'm accustomed to the space of a page and the solid flesh of paper and ink. I made therefore a mental inventory of the books piled by my bed at home. I discarded recent fiction (too risky because yet unproven), biographies (too crowded under my circumstances: hooked to a tangle of drips, I found other people's presence in my room annoying), scientific essays and detective novels (too cerebral: much as I'd recently been enjoying the Darwinian renaissance and rereading classic crime stories, I felt that a detailed account of selfish genes and the criminal mind would not be the right medicine). I toyed with the idea of startling the nurses with Kierkegaard's *Pain and Suffering: The Sickness unto Death*. But no: what I wanted was the equivalent of comfort food, something I had once enjoyed and could repeatedly and effortlessly revisit, something that could be read for pleasure alone but that would, at the same time, keep my brain alight and humming. I asked my partner to bring me my two volumes of *Don Quixote de la Mancha*.

Lars Gustafsson, in his moving novel *Death of a Beekeeper*, has his narrator, Lars Lennart Westin, who is dying of cancer, make a list of art forms according to their level of difficulty. Foremost are the erotic arts, followed by music, poetry, drama, and pyrotechnics, and ending with the arts of building fountains, fencing, and artillery. But one art form cannot be fitted in: the art of bearing pain. "We are therefore dealing with a unique art form whose level of difficulty is so high," says Westin, "that no one exists who can practice it." Westin, perhaps, had not read *Don Quixote*. *Don Quixote* is, I discovered with relief, the perfect choice for bearing pain. Opening it almost anywhere while waiting to be prodded and pinched and drugged, I found that the friendly voice of the erudite Spanish soldier comforted me with its reassurance that all would be well in the end. Because ever since my adolescence I've kept going back to *Don Quixote*, I knew I wasn't going to be tripped up by the prodigious surprises of its plot. And since *Don Quixote* is a book that can be read just for

the pleasure of its invention, simply for the sake of the story, without any obligation of studiously analyzing its conundrums and rhetorical digressions, I
could allow myself to drift peacefully away in the narrative flow, following the
noble knight and his faithful Sancho. To my first high school reading of *Don
Quixote*, guided by Professor Isaias Lerner, I have, over the years, added many
other readings, in all sorts of places and all sorts of moods. I read *Don Quixote*
during my early years in Europe, when the echoes of May 1968 seemed to
announce huge changes into something still unnamed and undefined, like the
idealized world of chivalry that the honest knight seeks on his quest. I read
Don Quixote in the South Pacific, trying to raise a family on an impossibly
small budget, feeling a little mad in the alien Polynesian culture, like the poor
knight among the aristocrats. I read *Don Quixote* in Canada, where the country's multicultural society seemed to me appealingly quixotic in tone and style.
To these readings, and many others, I can now add a medicinal *Don Quixote*,
both as a balm and a consolation.

None of these *Don Quixote*s can be found, of course, in any library, except
in the one kept by my diminishing memory. Karel Čapek, in his wonderful
book on gardens, says that the art of gardening can be reduced to one rule: you
put into it more than you take out. The same can be said of the art of libraries.
But the libraries of the material world, however great their hunger, can only
hoard existing volumes. We know that every book holds within it all its possible readings, past, present, and future, but its Pythagorean reincarnations,
those wonderful forms which depend on readers to come, will not be found
on our shelves. Paul Masson, a friend of Colette's who worked at the Bibliothèque nationale in Paris, noticed that the vast stocks of the library were de-
fective in Latin and Italian books of the fifteenth century and so began adding
invented titles on the official index cards to save, he said, "the catalogue's prestige." When Colette naively asked him what was the use of books that didn't
exist, Masson responded indignantly that he couldn't be expected "to think of
everything!" But librarians must, and wishful thinking cannot, unfortunately,
be granted room in a seriously run institution.

In the library of the mind, however, books that have no material existence constantly cram the shelves: books that are the amalgamation of other
books once read and now only imperfectly remembered, books that annotate,
gloss, and comment on others too rich to stand on their own, books written in dreams or in nightmares that now preserve the tone of those nebulous
realms, books that we know should exist but which have never been written,

autobiographical books of unspeakable experiences, books of unutterable de-
sires, books of once obvious and now forgotten truths, books of magnificent
and inexpressible invention. All editions of *Don Quixote* published to date in
every language can be collected—are collected, for instance, in the library of
the Instituto Cervantes in Madrid. But my own *Don Quixote*s, the ones that
correspond to each of my several readings, the ones invented by my memory
and edited by my oblivion, can find a place only in the library of my mind.

At times both libraries coincide. In chapter 6 of the first part of *Don
Quixote,* the knight's library of solid books overlaps with the remembered
library of the priest and the barber who purge it; every volume taken off the
shelves is echoed in the recalled reading of its censors and is judged according
to its past merits. Both the books condemned to the flames and the books that
are spared depend not on the words printed black on white in their pages but
on the words stored in the minds of the barber and the priest, placed there
when they first became the books' readers. Sometimes their judgment depends on hearsay, as when the priest explains that he has heard that the *Ama-
dís de Gaula* was the first novel of chivalry printed in Spain and therefore, as
fountainhead of such evil, it must burn—to which the barber retorts that he
has heard that it's also the best, and that for that reason it must be forgiven.
Sometimes the prior impression is so strong that it damns not only the book
itself but also its companions; sometimes the translation is condemned but the
original is spared; sometimes a few are not sent to the fire but merely removed,
so as not to affect their future readers. The priest and the barber, attempting to
cleanse Don Quixote's library, are in fact molding it to the image of the library
they themselves bear in mind, appropriating the books and turning them into
whatever their own experience made them up to be. It is not surprising that
in the end the room in which the library is lodged is itself walled up, so that
it appears never to have existed, and when the old knight wakes and asks to
see it, he is told that it has simply vanished. Vanished it has, but not through
the magic of an evil wizard (as Don Quixote suggests) but through the power
granted other readers of superimposing their own versions of a book onto the
books owned by someone else. Every library of the solid world depends on the
readings of those who came before us.

Ultimately, this creative hermeneutics defines the reader's supreme power:
to make of a book whatever one's experience, taste, intuition, and knowledge
dictate. Not just anything, of course, not the concoctions of a raving mind—
even though psychoanalysts and surrealists suggest that these too have their

validity and logic. But rather the intelligent and inspired reconstruction of the text, using reason and imagination as best we can to translate it onto a different canvas, extending the horizon of its apparent meaning beyond its visible borders and the declared intentions of the author. The limits of this power are painfully vague: as I have said before, Umberto Eco suggested that they must coincide with the limits of common sense. Perhaps this arbitration is enough.

Limitless or not, the power of the reader cannot be inherited; it must be learned. Even though we come into the world as creatures intent on seeking meaning in everything, in reading meanings in gestures, sounds, colors, and shapes, the deciphering of society's common code of communication is a skill that must be acquired. Vocabulary and syntax, levels of meaning, summary and comparison of texts, all these are techniques that must be taught to those who enter society's commonwealth in order to grant them the full power of reading. And yet the last step in the process must be learned all alone: discovering in a book the record of one's own experience.

Rarely, however, is the acquisition of this power encouraged. From the elite schools of scribes in Mesopotamia to the monasteries and universities of the Middle Ages, and later, with the wider distribution of texts after Gutenberg and in the age of the Web, reading at its fullest has always been the privilege of a few. True, in our time, most people in the world are superficially literate, able to read an ad and sign their name on a contract, but that alone does not make them readers. Reading is the ability to enter a text and explore it to one's fullest individual capacities, repossessing it in the act of reinvention. But a myriad of obstacles (as I mentioned in my essay on *Pinocchio*) are placed in the way of its accomplishment. Precisely because of the power that reading grants the reader, the various political, economic, and religious systems that govern us fear such imaginative freedom. Reading at its best may lead to reflection and questioning, and reflection and questioning may lead to objection and change. That, in any society, is a dangerous enterprise.

Librarians today are increasingly faced with a bewildering problem: users of the library, especially the younger ones, no longer know how to read competently. They can find and follow an electronic text, they can cut paragraphs from different Internet sources and recombine them into a single piece, but they seem unable to comment on and criticize and gloss and memorize the sense of a printed page. The electronic text, in its very accessibility, lends users the illusion of appropriation without the attendant difficulty of learning. The essential purpose of reading becomes lost to them, and all that remains is the collecting of information, to be used when required. But reading is not achieved merely by having a text made available: it demands that its readers enter the maze of words, cut open their own tracks, and draw their own charts beyond the margins of the page. Of course, an electronic text allows this, but its very vaunted inclusiveness makes it difficult to fathom a specific meaning and thoroughly explore specific pages. The text on the screen doesn't render the reader's task as obvious as the text in a material book, limited by its borders and binding. "Get anything," reads the ad for a mobile phone able to photograph, record voices, search the Web, transmit words and images, receive and send messages, and, of course, phone. But "anything" in this case stands dangerously near "nothing." The acquisition of something (rather than anything) always requires selection and cannot rely on a limitless offer. To observe, to judge, to choose requires training, as well as a sense of responsibility, even an ethical stance. And young readers, like travelers who have only learned to drive automatic cars, no longer seem able to shift gears at will, relying instead on a vehicle that promises to take them everywhere.

At some point in our history, after the invention of a code that could be communally written and read, it was discovered that the words, set down in clay or on papyrus by an author perhaps distant both in time and in space, could be not only whatever the common code proclaimed—say, a number of goats for sale or a proclamation of war. It was discovered that those goats, invisible to the senses of those who now read about them, became the goats of the reader's experience, goats perhaps once seen on the family farm, or demon goats glimpsed in a haunting dream. And that the proclamation of war could be read not merely as a call to arms but perhaps as a warning, or as an appeal for negotiation, or as bravado. The text inscribed was the product of a particular will and intelligence, but the reading of that text did not need subserviently to follow, or even attempt to guess at, the originating intelligence and will.

At that point, what readers discovered was that the instrument in which their society chose to communicate, the language of words, uncertain and vague and ambiguous, found its strength precisely in that ambiguity and vagueness and imprecision, in its miraculous ability to name without confining the object to the word. In writing *goats* or *war,* the author meant no doubt something absolutely specific, but the reader was now able to add to that specificity the reflections of vast herds and the echoes of a possible peace. Every text, because it is made out of words, says what it has to say and also volumes more that its author could ever have conceived, volumes that future readers will compile and collect, sometimes as solid texts that in turn will breed others, sometimes as texts written half awake and half asleep, fluid texts, shifting texts hoarded in the library of the mind.

In the thirty-second chapter of the first part of *Don Quixote,* the innkeeper, who has given the exhausted hero a bed for the night, argues with the priest about the merits of novels of chivalry, saying that he is unable to see how such books could make anyone lose his mind.

"I don't know how that can be," explains the innkeeper, "since, as I understand it, there's no better reading in the world, and over there I have two or three of these novels, together with some other papers, which, I truly believe, have preserved not only my life but also that of many others; for in harvest time, a great number of reapers come here, and there's always one who can read, and who takes one of these books in his hands, and more than thirty of us gather around him, and we sit there listening to him with such pleasure that it makes us all grow young again."

The innkeeper himself favors battle scenes; a local whore prefers stories of romantic courtship; the innkeeper's daughter likes best of all the lamentations of the knights when absent from their ladies. Each listener (each reader) translates the text into his or her own experience and desire, effectively taking possession of the story which, for the censoring priest, causes readers like Don Quixote to go mad, but which, according to Don Quixote himself, provides glowing examples of honest and just behavior in the real world. One text, a multiplicity of readings, a shelfful of books derived from that one text read out loud, increasing at each turned page our hungry libraries, if not always those of paper, certainly those of the mind: that too has been my happy experience.

I am deeply grateful to my *Don Quixote.* Over the two hospital weeks, the twin volumes kept vigil with me: they talked to me when I wanted entertainment, or waited quietly, attentively, by my bed. They never became impatient with me, neither sententious nor condescending. They continued a conversation begun ages ago, when I was someone else, as if they were indifferent to time, as if taking for granted that this moment too would pass, and their reader's discomfort and anxiety, and that only their remembered pages would remain on my shelves, describing something of my own, intimate and dark, for which as yet I had no words.

Sources

"I know *that!*" Alice cried eagerly. "You take some flour—"

"Where do you pick the flower?" the White Queen asked.

Through the Looking-Glass, Chapter 9

The pieces collected in this book have appeared, in a different form, in a number of publications, or were delivered as lectures, as follows:

"A Reader in the Looking-Glass Wood": Alberto Manguel, *Into the Looking-Glass Wood* (Toronto: Knopf Canada, 1998)

"Room for the Shadow": *Writing Life: Celebrated Canadian and International Authors on Writing and Life,* ed. Constance Rooke (Toronto: McClelland and Stewart, 2006)

"On Being Jewish": Published as "A Lost Sense of Belonging in No Man's Land," *The Independent* (London), 18 September 1994

"Meanwhile, in Another Part of the Forest": Foreword to *Meanwhile, In Another Part of the Forest: Gay Stories from Alice Munro to Yukio Mishima,* ed. Alberto Manguel and Craig Stephenson (Toronto: Knopf Canada, 1993)

"The Further off from England": *Bad Trips,* ed. Keith Fraser (New York: Vintage, 1991)

"Homage to Proteus": Lecture, Passa Porta Festival, Brussels, 26–29 March 2009

"Borges in Love": Alberto Manguel, *Into the Looking-Glass Wood* (Toronto: Knopf Canada, 1998)

"Borges and the Longed-For Jew": Published as "Borges and the Jews," *The Jewish Chronicle* (London), 9 February 2007, Literary Supplement

"Faking It": Published as "Contributing Editor's Column," *Descant 140 / Improvisations* (Toronto), vol. 39, no. 1 (Spring 2008)

"The Death of Che Guevara": Published as "Hero of Our Time," *Times Literary Supplement,* 2 May 1997

"The Blind Bookkeeper": Delivered as the Northrop Frye/Antonine Maillet Lecture, Moncton, New Brunswick, 26 April 2008

"The Perseverance of Truth": Hrant Dink Lecture, University of Ankara, 6 March 2009

"AIDS and the Poet": PEN International lecture, London, 1997

"The Full Stop": *New York Times,* 18 April 1999

"In Praise of Words": *The Spectator* (London), 10 March 2001

"A Brief History of the Page": Conference paper, *The Future of the Page,* University of Saskatchewan, Saskatoon, 20 June 2000

"The Voice That Says 'I'": Lecture, Turin Book Fair, 18–19 May 2009

"Final Answers": Published in French as an introduction to the Opera du Rhin, Strasbourg, 2006 season, Autumn 2006

"What Song the Sirens Sang": Conference paper, *Dante's Women*, Ravenna, September 2008

"Notes Towards a Definition of the Ideal Reader": Conference paper, *The Ideal Reader*, Maison des écrivains étrangers et des traducteurs de Saint Nazaire (MEET), Saint Nazaire, France, February 2003

"How Pinocchio Learned to Read": Conference paper, originally given in French as "Comment Pinocchio apprit à lire." *Et pourquoi pas un éloge de la lecture?* Actes des 13es Journées d'Arole, Bibliothèques de la Ville La Chaux-de-Fond, Lausanne, Institut suisse Jeunesse et Médias, 14–15 November 2003

"Candide in Sanssouci": Conference paper, originally given in German as "Den alles Fleisch es ist wie das Grass," Einstein Forum, Potsdam, 26 June 2003

"The Gates of Paradise": Introduction to *The Gates of Paradise: The Anthology of Erotic Short Fiction*, ed. Alberto Manguel (Toronto: Walter & Ross, 1993)

"Time and the Doleful Knight": Published in Spanish as "El reloj de Don Quijote," *Matador* (Madrid), vol. 50 (2008)

"Saint Augustine's Computer": Lecture, *Times Literary Supplement* Lecture, Hay-on-Wye, 29 May 1997; first published *Times Literary Supplement*, 4 July 1997

"Reading White for Black": Published as "No Minor Art," *Index on Censorship* (London) (March-April 1996)

"The Secret Sharer": *Saturday Night* (Toronto), vol. 102 (July 1987)

"Honoring Enoch Soames": Published as "The Writers' Wish List," *New York Times*, 8 September 1998

"Jonah and the Whale": Lecture, Banff Centre for the Arts Lecture, Banff, Alberta, 30 August 1996

"The Legend of the Dodos": Published in French in *Le Monde*, 23 March 2006

"In Memoriam": Alberto Manguel, *Into the Looking-Glass Wood* (Toronto: Knopf Canada, 1998)

"God's Spies": Introduction to *God's Spies: Stories in Defiance of Oppression*, ed. Albert Manguel (Toronto: Macfarlane Walter and Ross, 1999)

"Once Again, Troy": *Lebanon, Lebanon*, ed. Anna Wilson (London: Saqi, 2006)

"Art and Blasphemy": *Geist* (Vancouver), vol. 60 (Spring 2006)

"At the Mad Hatter's Table": Conference paper, *Folly*, The British Comparative Literature Association, Eleventh International Conference, 2–5 July 2007, Goldsmiths College, University of London

"Notes Towards a Definition of the Ideal Library": Previously unpublished

"The Library of the Wandering Jew": Published as "The Exile's Library," *The Guardian*, 21 February 2009

"The Library as Home": Published as "A 30,000-Volume Window on the World," *New York Times*, 15 May 2008

"The End of Reading": Lecture, Adam Helms Lecture, Stockholm University, Stockholm, 21 April 2009

Index